GREAT AIR BATTLES

GREAT AIR BATTLES

EDITED BY

Major Gene Gurney, U. S. A. F.

Bramhall House • New York

ACKNOWLEDGMENTS

The selections in this book are used by permission and special arrangements with the proprietors of their respective copyrights who are listed below. The editor's and publisher's thanks to all who made this collection possible.

The editor and publisher have made every effort to trace the ownership of all material contained herein. It is their belief that the necessary permissions from publishers, authors, and authorized agents have been obtained in all cases. In the event of any questions arising as to the use of any material, the editor and publisher express regret for any error unconsciously made and will be pleased to make the necessary correction in future editions of this book.

Doubleday and Company, Inc., for "How the Fighting Began" by Arch Whitehouse. This selection is from the book THE YEARS OF THE SKY KINGS by Arch Whitehouse. Copyright © 1959 by the author. Reprinted by permission of the publishers.

The Airpower Historian and Captain Raymond H. Fredette for "First Gothas over London" by Captain Raymond H. Fredette. This selection appeared in the October, 1961, issue. Copyright © 1961 by the Air Force Historical Foundation. Reprinted by permission of the author.

Cavalier for "The Day They Got Richthofen" by Gene Gurney. This selection is from the March, 1958, issue. Copyright 1958 by Fawcett Publications, Inc. Reprinted by permission of the author.

Random House, Inc. for "The Great Attack on St.-Mihiel" by Brigadier General William Mitchell. This selection is from the book MEMOIRS OF WORLD WAR I by Brigadier General William Mitchell. Copyright © 1960 by Lucy M. Gilpin. Reprinted by permission of the publishers.

For Men for "My Air Duel with Bruno Mussolini" by Captain Derek D. Dickinson as told to Edwin C. Parsons. This selection is from the February, 1939, issue. Copyright 1939 by County Press, Inc. Reprinted by permission of Edwin C. Parsons.

William Kimber & Co., Ltd., for "Three Against an Air Force" by Kenneth Poolman. This selection was condensed from the book FAITH, HOPE AND CHARITY by Kenneth Poolman and appeared in the October, 1955, issue of *Royal Air Force Flying Review*. Reprinted by permission of William Kimber & Co., Ltd.

Houghton Mifflin Company for "The Battle of Britain" by Winston Churchill. This selection is from the book THEIR FINEST HOUR by Winston Churchill. Copyright © 1949 by Houghton Mifflin Company. Reprinted by permission of the publishers.

Royal Air Force Flying Review for "Target: Amsterdam" by Leonard Trent. This selection is from the May, 1955, issue. Copyright 1955 by the Royal Air Force Review, Ltd. Reprinted by permission.

iv

Foreword

THE HISTORY of warfare is as old as the history of the human race. Down through the ages with club, spear, bow, and gun men have gone forth to defend themselves from attack, or to conquer the enemy. Weapons were improved but the basic strategies employed remained unchanged over hundreds of years. It was the airplane, an invention of the twentieth century, that radically altered the way wars were fought.

With the coming of the airplane, fighting could no longer be confined to the battlefield. An entire country and all its people were subject to attack. The ability of warring nations to launch and sustain all-out air attacks, or to survive them, became more important in determining victory or defeat than clashes between armies and navies.

Just as the airplane changed the way wars were fought, it was itself changed by war. The demands of the world's air forces for faster and more efficient planes resulted in technological developments that have converted the military airplane into something closely related to a missile. And guided missiles themselves are replacing airplanes.

It is unlikely that the air battles of World War I, World War II, and Korea will be repeated in a major conflict of the future. Speeds have become too great and thermonuclear weapons too powerful. In a future war it will not require repeated raids by vast fleets of bombers to destroy an enemy. It will not be necessary to send up squadrons of fighters to stop the bombers. Opposing groups of brave men will no longer fight battles in the sky to ensure victory on the ground.

The aerial combat of World War I, World War II, and Korea required great skill and courage. It meant facing the enemy directly to shoot him down or be shot down. It meant attacking the enemy over his own territory where he was strongest. And it meant fighting on, when both the plane and those who flew in it were mortally wounded.

This is a collection of true stories about air battles in World War I, World War II, and Korea and the brave men who fought them. Some of the selections are by the flyers themselves; others were written about them. They make an exciting account of how wars were fought in the air.

Contents

PART FOUR:
GREAT AIR BATTLES OF WORLD WAR II: THE PACIFIC

PART FIVE: GREAT AIR BATTLES OF THE KOREAN WAR

PART ONE

GREAT AIR BATTLES OF WORLD WAR I

Introduction

In June of 1914 Francis Ferdinand, the heir to the Austro-Hungarian throne, traveled to Bosnia to watch the summer maneuvers of the Imperial armies. It was a routine inspection trip until June 28. On that day Francis Ferdinand was assassinated, the first of a series of events that led to the outbreak of World War I.

After a month of diplomatic maneuvering, ultimatum, and troop mobilization, the battle lines were drawn — Austria-Hungary and Germany on one side; Russia, France, and Great Britain on the other. On August 4 the German army invaded neutral Belgium. It was the quickest way to get to France and the German army was in a hurry. According to the timetable drawn up by its General Staff, France was to be conquered in six weeks.

France refused to be conquered on schedule. Instead, she stopped the Germans at the Marne River. With the help of the British, and later the Americans, she held them off for the next four years. During that time fierce battles were fought across northern France from the coast to the Swiss border. This was the area known as the western front. On several occasions the German army was able to advance toward Paris. Each time it was driven back.

The United States entered the war in 1917. By 1918 thousands of American troops were in France and tons of supplies were moving across the Atlantic. The Germans who had no such fresh resources to draw upon were forced to retreat toward their own frontier. The armistice which ended the fighting was signed on November 11, 1918.

In the four years of war between 1914 and 1918 the airplane performed several military functions. It was first used for reconnaissance — to check up on the enemy's location and activities. Some of this work had formerly been done by cavalrymen. The trench warfare that developed after the German army was halted on the Marne ended the usefulness of the mounted soldier as a scout. The airplane, on the other hand, proved to be ideally suited to spying on the enemy behind his lines.

An airplane was used for bombing in the early weeks of the war. The first bombardier was a German pilot who dropped two bombs over the side of his ship as he flew over the outskirts of Paris. From this crude beginning there developed planes especially designed to carry bombs and special squadrons to fly them.

Neither side could afford to allow the planes of the enemy to fly about at will collecting valuable military information or dropping bombs on cities and troops. Fast, single-seater planes were given the job of driving off the unwelcome intruders. The result was that for the first time in history a war was fought in the air as well as on the ground. A new dimension had been added to military strategy.

All of the countries that went to war in 1914 had airplanes. Few, if any, of the planes had been built for strictly military purposes and some of them were already outmoded, even by 1914 standards. France, Great Britain, and Germany had each organized an air force of sorts and given some thought to how the still-new flying machine could be used in a war.

It was generally agreed that the airplane, with its ability to move above and beyond the battle lines, was a better means by which to check up on the enemy than the stationary observation balloons that had been used in past wars. There were the usual diehards who doubted this. They saw no use whatsoever for the "flying birdcages" and they were often military men of high rank. In spite of dire predictions that the airplane would be useless, or worse, in combat, when war was declared planes and pilots moved to the front along with the armies of Germany, France, and Great Britain.

Here is an account of how the British Royal Flying Corps went off to war. It lacked equipment and training but its men were brave and ready to battle the enemy in the air.

How the Fighting Began

Arch Whitehouse

IN COMPARISON with the aviation equipment and training of France and Germany, the British Royal Flying Corps had no right in the war. On paper they claimed 450 planes and 750 pilots, but when war broke out early in August the best they could do was to assemble four skeletal squadrons. They had less than 50 machines that would fly. Under the command of Brig. Gen. Sir David Henderson, who had learned to fly at the age of 49, the RFC actually started for France on August 13, 1914 — nine days after war was declared. Henderson's chief of staff was Acting Col. F. Sykes, a Boer War veteran who had been floating

about in free balloons since 1904. In 1911 he took his ticket on a Bristol biplane — presumably the early Bristol Bullet.

Some prewar emergency plans had been drawn up and these stated that each squadron would be allowed three days to mobilize. On the fourth they were to proceed to Dover and over the next 48 hours were to "do a Blériot" and fly across the Channel to France. Their motor transport was to go by ship.

At this point history becomes very confused. Those who took part have stated that few planes actually made the overwater flight, but professional

5

historians claim that practically all but one made the trans-Channel flutter safely. One plane crashed on taking off, killing Lt. R. R. Skene and Air Mech. R. K. Barlow. Each pilot carried a revolver, field glasses, spare goggles, a water bottle, a small stove, biscuits, cold meat, a piece of chocolate, and some soup cubes. It was just as well as most of them spent the next few days and nights huddling against French haystacks awaiting the arrival of their transport and spare parts. Nos. 2, 3, 4, and 5 squadrons and a variegated outfit called an aircraft park went over first.

It was a real musical-comedy effort. No one had any idea where the war was or what uniforms the German soldiers would be wearing. They had no military maps of France or Belgium until M. Michelin, the famous tire manufacturer, provided them with a few automobile road guides. These profusely illustrated charts were most interesting to auto tourists but of little use to aviators. Still they had to suffice for weeks and weeks. Later a London newspaper obliged with a few sheets of gaily colored "war maps" which were being given away to subscribers as premiums.

The equipment assembly provided some burlesque situations. Blériot tails were bolted on Avro fuselages. Undercarriages designed for Morane Parasols were "bent a bit" and affixed to a BE-8 aircraft. Engines intended for Farmans were blandly attached to RE-2's — but everything seemed to fly.

What didn't was hauled over by channel packet steamer, unloaded, and towed through French streets to the nearest cow pasture and flown to the battle areas.

Nos. 2 and 4 squadrons were equipped with BE-2's. These machines were said to be Blériot-inspired — a real slur on M. Blériot — and were registered as Blériot Experimental. They were manufactured at the Royal Aircraft factory at Farnborough. No. 3 Squadron had a mixed bag of BE-2's and Henri Farmans. Avros, Maurice Farmans, and BE-2's, affectionately known as "Bloaters," were the mounts of No. 5 Squadron.

This heterogeneous collection took off at two-minute intervals and eventually arrived in France. One plane even got as far as the final destination — Amiens — the first night, and its pilot, Lt. H. D. Harvey-Kelley, got a severe reprimand for taking a shortcut and arriving on French soil before his commander, Maj. J. C. Burke, formerly of the Royal Irish Regiment. Lt. R. M. Vaugh was forced down by engine trouble at Boulogne and was arrested by the French authorities and kept in confinement for a week. At any rate, by August 16, Nos. 2, 3, and 4 squadrons left Amiens for Maubeuge, and four more casualties were suffered en route. Two Bloaters crashed.

Transport was composed mainly of borrowed furniture vans, commercial delivery vehicles, and one odorous tumbrel that had been used in the collection of garbage. A bright red truck was commandeered from a renowned provision firm and was used by No. 2 Squadron as its mobile service unit. During the retreat from Mons this gaudy vehicle was better than any electronic guidance system — for both sides! After all, it could be easily seen and it could travel almost as fast as the military aircraft it was serving.

The flying equipment was particularly prehistoric, much of it consisting of Maurice Farman "Shorthorns" and "Longhorns," BE-2 biplanes, a parasol-type Blériot only a few bolts removed from the contraption that had mastered the English Channel five years before, and some nebulous R.E. (Reconnaissance Experimental) airplanes of doubtful parentage and performance. The Farman Longhorn was a pusher biplane encumbered with a Wright elevator mounting which projected out in front on a pair of skilike landing skids. In the rear was a tail assembly large enough to be employed as a billboard. The Shorthorn was equally ungraceful, but came minus the frontal grape-arbor equipment and had a simple monoplane tail.

The Farman brothers, who were responsible for these aeronautical creations, were the sons of a Mr. Richard Farman, British correspondent for the *London Daily Telegram* in Paris. Henri, Maurice, and Dick were all of English descent but were born in France and acquired French nationality. Henri studied painting and was exceptionally good. Along with his brother Maurice he was also a champion tandem cyclist. Dick was an automobile nut and as early as 1896 had written a book about motorcars. Maurice devoted himself to astronomy, meteorology, and ballooning, but Henri was the first to take up airplane flying. In 1907 he bought a Voisin biplane and learned to fly at Issy-les-Moulineaux. He was still flying antiquated biplanes in 1937, doing wild cross-country flights with a tomboy daughter.

In 1908 Henri built a pusher biplane that captured some lucrative prizes for covering a few hundred kilometers under the watchful eye of the French Aero Club officials. In fact, Henri is credited with several respectable records.

For a short time Maurice and Henri were induced to set up a shop in Bradford, England, to supply the British army with equipment that would fly. Maurice did the drawing-board work, Henri built the machines, and Dick took over the business end of the project. At Bradford and at another factory they set up at Billancourt in France they turned out 1,084 of their bathtub pushers for the Royal Flying Corps. These aerial dreadnoughts stayed in the service until well into 1916. The Shorthorn biplanes of No. 4 Squadron, which arrived in France early in September of 1914, were the first active-service aircraft definitely armed for aerial combat. They were, indeed, armed with a Lewis gun, but unfortunately the machine would not leave the ground if a gunner was included in the pay load.

One of these old warbirds turned up and actually flew again in the Old Crocks Parade of the 1936 Royal Air Force display at Hendon, England. The effect was terrifying.

The engines available for RFC airframes were mostly 50-, 70-, and 80-hp Gnome rotaries. There were a few 70-hp Renaults and a government factory product known as an RAF (Royal Aircraft Factory) air-cooled engine. This monster had eight cylinders which "blew off in the order of firing" — according to one irrepressible gunner who served with me — and what was probably the world's most elaborate exhaust-pipe system.

Most of the flying personnel were sportsmen-flyers who had worked out some fraternal association with this new aviation arm, and when the call came they simply donned a double-breasted uniform, borrowed a motorcycle, and rode around until they found a covey of aircraft. Many of the airmen were boisterous types who had been deprived of their motorcar licenses because of frequent speed infringements, so they had taken to flying to avoid the frowns of the highway bobbies. Lt. W. B. Rhodes-Moorhouse, the first Britisher to win the Victoria Cross in the air, was such a culprit.

The observers and gunners were at first blindly selected from the ranks of mechanics or orderly-room officers if they were not otherwise engaged that day. None had had any air or gunnery training, their chief qualifications being the ability to load and fire a cavalry carbine, drop fléchettes (metal darts), and have jacket pockets that would accommodate two half bricks for dropping on unsuspecting enemy aircraft. One of Britain's finest war airmen, Maj. James McCudden, began his career in this way. It seems he knew how to load and fire a Parker shotgun.

While a few rollicking characters had considered the possibility of "having a go" at enemy aircraft with small arms of some sort, nothing deliberate or premeditated had been thought of. A Maurice Farman biplane of No. 3 Squadron had allegedly taken to the air carrying a Hotchkiss machine gun — but not for shooting purposes! It was simply an experiment in weight carrying.

There was nothing offensive in the way of aerial armament until scouting pilots noticed the air was becoming crowded. Everyone went about his business, checking the movement of troops, photographing the real estate, and wondering what the devil was burning down there.

Of course these idyllic conditions couldn't last forever. There is always some uncouth oaf who has to spoil the sanctity of harmless routine patrols. As stated above, half bricks were tossed; lengths of rusty chain were flung; large lead weights dangled from lengths of wire with the idea of fouling some Rumpler's propeller. Another ill-man-

8

nered type amused himself by firing a Webley pistol at passing Aviatiks. The Parker shotgun idea finally broke down the entente cordiale completely.

The Germans retaliated with rifle fire, and during the first week of the war a Lt. Waterfell was shot down and killed over Ath in Belgium. He was the first such casualty of the 7,589 who died in the British flying services during the more than four years of air action.

Then within a few days special clips to mount army rifles were fitted to all available aircraft. Air fights of varying decision were being reported from all fronts. In most cases the gunners or observers who manned these weapons sat in the front seats of the biplane types and as a result were somewhat handicapped in having to aim and fire through a network of struts, stays, flying wires, a whirling propeller, and fluttering wing tips. On several occasions overanxious gunners shot their own struts away and returned to enjoy the concern of their squadron mates until the details of the self-inflicted escapade were revealed.

Toward the end of September two Bristol Scouts were delivered, one to No. 3 Squadron and one to No. 5 Squadron, both armed with a rifle on each side of the pilot's cockpit and set to shoot at an angle of 45 degrees to avoid hitting the propeller tips. Whether they ever went into action with any success has not been related.

Rifles, shotguns, and carbines gave the aircrews some small measure of satisfaction, but the German aircraft were so superior in gaining and maintaining height that it was impossible for British or French planes to get at them. German Rumplers would be buzzing over the Allied areas while their observers drew maps, took photographs, or wrote out detailed reports, completely undisturbed. Frustrated British airmen floundered about 3,000 feet below, vainly shooting off carbines at the nosy Jerries.

Since they couldn't vent their wrath on the enemy airmen above, the Britishers took it out on the ground troops below. Cardboard boxes of steel darts were poured over the side, and it was claimed that these missiles could drill a man from his skull to his crotch. Multipointed variations of these darts were dropped along roads to cripple enemy cavalry or transport horses. I never met anyone who ever admitted taking part in this kind of warfare, but I have seen boxes of the frightful devices.

There were several variations of aerial bombs during those early days. The first was a streamlined canister of gasoline which was presumed to ignite on impact with the ground and was often used against German hangars and airship sheds. Another incendiary bomb was a simple can of explosive which was wrapped with sticky tarred rope. Burning rope was supposed to fly in all directions and do the arson job. Then there was a treacherous melinite shrapnel bomb, actually a converted French shell fitted with

9

an unpredictable nose-striker. These would sometimes explode while being hung in the racks and eventually had to be discarded. Later parachute-braked bombs were tried, the parachute to delay the fall and give the airman a chance to escape from the explosion and debris. Some shell bombs were tied to the upper longerons with wrapping cord, and when the airman wished to release them over the target he used his pocketknife.

The first real bomb raid was carried out against Brussels early in the war. All available RFC aircraft took part, with each plane carrying six 20-pound bombs which were dumped over the occupied city. Several of the planes were damaged and had to land in Holland, but instead of being interned for the duration, the aircrews signed on as ships' firemen in Rotterdam and worked their way back to England.

Meanwhile, on the Continent, the RFC and the German air force were developing the rivalry and competition that were to mark their activities over the next four years. Musketry was exchanged whenever possible, and each day provided new variations of war in the air. Among the first of the British casualties was a Sgt. Maj. Jillings, who was flying as an observer with a Lt. Noel. Jillings was credited with actually downing a German two-seater Albatros with a single rifle bullet, but on the way home from his success someone on the ground took a shot at Jillings and hit him "where he sat down." According to official reports,

the sergeant major had to be assisted out of the machine, but later he went on to glory, became a squadron leader, and was awarded the Military Cross.

During this time the German army under von Kluck was storming across eastern Belgium and northeast France practically unopposed. The French army had consumed two weeks getting mobilized and only the heroic delaying actions of the Belgians held the Germans in check. During August the field-gray hordes had practically encircled Paris, and Britain's little army had been shoved to the area around Meaux. It looked like a walkover for the Germans.

Britain's air squadrons were scattered about between Amiens and Compiègne. The toughest battles they fought whenever they landed on any stretch of open farmland were with outraged French peasants. The rustics mistook them for the enemy and usually made gallant pitchfork attacks before asking questions. The result was the British decided to identify their aircraft by painting Union Jacks on the wing tips. Later this insignia was simplified by daubing on a design of red, white, and blue roundels. The French reversed the British sequence of colors, making the outer circle red and the inner spot blue. Out of that simple precautionary measure came the first military airplane insignia. Before 1914 was ended the Germans selected their Iron Cross design — each airman hoping he would one day be awarded the coveted honor.

During the opening period of the campaign, the RFC often found themselves further ahead than their own infantry. On several occasions No. 3 Squadron had to stand by with loaded rifles resting against the undercarriages while they made routine repairs. Once a patrol of Uhlans was driven off just as the last of the squadron's motor transport was being cranked up to move out.

Antiaircraft gunnery — particularly from the German side — was not to be taken lightly. The Krupp factory had produced a very good high-angle weapon, and with targets of limited altitude they kept the British and French airmen busy darting in and out of sheltering cloud layers.

Americans have long been puzzled by the British term "Archie" which was applied to enemy antiaircraft fire. This is how Archie came into being. Back in London the famous comedian George Robey had been singing a rather risqué ballad in a musical comedy which was being whistled and sung by all the playboys haunting London's theater district. The various choruses always ended with the words, "Archibald, certainly not!"

Many of these playboys were now in action with the RFC, and whenever a Jerry shell burst uncomfortably close the British pilot would raise one hand in remonstrance, assume the George Robey leer, and exclaim, "Archibald, certainly not!" This soon became "Archibald!" and with the weeks the catch phrase was eventually whittled down to the single word, "Archie." During World War II the more ominous term "flak" replaced it — but that was a more ominous war.

Regardless of the apparent ragtime behavior of Britain's air arm, they were doing an amazing job of observation and reconnaissance. So well, in fact, that on August 22 Sir John French held a conference at Le Cateau with Gen. Lanrezac, commander of the 5th French Army, and decided to fight a defensive action and hold on for at least 24 hours. RFC reports had given a reliable hint that von Bülow was massing across the Sambre River and that an enveloping movement was expected from Grammont. The next day the Battle of Mons was fought along a 25-mile front. Allied artillery was on hand — but they had no shells — so all available planes of the Royal Flying Corps flew unceasingly, marking enemy movements and locating enemy batteries. That night the retreat began, and for the next nine days RFC pilots and observers were in the air almost continuously, writing a gallant chapter to the history of that glorious military movement that was to save Paris and the French army.

The outstanding hero of this "Eyes of the Army" air service was Second Lt. William Bernard Rhodes-Moorhouse of No. 2 Squadron. He was the first of 19 British airmen to win the Victoria Cross. Prior to the outbreak of the war Rhodes-Moorhouse had been a devil-may-care young man and his driver's license carried many red-ink citations because of his disregard for his neck on the public highways. Since moody officialdom frowned on such motoring, this slim athletic character with the toothbrush mustache turned to civilian flying at Brooklands. Being the experimental type, he had often speculated on what would happen if one zoomed an airplane steeply and then shut off the engine.

Would it come back and do a sort of tail slide? he wondered.

He tried it, and the plane slid back on its tail, driving his onlookers into nearby cellars. However, William Bernard managed to recover in time and another stunt was added to the primitive book of aerobatics.

He had been flying for two years before he bothered about applying for an official certificate, his theory being that if you consorted with officialdom you were likely to come under its ridiculous jurisdiction. He simply wanted to fly and damn the red tape. However, he took his pilot's certificate in October, 1911, and by then was considered a first-class cross-country pilot. In 1912 he finished third in Britain's Aerial Derby and afterward established a record by carrying two passengers across the English Channel in an ancient Bréguet. He enlisted in the Royal Flying Corps when war was declared and was posted to Farnborough, where he fretted and stewed until March, 1915. He then joined No. 2 Squadron at Merville and immediately began active-service patrols. During the Second Battle of Ypres

on April 26 — a few days after the first poison-gas attack — a message was received from Air Headquarters that the Courtrai railroad junction and station were to be bombed at all cost. German reinforcements were said to be pouring through the station. With a hole two miles wide in front of Ypres, where the Allies had been driven out by chlorine gas, the situation was most precarious.

Four aircraft — presumably B.E. 2's — were assigned the job, but only Rhodes-Moorhouse succeeded in getting to the target. He was carrying a 100-pound bomb slung between his wheels and before takeoff was told to use his own discretion as to how low he would go in for the attack. He went in at 300 feet, bombed the station, and scored a direct hit on the all-important signal box. He could have zoomed into the smoke and cleared off, but instead he circled and circled the area, picking up all the information possible. What he saw convinced him that Ypres was in for a rough time.

(It is a historical fact that Germany's failure to get reserves into the poison-gassed area in time completely sacrificed what initial surprise the gas attack had established.)

During the minutes that Rhodes-Moorhouse was over the Courtrai area he came under heavy rifle and machine-gun fire, but he continued to "spot" the enemy. Then a bullet went through the fingers of his left hand, so he decided to head home. Flying low over the city, he roared past the belfry of a Courtrai church. The Germans had set up a machine gun in that tower, and as Rhodes-Moorhouse buzzed past, a savage burst caught him cold. One bullet smashed his thigh and another tore through his stomach. His base was 30 miles away, and below were many suitable landing areas where he might have dropped down and requested medical assistance, even though he was well inside enemy territory. But he thought only of the hordes of Germans moving toward the Courtrai station that might make the difference between hanging on or losing the war at Ypres. The General Staff should know of this concentration — and the fact that he had damaged the signal box.

No one knows what Rhodes-Moorhouse suffered over those 30 dreadful miles. Once he was inside his own lines, he did not land but flew on to the rear area and dropped down near the British headquarters. There he huddled in his bullet-torn plane and dictated his report to an infantry officer, and then added before he fainted: "I didn't want them to get my machine. It's not too badly bashed about, is it?" He died in the hospital 24 hours later without ever knowing he had been recommended for the Victoria Cross. In his citation someone had written, "The bomb he dropped perhaps did more definite service on a great scale than any bombs released during the war, but his last act set a standard of courage which others may hope to equal but can never excel."

The first planned, long-range bombing attack of World War I took place in November, 1914, when the British sent three of their Avros after the Zeppelin sheds at Friedrichshafen in southern Germany. The attack did little damage but it caused Germany to form a bombing squadron of her own with the intention of sending it to England.

The first mass attacks on England came not from airplanes but from the much-feared Zeppelins. The early German bombers were not able to cross the Channel and carry a load of bombs too. By 1917 the Zeppelin menace was fading thanks to the defense put up by British fighters using incendiary and explosive ammunition. To replace the Zeppelin, Germany had the Gotha, a plane that was to terrorize England for months.

The first Gotha raid took place on May 25, 1917; the target area was the British Channel coast. This was followed on June 13 by a big raid on London in which 14 Gothas dropped 118 bombs. The resulting damage was extensive; there were 162 persons killed and 432 wounded. Here is the story.

The Gotha G-IV, one of the first airplanes to be designed primarily for bombing, went into service in May, 1917. Because of its frail superstructure and gear it was a difficult plane to land and its accident rate was high. The Gotha was manufactured by Gothaer Waggonfabrik.

First Gothas Over London

Capt. Raymond H. Fredette, USAF

EVEN BEFORE the first gray light of dawn, the Gotha nests about medieval Ghent were stirring with feverish activity. Capt. Ernst Brandenburg, commander of Battle Group III of the German Army High Command, had alerted his squadrons the day before. London, still sleeping and unsuspecting, was to be the target.

A frantic round of last-minute preparations had been set in motion by the order. Observers had pored over their maps to study once more the snaking course of the Thames, and the jumbled pattern of London's landmarks. The bombers had been taken aloft locally for final trial flights. Engines, bomb release mechanisms, signal lights, all had been checked and rechecked with exhausting thoroughness.

A new day, June 13, 1917, was now breaking. In the chronology of what was the greatest war, the date would merit an asterisk. For on this day a small armada of bombers, leaving consternation and casualties in its wake, would reach Britain's capital city for the first time.

Brandenburg and his crews were itching for their first long look down the British lion's throat. Beginning in late May, they had made two starts without getting through to London.

But, this time, there was every expectation that the attack would be consummated. The weather, which had blanketed the city earlier, finally turned in the raiders' favor. Clear skies, announced the bombing unit's weather service, could be expected to prevail over England during the next few days. With this report, the *England-Geschwader*, as Battle Group III commonly became known, could be certain that the promise of battle would be fulfilled at last.

In a broader sense, the promise of reaching London in strength really depended on the Gotha G-IV. The machine arrived in Belgium just in time to revive the fading air campaign against England, waged up to now by the highly assailable Zeppelins. This remarkable airplane, one of the first true bombers, carried a crew of three in open cockpits. Even though its two Mercedes engines generated only 520 hp, the Gotha's dimensions were impressive. Its upper wing was longer than the span of the B-25 Mitchell of World War II by over ten feet.

Unlike the Zeppelins, however, the Gothas had no radio equipment, but at least some of them carried homing pigeons. These were released to get word back to base in an emergency. After reporting its position, a crew had some chance of rescue by submarine, or some other craft if downed at sea. Vents and other openings in the Gotha's fuselage could be closed tightly to delay sinking after ditching.

On the minus side, the Gotha was hopelessly slow and sluggish in flight. Its top speed was little more than 90 mph. These disadvantages of the machine as an air weapon were compensated for, in part, by three machine guns. The most unique of these was the rear gun defending the bomber's tail against low attacks. When aimed straight to the rear, the gun's fire cleared the machine through an open, arched depression or tunnel in the underside of the fuselage. The Gotha crews were very much intrigued by this gun. They felt confident that its fire would claim many unsuspecting victims among attacking pursuit planes. The existence of just such a gun did become, in fact, a matter of intense British curiosity which was unsatisfied until the first Gotha fell into their hands.

The Gothas, which finally will make it all the way to London this June day, are rolled out from the hangars in the dawn's half-light and lined up on the dewy field. Straining ground crews hang bombs up into position and install the machine guns. Mechanics manipulate the controls and "rev up" the engines. Only later, after the sun is well up, do the aircrews themselves begin to arrive.

One of the gleaming white Gothas stands out from the others. It is decorated with large, painted snakes, undulating from nose to tail on each side of the fuselage. Because of its bizarre markings, the bomber is called the "serpent machine."

The Gotha's commander and observer is Oberlt. Walter Aschoff, who strides up confidently with a battered oak cane under his arm. Aschoff would not think of going to London without his walking stick. Since it has seen him safely through months of deadly patrols over the Somme, the staff has become an indispensable good-luck charm. Close behind appear the pilot, 19-year-old Lt. Erwin Kollberg, and the rear gunner, Reserve Sgt. Mayer.

The squadron commander rushes from machine to machine for one last check. With each crew he quickly reviews the assigned targets, the anticipated winds aloft, and the heading to be flown on the bombing approach. As the time for takeoff draws near, the crews struggle into their cumbersome, fur-lined flying suits. The bundled airmen climb aboard. They begin to sweat as they sit waiting in the warmth of a bright, midmorning sun.

At ten o'clock the air is filled with the roar of engines. Lined up side by side, the Gothas vibrate and shake as if anticipating the straining effort needed to leave the ground. At the signal each bomber lurches forward in turn. Engines groan deeply as one machine after another picks up speed and then hesitantly rises into the air. Two of the Gothas are forced to land almost at once with faltering engines. Their crews will have another chance later, but this time they stay behind, the forsaken victims of a new weapon's imperfections.

Twenty-one Gothas in all manage to break away with their heavy loads from the earth's resisting tug. Slowly, they begin to wind and turn over Ghent in their long struggle for altitude. The noisy machines eventually form into a formation of three elements and then head for the coast. The sea is reached at Zeebrugge which is easily recognized from 10,000 feet. German gunboats emit dense, black smoke as they stand by below with full steam in case any of the bombers are forced down into the cold sea.

The German airmen leave this reassuring sight behind as the formation advances westward over the unfriendly waters. The bombers continue to climb in a brilliantly clear sky. Each pilot is forced to fly with wearying concentration as other planes in the formation weave and bob in the turbulent air. Tension mounts even higher as the dark outline of hostile coasts rise up out of the sea. The raiders' view stretches from Dover's white cliffs to Harwich, some 60 miles to the north. Looking back and off to one side, the airmen also can see the French coast clearly, noting the Allied ports of Dunkirk and Calais.

As the droning Gothas near the English coast, a multitude of ships, large and small, respond excitedly to the overflight of the enemy planes.

Warships go into zigzag courses, churning the calm sea into white foam. Further away, a convoy of some 20 ships heads northward under destroyer escort.

The bombers ignore these tempting targets and press on toward the shore. While still over the sea, one lone Gotha suddenly breaks away from the formation and turns southward. It is headed for Margate on a diversionary attack which the Germans hope will confuse and disperse the defense efforts. Five bombs are dropped on the seaside resort. Two fail to explode, but the others injure four persons.

As the main force flies over Foulness Island, three more machines drop away. Their target is Shoeburyness just to the south on the Thames estuary. From the air the town hardly seems worthwhile attacking. But, actually, Shoeburyness is a large gunnery center with proving grounds for all types of weapons and munitions. Two of the Gothas drop six bombs which wound two persons and cause some slight damage. The third machine is observed to be headed toward Greenwich.

The Gotha formation itself flies straight into the mouth of the River Crouch to be greeted by the first opposing fire. Four picket ships, posted near Southend, have let loose with a barrage. To the German airmen the exploding shells resemble small, gray clouds. Anticipating worse to come, the Gothas climb still higher and tighten their ranks. Then, by follow-

17

ing the Thames, they set a direct course for London some 40 miles away.

It is just before 11 o'clock. The entire area resounds with the loud, throbbing hum of airplane engines. This causes wonderment in many villages and towns where the bombers are heard for several minutes before they can be sighted. At other places people peer from windows or run into their gardens to see a diamond-shaped formation flying nearly three miles up. To some the white Gothas in the bright sunlight look like "a shoal of little silverfishes." Others report that the enemy bombers were like large, white butterflies.

If any of the raiders are reminded of butterflies, it is, very likely, of those fluttering in their stomachs as they approach London. After penetrating the city's outer gun defenses, they are forced to fly through light but persistent antiaircraft fire. But what really fills the Gotha airmen with excitement and awe is the breathtaking sight of mighty London, stretching out in all directions beneath them like a vast, hostile sea.

The first bombs fall on the eastern suburbs at 25 minutes to 12. They strike in a cluster north of the Thames between the Royal Albert Docks and the borough of East Ham. But the formation retains most of its bombs, and bears on toward the center of the capital for the main attack.

Slipping past the Gothas' wings are shipyards, docks, factories, and railroad stations. Arising below is the gray, walled, Tower of London, the majestic dome of St. Paul, the Tower Bridge, casting its shadow on the Thames.

In the full light of noon, the heart of an empire lies exposed to the bombers. Down below are the finally attainable vitals of a stubborn enemy so long protected from attack by the Channel moat. German airmen, with the power of releasing high explosives at their fingertips, have reached London in numbers at last. Theirs is a dream of war realized, and because of it, warfare would never be the same again.

Although much distressed, the great city is not entirely without the means for showing its annoyance and anger. Deadly, dark blossoms fill the sky. The Gothas bank and curve as they fly the gauntlet of the guns. At times, the angry crunch of the shells reaches the ears of the airmen, even above the roar of their own engines. Still, the bombers go on their prearranged course without losses.

For the Londoners, the barrage becomes a rain of shrapnel pelting rooftops and the streets. Before the guns stop, 20 persons are wounded, not by the bombs, but the shell fragments. One victim dies.

Near the center of London the formation wheels at the firing of a white flare. The sign came from the lead machine occupied by Capt. Brandenburg. Another signal follows, and many Gothas drop their bombs. Liverpool Street Station, one of the city's largest rail terminals, is the objective for this principal attack.

Seventy-two bombs strike within one mile of the station in a two-minute period beginning at 1140 hours. But only three hit the station, where they kill 16 persons and injure twice that number. Two of the bombs come crashing down through the high, arched roof and explode on the concrete waiting platforms. The third scores a direct hit on a train about to leave for Hunstanton. A dining car is wrecked and two coaches are set afire. Away from the station, still another bomb falls on the Royal Mint. The blast kills four workmen and injures 30 more.

After having rocked the Liverpool station area, the formation splits into two groups. One element of six Gothas turns south to cross the Thames near the Tower Bridge. Its task is to bomb the warehouses and railroad stations in the Southwark area.

Lt. Aschoff aligns the target in his sight aboard the serpent-striped Gotha, and signals the pilot who reaches for the bomb release. After what seems to be an endless pause, the projectiles tumble from the machine. Relieved of its load, the Gotha rises into the air with a sudden jerk. Aschoff hangs on tightly to his seat in the open nose position, and waits breathlessly for his bombs to detonate below. Warehouses absorb the brunt of the hits. Fire breaks out, and heavy smoke rises in the clear sky. Tooley Street, the scene of nineteenth-century London's great-est fire, becomes the setting for still another spectacular blaze.

Meanwhile, the other wing of Gothas has gone northward to bomb Dalston, another suburb and important rail junction point. After this attack, these bombers pivot again in the direction of the Thames to rejoin the other element. As they near the river, the Gothas pass over Poplar, scene of the greatest single tragedy of the raid.

The North Street School in that borough is hit by a bomb weighing 100 pounds. Without immediately exploding, the bomb breaks in two as it strikes the roof of the school. One piece of the missile continues on its fateful journey, penetrating three floors. It detonates at ground level in a kindergarten classroom. In a split second the peaceful scene of 64 very young children busy with their lesson is changed into one of horror. Scattered amidst the debris are tiny, mangled bodies and torn limbs. Other children, somehow miraculously untouched, scream and struggle to escape from the wreckage.

The war has struck Poplar like an unexpected bolt of lightning. As word of the calamity spreads like wildfire, pandemonium breaks out in the neighborhood. Distraught mothers converge on the school, and tear at the gathering crowd to claim their children. Five gruff sailors, who happened to be nearby, are driven to tears as they help in the rescue work. But, for the most part, the people are too stunned to panic or show any emotions. The high-flying Gothas are all but forgotten for a moment. Full realization of this new aspect of the war, and the anger it would provoke, will come later.

When the gruesome sifting is over, the toll is set at 16 dead and 30 injured. Fate, which had guided the wayward missile into the midst of these children, might have been even more cruel. Very likely none in the classroom would have survived if the bomb had exploded there intact, instead of breaking in two. Elsewhere, still another school is hit by a bomb which goes through five floors without exploding.

From naval air stations and the aerodromes of the home defense squadrons, nearly 100 planes race into the air to battle the Gothas. But most of the defending machines do not even see the enemy. The German bombers are able to penetrate all the way to central London without fighter opposition. It is only as the formation withdraws that it has to deal with some daring but futile attacks by single planes.

The "serpent machine" is one Gotha which does come under fire. Upon hearing a sharp staccato, Lt. Aschoff turns quickly to see a British fighter converging upon him. The German crew returns the fire, crisscrossing the sky with the smoking streaks of phosphorus bullets. With one ammunition drum soon expended, Aschoff fumbles nervously as he tries to reload.

But, suddenly, the fighter goes into a steep turn and the fight is broken off.

The German observer watches with mixed feelings of relief and disappointment as his adversary drops far below. The Gotha crew is left wondering whether their opponent lost heart in the face of concentrated fire, or whether he suffered some crippling hit.

The repulsed attacker may have been a Bristol Fighter from No. 35 Training Squadron. This machine returns to its aerodrome at Northholt with the observer-gunner, Capt. C. H. C. Keevil, sitting dead behind his twin guns. The pilot, Capt. C. W. E. Cole-Hamilton, reports having engaged three straggling Gothas over Ilford. He explains that after Keevil was killed by the bombers' raking fire, his own guns became jammed. There was nothing to do but let the Gothas, now hell-bent for the coast, go their way.

The raiders are relieved indeed, as they leave the sprawling patch of London behind. A cloud of black smoke rising from the city satisfies them that the British have been hurt. But now that the bombs have been dropped, the return flight over an alerted and angry England is all the more perilous.

Flying over airfields, the Gotha crews can see even more fighters rising to take up the pursuit. But it is far too late for the defenders to reach sufficient altitude. Near the coast, the guns throw up a sporadic fire at the escaping bombers with no effect. All safely regain the neutral sea.

Some anxious moments still lie ahead, however, for the wearying Germans. As he scans the skies, the "serpent" Gotha's rear gunner spots another fighter. He excitedly alerts the observer. Lt. Aschoff's heart sinks as he sees a British triplane approaching from the direction of Southend. This fast machine is something to be feared by anyone in a slow, cumbersome bomber, such as the Gotha.

But for all its deadliness, the "Tripe" is apparently flown by an untried pilot. He fails to press the attack, limiting himself to firing a few rounds at long distances. The Gothas leave the halfhearted defender behind to fly on over the North Sea.

The German airmen anxiously measure the distance back to the Continent. After several hours at higher altitudes, time itself becomes blurred. The early morning preparations, the takeoff, all seem to have occurred long ago. In their fatigue, some of the crew members are almost insensitive to the discomforts of being cramped in open, wind-lashed cockpits. Though their bodies shook and tingled at first from sitting between two roaring, vibrating engines, most feel nothing now but a wooden numbness. As for the loud noise, the airmen mercifully hear it no more after its unrelenting pounding on their ears for hour after hour.

As the coast takes shape, tension is replaced by the exhilaration that comes from having met a great challenge successfully. Ahead lies Ostend with its beach and seafront facade of hotels and summer houses. To the crews of the *England-Geschwader* it is a friendly, familiar sight.

On to their right, and extending inland from Allied-held Nieuport, are the flooded lowlands which separate opposing armies along the western front. For the Germans, who had hoped to bomb England from Calais in 1914, the waters were once an unsurmountable barrier. But for the Gotha crews, the inundated area is but an interesting landmark which serves to guide their landfall.

The airfields of Ghent, the tired airmen's secure havens, are reached at last. Buildings and trees loom larger as the "serpent machine" drops down for a landing. The Gotha glides smoothly over the grassy expanse, and finally settles on the ground with a hard bump.

While the plane still taxis, Lt. Aschoff tears off his uncomfortably warm goggles and helmet. Mechanics run joyfully toward the Gotha which they easily recognize as their own because of its gaudy markings. As the machine bounces lightly across the field, the men hold on to its wings until it is safely inside the hangar.

Lt. Aschoff files his report, and hurries to his quarters to change before going to the newly built officers' casino. Food, drink, and good cheer await the Gotha airmen there. Endless toasts will be drunk to their first attack on the English capital. The daring raid will swell German pride and hopes of victory everywhere.

Up and down the front, and to the

war-weary people at home, the official German communique will announce triumphantly, "Today our airmen dropped bombs on the Fort of London . . ."

The aerial battles of World War I produced a group of men who became famous as no military pilots have since. These were the aces, the flyers who shot down five or more enemy aircraft. Each of the warring countries had its list of aces. The top ace of them all was Baron Manfred von Richthofen, the "Red Knight" of Germany, whose 80 victories in aerial combat were never equaled.

Manfred von Richthofen and Moritz, the dog he acquired as a puppy early in the war.

Success in aerial combat required skill and courage. The mortality rate was high. Only the sharp-eyed, the fast thinker, and the expert strategist could hope to survive for long. Von Richthofen was all these things and a talented aerial commander as well. The "Flying Circus" that he organized and led controlled the skies above the western front. Allied airmen had ample reason to fear the gaily painted planes of the Richthofen "Circus."

Very few of the great aces of World War I survived the conflict. The planes they flew offered little protection from the gunfire directed at them by enemy pilots and antiaircraft gunners. This is the story of the last aerial battle of the great German ace, Manfred von Richthofen, and of the man who shot him down, Capt. Roy Brown of Britain's Royal Air Force.

22

The Day They Got Richthofen

Gene Gurney

THE SPRING RAINS had finally stopped and the faint light of dawn poked through the scattering clouds. In the distance the cannonading at the front continued. Capt. Roy Brown of the Royal Air Force slowly rose from his bunk, walked to the window and studied the clearing skies. It was April 21, 1918, and today he would again do battle with the enemy.

Donning his flying togs he walked wearily toward the Officers' Mess for breakfast. He had been in combat for 18 continuous months, and had shot down 12 enemy aircraft. War, then, was not new to this aviator, but at 24 years of age he felt very old, very tired. Each day the pains in his stomach became more intense. "Nervous stomach" they called it: war killing and the constant tension of aerial combat were the harassment of his easy good nature and soft manner. He longed to return to his Canadian home, but he had a job to do and he knew he must stay to finish it. He was a good pilot, a superior marksman, and a leader his men could rely upon.

He forced himself to eat his breakfast, washing it down with the military ration of milk and brandy, a combination which, unknown to Roy Brown, did great damage to his weary stomach. A few of his men had openly noted that Roy was looking thinner,

The leading ace of World War I, Manfred von Richthofen .The medal at his neck is the *Ordre Pour le Mérite*, Germany's highest decoration for gallantry in battle. It was awarded to him when he had won sixteen victories in aerial combat.

but Roy kept to himself the pain that was sapping his strength. He had to hang on for just a while longer.

Twenty-four miles away, on the other side of the bursting shells, the rattling machine guns and the maze of muddy, rain-soaked trenches, another airman rose from his bed to greet the slowly dawning day. Manfred, Baron von Richthofen, leader of the famous German *Jagdstaffel* — the

"Flying Circus" — viewed the clearing skies with anxiety and good cheer. For weeks the spring rains had grounded the flyers, and although it had let up sufficiently the evening before to allow the German ace to down two more Allied planes to bring his total to 80 kills, he still viewed happily the prospect of a bright, clear day. Today, he felt, there would be new glory.

Richthofen was tall, straight, and dashingly handsome in his always correct uniform. His flying prowess was famous throughout the world. He was the Red Knight of the German Empire, and the living symbol of the glory of the Fatherland.

He had slept well that night. The freshness of the dawn and the distant pounding of the guns at the front sent the thrill and excitement of the hunt and the kill surging through his veins. Breakfast was served to him in his room and he ate a regal meal.

The son of a Prussian military man, the young, 25-year-old German ace had made history in his meteoric rise to fame. It was only yesterday that, having reached the fantastic tally of 80 victims for his deadly guns, he had been personally decorated by Kaiser Wilhelm. He was soon to be given the title of *Rittmeister*, Commander in Chief. Not only had he personally destroyed fourscore Allied aircraft, but his brilliant leadership and ingenious aerial tactics had been responsible for the death of hundreds more of the enemy.

Among his many stratagems was the plan he devised to move his squadron quickly from one area at the front to another by loading his planes on railroad flatcars.

Seeing his brightly colored aircraft rolling down the rails on top of the flatcars, the Germans, reminded of a traveling circus, had adopted the nicknames, "Flying Circus" and "Tango Circus," for Richthofen's squadron. His own plane was painted a bright red, the only ship in the German Air Corps to have that distinctive color. The Allies referred to him as the Red Baron.

Richthofen was a remarkable hunter as well as the world's leading combat flyer. The hunt and the kill were always moments of great joy and personal triumph for the baron. He killed in the forest for sport and in the air for glory. For each enemy plane he shot down he ordered an engraved silver loving cup. He piled up his victories so rapidly that the silversmith was still a dozen cups behind when he lost his most valued customer.

The secret of the baron's amazing success was, to no small extent, his ability to single out the inexperienced flyers, pounce upon them and send them crashing to earth. Among his 80 confirmed victories were included 69 green, young lieutenants and five sergeant-pilots. His 80th victim, Second Lt. D. E. Lewis, who lived to tell the story, later wrote of his experience:

"On the evening of April 20, twelve of us left the airdrome on an offensive patrol. . . . The day had been a stormy

24

one, with intermittent squalls, and there were still heavy clouds in the sky when we reached the German lines.

"I was attacking a bright blue machine, which was on a level with me, and was just about to finish this adversary off when I heard the rat-tat-tat of machine guns coming from behind me and saw the splintering of struts above my head.

"I left my man and wheeled quickly to find that I was face to face with the renowned Richthofen. . . . The baron always flew a bright red machine, that is how I knew it was he.

"I twisted and turned in the endeavor to avoid his line of fire, but he was too experienced a fighter, and only once did I manage to have him at a disadvantage, and then only for a few seconds, but in these few ticks of the clock I shot a number of bullets into his machine and thought I would have the honor of bringing him down, but in a trice our positions were reversed and he had set my emergency petrol tank alight, and I was hurtling earthward in flames.

"I hit the ground . . . at a speed of 60 mph, was thrown clear of my machine and except for minor burns, was unhurt."

Richthofen pulled his spotlessly clean flying togs over his blue silk pajamas and walked briskly from his quarters. The three-winged Fokker airplanes were lined up in flawless rows. Called Tripes, the German fighter planes of the Flying Circus had scored impressively against the Allied airmen. Richthofen's own ship, a special gift from the manufacturer, Anthony Fokker, was in perfect condition. Its bright red color stood out even among the other brightly painted ships of the squadron.

At the airplane an orderly handed the Red Baron sealed papers. He tore open the seal and read the contents. They were his battle orders for the day: their mission was to destroy all Allied reconnaissance planes in the sector. The army was preparing for a big push, and the enemy must be denied the valuable information that the darting reconnaissance ships could provide. None must get through!

The baron stuffed the orders in his tunic, and went to the briefing room to see that his men were made aware of their mission for that day.

Just before 10:00 he was back at his plane. From behind the hangar came running his pet hunting dog, Moritz. The large dog made a dash to jump on the bottom wing of the baron's airplane. Richthofen smiled, leaned over and patted the happy animal. One of the mechanics watching this little incident approached the famous ace.

"I beg your pardon, sir," said the man, "but may I take a picture of you and your dog beside the plane? I would be very proud to own such a picture."

The baron nodded.

"Oh, no, sir," cried another mechanic, his face paled with fright, "you mustn't allow a picture. It will bring you bad luck!"

The baron scowled at the man. "Silly superstition," he said, waving to indicate that he was ready for the picture to be taken.

The superstition to which he had referred was one that had existed among the German flyers since Richthofen's good friend, the great German ace, Oswald Boelcke, had allowed himself to be photographed just prior to taking off on what turned out to be his last mission.

The picture was snapped: the last picture ever made of Baron Manfred von Richthofen.

He climbed aboard his Fokker triplane, signaled his squadron, and easing the throttle forward bounced down the soggy field and felt the rush of the wind lift him into the clear blue sky. The time was 10:26.

Twenty-five minutes earlier, from the Bertangles field, Capt. Roy Brown had similarly eased forward the throttle of his cherry-nosed Sopwith Camel. Just prior to takeoff, after briefing his men on the mission that day, he had watched the ground crew roll his airship out of the repair tent and into position on the wet flying field. His stomach still ached and it was without enthusiasm that he signaled his flight of five planes for takeoff and roared across the field into the air. Climbing eastward, 15 Camels headed toward the front — three flights of five with Maj. Charles Butler commanding the lead flight, and Capt. Roy Brown leading the flight on the right. They climbed steadily to 15,000 feet and there leveled out for their scouting back and forth across the enemy lines. They had no oxygen equipment, and at that extreme altitude the exhaust fumes in the open cockpit were causing Brown to suffer severe nausea. He tightened his safety belt and tried to ignore the volcano boiling inside him.

From the German airfield at Douai, Richthofen, leading 15 planes of *Staffel* 5 and *Staffel* 11 — his other squadron — had taken off and joined the formation. The ground crews watched the join-up and the long, steady climb to altitude. The Germans leveled off at 17,000 feet and headed westward to seek out the enemy's reconnaissance planes. The deadly squadron of multicolored hawks soared along the front awaiting their prey.

They did not have to wait long.

Below, two lumbering British RE-8's came chugging along, reconnoitering the German entrenchments in the French village of Hamel. The Red Baron signaled for four Tripes to go down and get them. The Fokker triwinged pursuit planes peeled off with an easy grace and swooped earthward for the unwary scouts.

The baron smiled. Hunting would be good today. When the conditions were just exactly right, he himself would scream down for added glory. He was a superb pilot, but he took no unnecessary chances. He could well afford to wait until the conditions were perfect. But unknown to him there was now less than a half a mile

26

separating him from Capt. Roy Brown and death.

Suddenly the pain in Roy Brown's stomach seemed to relax and his mind snapped clear of the fog that the pain had forced upon it. In that same instant he noted that his flight and the flight on his left had become separated from Maj. Butler's lead flight. He made a three-sixty — a complete circle — but could not spot the other formation. The leader of the left flight looked over at him, and Capt. Brown made a T signal with his hands, advising the other flight to join in behind him. Thus, regrouped, he turned his airmen in toward the front lines.

As he turned he caught in the corner of his eye the flicker of a motion. Looking down he spotted the two RE-8's turning, too late, to escape the German hawks that were screaming down upon them from above. In that same instant he saw several thousand feet above his own group, a bright red Fokker and the distinctive colors of the Flying Circus.

For an instant Brown hesitated, as he eyed the enemy far out and above. He paused, but for a second, for the two RE-8's were in trouble. He signaled his men for a "dive and cover" tactic, and eight cherry-nosed Camels plunged into a 200-mph descent with two ships remaining aloft as cover. The wind whistled through the struts and around the open cockpit. Brown pressed the throttle to the firewall, but he could see that his flight was not going to arrive in time to meet the onrushing Germans.

The two British scouts twisted and turned to avoid the German pursuits, but it appeared that the Germans would arrive well ahead of the racing R.A.F. fighters.

Watching from below, the Australian antiaircraft batteries were not unmindful of the drama that was taking place above them. The "Archies" threw up a murderous barrage at the four incoming Tripes. The Germans heeled over quickly to dodge the sudden volley from below, and in that priceless moment of time the British scouts were able to make a quick, last-minute break for the safety of their own lines.

From above Richthofen watched gloomily the unsuccessful attack below. His orders were that no British reconnaissance ships were to return to their bases with information. He held up his arm and signaling his men, he sent down his entire outfit — Fokkers and Albatroses — to crush the stubborn enemy.

Flying with Capt. Roy Brown, as a wingman for one of the veteran pilots of Brown's command, was Lt. Wilfred R. May. This was May's first flight over the front lines, and Brown had made clear his orders: "Stay out of the dogfights"; "Combat only a stray or inexperienced or wounded plane"; "Concentrate more on formation flying than visual scouting." Brown had been most emphatic in his order. More young flyers on their first mission were lost in air collisions with brother

27

planes than in combat. Lt. May, like all new pilots, had much to learn, and Brown wanted him to take his lessons in easy stages, lest there be but a single lesson.

Lt. May was in the flight behind Brown when they streaked down upon the enemy.

Meanwhile the four Fokkers had been so anxious to flame the two British scouts that without noticing they had slid past their own lines and into Allied territory. Brown noticed their frantic efforts to reach the British planes, and he realized that today the enemy was not interested in the usual air duel, but was out for a purpose: to stop Allied aerial intelligence. Something big must be in the wind.

Looking around for the two RE-8's, he saw them returning once again to the German lines. The Fokkers banked in toward the scouts. Brown and his flight had now made the distance into position to meet the enemy fighters, and immediately engaged them. The Fokkers turned with the Camels and tried to get by them to the safety of their own lines. Outnumbered, the Germans were cut off in enemy territory. The whine of the engines and the chatter of machine guns filled the morning air.

Lt. May, falling back from the fight, dropped lower and lower. A single Fokker shook loose and, slipping toward the deck, scooted for safety. May saw the enemy. The temptation was too great and the setup too perfect. His orders said that he could do com-

bat with a single ship. Down he went toward the German. He held forward pressure on the stick in a steady dive to a converging point just ahead of the enemy plane. The Tripe came into his sights. May squeezed his trigger. One short burst. The plane exploded in a ball of flame and spun crazily toward the earth. His first kill.

Brown had instructed him: "If you get your first kill, hard-rudder and fire-wall it for home, and that is an order!" Lt. May, elated at his victory, racked his plane upon a wing and horsed back on the stick, bending around toward home. He opened full throttle and scurried across the tree-tops for his home field.

The big dogfight continued with renewed fury with the arrival of the main body of the German fighters. The air was filled with twisting, turning, diving planes. Lt. F. J. W. Mellersh pegged a blue-tailed triplane. Mackensie flamed a red-tailed Fokker and Taylor snuggled up behind another tri-winged enemy and laced it with a fatal flurry of lead. A German scored on Mackensie who, fighting his half-shot-away controls, headed down toward the British lines. Planes were going down all over. In the mad tangle of the battle there was no way to tell which side held the advantage.

Capt. Roy Brown had two Fokkers on his tail firing lethal bursts at him. He headed for the deck, slipping and skidding as he went. He bottomed-out just above the trees, and the two ships pressed in. Horsing back on the stick, he felt his plane fall over on a wing and begin to spin. The Germans did not care to follow. Kicking opposite rudder and pepping his stick forward he broke the spin just above the trees and leveled out.

At that instant he caught sight of Lt. May heading for home. To his right he saw the unmistakable bright red Tripe of the Allies' most feared enemy. His heart jumped into his throat. The Red Baron was rapidly bearing down upon young Lt. May. Brown pressed his throttle forward as far as he could and started a climb toward that invisible junction where the world's greatest living ace would bring quick death to the inexperienced boy.

Brown could feel pain gripping his stomach as he urged his ship to greater speed. The baron's plane seemed almost to have dropped from nowhere.

At better than 200 mph the Red Knight of Germany bore down upon the unsuspecting May. A few minutes earlier the baron had been at altitude with his flight commanders, surveying the battle. His job was to get the reconnaissance planes and safeguard the German movements for the "big push," but the temptation of the lone ship had been too great. He could tell from the way that the pilot handled his Camel that inside the cockpit was a green flyer. This would be quick. One pass, a flaming wreck, and then a steep, climbing turn back to altitude to wait and watch for more single wrens.

Brown had reached 2,000 feet and was closing on May and Richthofen, but he might be too late. Richthofen slid into position behind and slightly above May's Camel. He fired one short burst. The slugs struck May's engine cowling and snapped several wing struts. The surprised May kicked left rudder and side slipped. His startled face looked back, and turned an ashen white as he stared into the cold, steady eyes of the Red Baron of Germany. The "Red Death" seemed almost in the cockpit with him; and it appeared that no human force could turn aside the inevitable doom that awaited him from inside the dark guns. The twin Spandaus spit fire and a short burst of German lead tore into the cockpit. In an instant his right arm was ripped with pain, and blood oozed down his sleeve.

Richthofen slowed his plane to stay on May's tail and to steady his flying platform for a better shot at the doomed aviator.

Brown, his engine straining on its mounts, had reached 5,000 feet, and was now closer to the two airmen. He could see the baron drawing a final bead on the young May. Brown touched his right rudder slightly and added a breath of forward pressure on the stick. Nausea crept over him as the Red Baron slid into his sights. Brown was an experienced aerial gunner and he knew that he was still too far out for accuracy. If he waited just a few seconds more he would close the 1,000 feet that separated him from his enemy, and Germany's most valued flyer would be a certain victim of his guns. But he could not wait. A second's pause and Richthofen would claim his 81st victim. He must swat at the fly to drive him off. He squeezed his trigger. A sharp pain shot through his stomach and he fought off an almost overwhelming dizziness. The tracers struck the tail of the baron's red Fokker. Bullet holes began to march down the fabric. Richthofen jerked his head around in amazement. It all happened in the smallest fraction of a second, but in that time Richthofen had full cognizance of what was taking place. He turned forward to give May one more quick burst before breaking hard over to roll away from the intrusive Capt. Brown. Brown added the faintest pressure to his control stick and the bullets continued in their solemn procession along the baron's fuselage — in a broken, uneven stitch across the cockpit. A bullet struck home and Richthofen slumped forward as Brown's Camel swept past. The bright red Tripe nosed over and dove straight for the ground. The Aussies who had been firing at the Red Baron as he closed on May's Camel, suddenly ceased their fire. All eyes turned toward the earthward-twisting red Tripe. At 50 feet the German ship broke its sharp descent, made a last, futile half sweep, and dropped suddenly to the turf. It hit hard, bounced and stopped.

It was little more than an hour after his takeoff that Capt. Roy Brown was sitting in the briefing shack signing his name to one of the most important combat reports of World War I. Maj. Butler, who had certified Brown's report, picked it up and read it once again:

Date: April 21, 1918
Time: 10:45 A.M.
Place: 62D, 2. (Map designation)
Duty: High Offense Patrols
Altitude: 5,000 feet
Engagement with red triplane
Locality: Vaux sur Somme.
Fokker triplane, pure red wings with black crosses

(1) At 10:35 I observed two Albatroses burst into flames and crash.

(2) Dived on large formation of 15 to 20 Albatros scouts, D-5's and Fokker triplanes, two of which got on my tail, and I came out.

(3) Went back again and dived on pure red triplane which was firing upon Lt. May. I got a long burst into him, and he went down vertically and was observed to crash by Lt. Mellersh and Lt. May. I fired on two more but did not get them.

Signed: A. R. Brown, Capt.
Certified: C. H. Butler, Maj.
209th RAF

Back at the scene of the crashed triplane, Lt. Mellersh, who earlier in the battle had been forced down near the very same spot, was on hand to join the Australian gunners as they retrieved the wreck. The occupant was removed from the downed Fokker, and laid out on the ground. A single bullet had entered his right side and had come out the left.

Mellersh opened the dead pilot's tunic and removed his papers and identification cards. Reading them, he turned toward the anxiously waiting Aussies, and nodded his head.

"Blimey," whispered one, " 'E gawt the bloody Baron!"

When the word reached Brown that the death of Baron von Richthofen had been confirmed, he sank into a half stupor as he finally allowed himself to realize the significance of his victory. He gave in a little to the abdominal seizures which he had been fighting off since his landing. The pain seemed to swell up in him, and at last he realized that the job he had really come to do was done. The war was over for him now — he had flown his last combat mission.

The doctors finally insisted that Roy Brown return to his home. Their diagnosis: advanced ulcers. And so the quiet unassuming, unpretentious Canadian, who had stayed in combat long enough to score the most important single victory in the Great War, returned once again to the peace and quiet of the Canadian country that he loved. But as long as he lived, he was always known as the man who downed the Red Knight.

Brigadier General William Mitchell, who won fame as an air commander during World War I. After the war his aggressive campaign for a strong United States air arm made him a center of controversy and led to his court-martial in 1925. He resigned from the service and as a civilian continued his fight for air power until his death in 1936.

When the United States entered World War I in April, 1917, William Mitchell, the man who was to become the outstanding commander of its Air Service, was in Spain. He went at once to France to study Allied air operations. The result was a series of plans and reports that had much to do with the development and organization of United States air power. One of Mitchell's recommendations was that two types of combat aviation should go into action — one to directly support ground troops and the other to attack the enemy in his own territory.

The United States Air Service developed slowly during 1917 because pilots had to be trained and planes procured. It was not until the spring of 1918 that the first American squadrons were ready for combat.

In August, 1918, William Mitchell was named commander of all the American air units at the front. He was also given command of a number of French squadrons. The Allies were preparing an attack on St.-Mihiel where the German lines bent deep into Allied territory. Col. Mitchell was in charge of the air phase of the operation. When the attack began on September 12, he had at his disposal the largest air force that had ever been assembled. It numbered almost 1,500 planes.

In the battle of St.-Mihiel Mitchell demonstrated that his theories about combat aviation were sound ones. He used one-third of his force to support ground troops. The rest attacked targets behind the German lines. The Germans were placed on the defensive and their losses were heavy.

Here is Mitchell's own account of the air operation he directed at St.-Mihiel. It proved beyond a doubt that battles could be won or lost in the air.

The Great Attack on St.-Mihiel

Brig. Gen. William Mitchell

SEPTEMBER 1, 1918 saw my headquarters permanently organized and a force of 1,476 airplanes and 20 balloons, under my command, concentrating to join battle with the Germans.

Thirty thousand officers and men handled the airplanes. They were disposed on 14 main flying fields and a great many substations, while three large supply points handled the materiel for the Americans, French, British, and Italians. It was the greatest concentration of air power that had ever taken place and the first time in history in which an air force, cooperating with an army, was to act according to a broad strategical plan which contemplated not only facilitating the advance of the ground troops but spreading fear and consternation into the enemy's line of communications, his replacement system, and the cities behind them which supplied our foe with the sinews of war.

In addition to the American, French, and British units, I had some squadrons of Italian bombardment aviation, who did all they could in their sphere. Here we were, a force of four nations, acting together with no discord, misunderstanding, jealousy or attempt to shrink or escape the maximum duty or losses which may be required. Such a thing could not have occurred with ground troops. I say this because the game on the ground is such an old one, and the element of novelty and development has ceased to exist in it. In aviation, there is an entirely different feeling between the persons engaged in it. It is an extremely dangerous and hazardous occupation and every man who is a real pilot is looked up to and appreciated by his fellows.

Most of the officers on our general staff, with a few marked exceptions, had no appreciation of what this great air force meant. Not a single one, however, except Maj. Bowditch, had shown any inclination to go up in the air and see what was going on. Just think of such a thing! Here was a great military operation about to be undertaken, the success or failure of which meant everything to American arms. A tour in the air by the commanding general or the chief of staff would have given them an insight into the positions and locations of the enemy and our own troops which could have been obtained in no other way. I could have taken them myself and protected them so that there would have been 99 chances out of 100 of their getting back unscathed (even if they did get killed, there were plenty of people to step into their shoes); but out of all this group only one chose to go up in the air.

There are a great many points of difference between the management of an air force and that of an army or navy. An air force operates in a new medium, the air, which offers a wider scope for action than either land or water. They must be communicated with through the air, that is, by radio or visual signals. When air forces are committed to a combat they cannot be withdrawn and redisposed ordinarily, but must come back to the airdromes to refuel and replenish before renewing the fight. Air forces cannot dig holes in the air and get into them where the enemy will not see them, and where they may sit in safety and comfort. The premium of successful combat is shooting down the enemy and the forfeit when unsuccessful is to go hurtling to earth in a flaming coffin. Air forces are the eyes of the army, and without their accurate reports, ground forces cannot operate.

We had three tasks to accomplish: first, to provide accurate information for the infantry and adjustment of fire for the artillery of the ground troops;

second, to hold off the enemy air forces from interfering with either our air or ground troops; and third, to bomb the b ck areas so as to stop the supplies for the enemy and hold up any movement along his roads.

The shape of the St.-Mihiel salient furnished an interesting situation. It projected into our line in the shape of a horseshoe, rather a sharp one at the toe, the point of which was located at the city of St.-Mihiel. The Germans pushed in here in 1915 and occupied it in an attempt to surround Verdun.

It must be remembered that the most direct line of advance from Germany into France is through Koblenz, Treves, Verdun, Nancy and then straight toward Lyons, where the centers of population and factories of France are located. Conversely, if we could advance into Germany by way of Treves and Koblenz, we would have the shortest line through this great gateway into the country of the Teutons. Now our American Army, acting under its own chiefs and holding its own sector of the line, was charged with the duty of advancing into the Treves gap, and by pushing on, to threaten this great open portal into Germany.

Our line at most places was more or less straight and the Air Service acted out from it more or less homogeneously all along the front. Now we were attacking a salient, so I intended to change the ordinary procedure and employ massed air attacks against the vital points in the enemy's rear. In this case, we could hit first from one side of the salient, then from the other, just as a boxer gives a right hook and a left hook successively to his opponent.

In the present case, I would have a preponderance in the air for at least two days before the Germans could concentrate. I had therefore issued orders to the French Air Division that they would attack entirely by brigades, nothing smaller. There were two brigades of about 400 airplanes each in the division. One brigade would habitually attack twice a day on the right of the salient, entering it from west of Pont-a-Mousson. The bombardment would attack Vigneulles, Conflans, and Briey.

At the time their gas was beginning to run out, the second brigade of the Air Division would attack the same places from the left of the salient, crossing the lines in the vicinity of Genicourt and Fort Haudainville. In this way, while the Germans were resisting and fighting one of our brigades, I would catch them in the rear with the other brigade. I would time it so there would be sufficient gas left in the airplanes of the first brigade for them to continue the combat for about 30 minutes after the second arrived.

Nothing like this had ever been tried before. It marked the beginning of the great strategical air operations away from the troops.

Our own observation squadrons were assigned definitely to the troops on the ground. For their local protection at low altitude, we had our own

American 1st Pursuit Group, under Maj. Harold E. Hartney. I considered this group the peer of any fighting organization on the front.

Our bombardment wing, consisting of the 2nd and 3rd Pursuit Groups, with the bombardment group, would act out from the head of the salient and attack Vigneulles. We had done everything we could with this new bombardment organization but they had not yet had the experience required to make them proficient.

Our bombardment group was not in good condition. It was poorly commanded, the morale was weak and it would take some time to get it on its feet. This was largely due to the fact that when I was away in Chateau-Thierry, the 96th Squadron was left behind in the Toul area. The major who was then in command of the 96th flew over into Germany with what ships he had available for duty. He lost his way in the fog and landed in Germany with every ship intact. Not one single ship was burned or destroyed and the Germans captured the whole outfit complete. This was the most glaring exhibition of worthlessness we had on the front. The Germans sent back a humorous message which was dropped on one of our airdromes. It said, "We thank you for the fine airplanes and equipment which you have sent us, but what shall we do with the major?"

I know of no other performance in any air force in the war that was as reprehensible as this. Needless to say, we did not reply about the major, as he was better off in Germany at that time than he would have been with us.

The day for the attack drew near. Maj. I. B. Joralemon had done wonderful work in locating our great air host, preparing its airdromes and getting its supplies. Col. DeWitt, G-4 of the General Staff, had helped us to the limit. On September 7, the French Air Division reported and took its place.

We moved the air forces into their airdromes with the greatest secrecy possible so as not to let the Germans know how many airplanes we were assembling. We were careful not to make too great a display over the front; but on the other hand, we kept our pursuit patrols working up as high as they could go, about 20,000 feet, so as to prevent German reconnaissance.

In our advance airdromes for the observation groups, such as at Souilly, I had camouflage or fake hangars constructed with fake airplanes in front, so that if the Germans took pictures of them, it would look as if a certain number of aircraft were there. Each day I had the position of these camouflage airplanes changed so as to make it look as if the place were active.

I issued orders to the 88th Squadron, among others, which was commanded by Maj. Christy, to occupy the airdrome at Souilly. They were to come up from Luxeuil, near Belfort, and arrive just before dark, so as to put their airplanes into the hangars immediately and in this way escape observation from the enemy. During the night of September 9, I had real hangars put up exactly where the camouflage hangars had been. This same system had been followed on the other airdromes. In every other case, the organizations, flying low, arrived just before dark and immediately hid themselves. Christy, however, apparently did not get the spirit of the order. He arrived with his squadron in broad daylight, leading it himself, lined it up on the airdrome, then took his own ship with the best observer and actually made a reconnaissance away over Metz and got away with it. He was lucky not to have been killed but it disclosed our whole position at Souilly. The enemy then knew exactly what was there. It was a very brave act but absolutely the wrong thing to do. I told Christy what I thought of it. (Christy never did anything like that again; in fact, he developed into one of the best commanders that we had on the front.)

September 12 had been decided upon as the day of our grand attack. It was the greatest army ever assembled under the American flag; facing the enemy were 400,000 men with over 3,000 cannon. Our air force consisted of nearly 1,500 airplanes.

Of course the Germans knew that we were going to attack them in the St.-Mihiel salient. Their power of offensive and initiative passed after the battle at Soissons. St.-Mihiel was a dangerous place for them to hold; in fact, they could not; all they could do was to delay our operations. They therefore had no intention of holding it and had put in, in addition to a few of their first-line organizations, a lot of second-line troops and Austrians, in which were included many Hungarian regiments.

In my personal reconnaissance with Maj. Armengaud over the lines on September 10, I had noticed considerable movement to the rear which indicated that the Germans were withdrawing from the St.-Mihiel salient. To my surprise and consternation I found at the meeting of General Pershing's staff on the evening before the attack that our chief engineer recommended that we delay the attack because there had been considerable rain. This, he said, held up our light railways used for getting up artillery ammunition. The question of adequate water for some of the troops would be difficult, and a thousand and one things which could not be done were mentioned. I was surprised to see that several of the old fossils there agreed with this foolish view. You can always trust an engineer officer to go on the defensive wherever it is possible. I was the junior member of the staff and when it got to me for my opinion, I told them very plainly that I knew the Germans were withdrawing from the St.-Mihiel salient as I had seen them personally, that our troops were now in position for the attack and were keyed up to it; furthermore, I said, there was not going to be much of a battle at St.-Mihiel anyway, and our troops might be better off without artillery, as they would probably shoot a good many of our own men anyway; and all we had to do was to jump on the Germans, and the quicker we did it, the better.

General Pershing smiled, and ordered that we attack.

On September 11 I assembled the officers from every major organization of the Air Service within our great force — British, French, Italians, and Americans. I read them the orders myself and asked each one individually what he could do to comply with them. Each one went back to his organization thoroughly conversant with what he was to do for each day of the attack.

The morning of September 12 dawned dark and cloudy, with intermittent rain. Clouds hung low and the visibility was very poor. Nevertheless, our Air Service with that of the Allies went over the lines, and I was much pleased with the fact that virtually no German airplanes got over our ground troops.

We forced the German airmen to fight away back of Vigneulles and Conflans, 30 miles away from our ground troops. We had many combats at these places during the day.

On September 13, we could see that the enemy was concentrating all his available air power against us because he was losing too many prisoners. The Germans did not care whether we took the St.-Mihiel salient or not, as they knew they were incapable of taking the offensive in the Verdun and Metz areas, but they did not want to lose a lot of prisoners and equipment. Our air force, however, by attacking their transportation trains, railroads and columns on the roads, piled them up with debris so that it was impossible for many of their troops to get away quickly, resulting in their capture by our infantry. We had forced them to measure strength with us in the air with their main forces, and if they did not come and attack us, we intended to destroy Metz, Conflans, Diedenhofen, and even Treves.

The British, under Gen. Trenchard, tore into their airdromes, smashed up their hangars and forced them to fight at all points. An airman may stay on the ground if he wants to and let the other fellow go ahead, but if the other fellow starts blowing up everything, he will have to get up in the air and fight him, or allow complete destruction. We were constantly forcing them to fight in the air; of course, it was a walkover on the ground for the army.

By September 14, the German air service began to appear in great numbers and we had a tremendous number of combats. There was one fight which I wish to mention particularly, because it illustrates the terrific destructive power of pursuit aviation when acting against bombardment aviation.

On September 14, one of our bombardment squadrons, belonging to a French group, failed to meet the pursuit aviation detailed to protect it, on account of poor visibility in cloudy weather. Nevertheless it proceeded in the direction ordered, to bombard the objective. There were 18 airplanes in the squadron, 15 being two-seaters and three being three-seaters. The three-seaters were equipped with six guns each, and, as far as volume of gunfire was concerned, were the most powerful airplanes on the western front. They were unable to maneuver as rapidly as the single-seaters, however, and therefore did not fulfill the ideas of their originators who thought that through volume of fire alone they could defend themselves against small, highly maneuverable single-seaters. The three-seaters were supposed to be for the protection of the two-seaters; that is, these powerfully gunned airplanes were expected to fight off the enemy pursuit while the bombers concentrated their whole attention on dropping their bombs on the targets.

The squadron flew in a V formation, like a flock of ducks. One of the great three-seaters was on each flank and one in the opening behind. When this squadron crossed the line on the way to its objective, it was passed by a patrol of 12 German pursuit airplanes flying one behind the other, about 500 meters above it. The German patrol deployed in line formation behind the bombardment squadron. Four of the enemy planes attacked the three-seater which was behind and sent it down in flames. The other eight kept up a long-range fire at the squadron so as to derange its aim while dropping its bombs on the city of Conflans. At the same time, antiaircraft artillery opened fire at the vanguard of the squadron while the German pursuit ships attacked the rear. While antiaircraft guns failed to hit any of the airplanes, their bursting shells allowed the German pursuit organizations, which were now concentrating for an attack on the squadron, to see where they were. During this time, the commander of the bombardment squadron noticed German airplanes rising from Mars-la-Tour, the airdrome close to Conflans.

All the bombs were dropped on the objective and the return flight was started to our lines. Just as the turn was made, a fresh enemy pursuit squadron joined the former, immediately deployed and attacked the rearmost plane and shot the observer through the leg. He continued to battle, however, and hit one enemy plane which fell in flames. The formation was now well on its way back when a third enemy squadron attacked ours in front and to the left. The bombing squadron was now being attacked in three dimensions, from underneath, above, and on the same level.

The great lumbering bombing machines huddled together as a flight of geese might when attacked by falcons. The pursuit planes dived at them from all directions, firing their machine guns, then zooming up in the air or turning over on their backs at a speed of about 200 mph, taking an erratic course to avoid the fire of the big ships and then resuming their position for attack again.

By this time the big three-seater protection plane on the left had been shot in one of its engines and started slipping down. Immediately when it left the formation, it was jumped on by three German machines. In a moment, it was shot to pieces and disappeared in flames. The fighting had now become terrific. More German machines were constantly joining their comrades. The signals made by the artillery projectiles bursting in the air and the radio on the ground told the German aviators that our bombardment squadron had no pursuit protection and was an easy victim. The attacks of the German pursuit ships were carried on up to within 50 feet of the bombardment planes.

The next airplane to be hit was No. 13; a two-seater, which caught fire and dropped its movable gasoline tank. It dived at a sharp angle, turned over on its back about 200 meters below the squadron, lost its left wing and then crashed to the ground.

At this same moment a German pursuit ship was shot down, on fire. No. 2 bombardment airplane was hit in the gasoline tank in the upper wing and caught fire; but the machine, flaming like a torch, kept its position in the formation. The machine gunner was magnificent in his courage, fighting the hostile airplanes while the flames slowly crept up around him. The plane continued to fly for about 200 meters, leaving behind it a trail of fire about twice as long as the ship itself. Pilot and observer by this time were consumed and the airplane dived

to its doom.

At about that time a German Fokker plane, diving vertically with its engine full on, lost both its wings. Now the whole right wing of the squadron had been shot down and a rearrangement of formation was made so as to get the remaining machines into V formation again. Machines Nos. 9 and 14 were then both hit at the same time, No. 14 catching fire. The pilot of No. 14 stretched out his arms toward the sky, and, waving his hand and saying farewell to the remainder of the squadron, went to eternity. No. 9 machine disappeared and, as it did, an additional German pursuit machine retired from the combat, crippled. No. 15 machine was now having a hard time keeping up with the formation. Its gasoline tank had been perforated by bullets, its aileron control cut and its rudder hit. However, it kept up.

By this time the squadron had come back to our lines and was joined and protected by our pursuit aviation. The combat in its intensity lasted for 40 minutes, and of 18 airplanes which had constituted the squadron, only five remained. Most of the crews were wounded and their planes perforated in all parts by bullets. They had never once broken their formation or failed to obey the orders of their leader. They furnished an example of military precision and bravery which is required of all airmen.

General Pershing was tremendously pleased with our operations at St.-

Mihiel. He told me that we had been the eyes of the army and led it on to victory. He wrote me the following letter:

AMERICAN EXPEDITIONARY
FORCES
Office of the Commander-in-Chief
France, Sept. 1, 1918.
Col. William Mitchell,
  Chief of Air Service, First Army,
  A.E.F., France.
My dear Colonel —
  Please accept my sincere congratulations on the successful and very important part taken by the Air Force under your command in the first offensive of the First American Army. The organization and control of the tremendous concentration of air forces, including American, French, British, and Italian units, which has enabled the Air Service of the First Army to carry out so successfully its dangerous and important mission, is as fine a tribute to you personally as is the courage and nerve shown by your officers a signal proof of the high morale which permeates the service under your command.
  Please convey to your command my heartfelt appreciation of their work. I am proud of you all.
                    Sincerely yours,
                    JOHN J. PERSHING

PART TWO

INTERLUDE IN SPAIN: THE CIVIL WAR

Introduction

WHEN WORLD WAR I ended it was apparent that the airplane would be used in any future conflict. The only question not completely answered was how it could be used to the greatest advantage. The 1920's and 1930's were years of rapid aeronautical development. In every country theories about aerial combat had to be revised over and over again to keep pace with the growing potential of the airplane.

In 1936 a civil war that broke out in Spain provided three countries with an opportunity to test new warplanes in actual combat. The Soviet Union sent planes and pilots to Spain to help the government, or Loyalist, forces. Germany and Italy sent similar help to Gen. Franco's Insurgents.

Most other nations remained neutral during the struggle in Spain, but some of their citizens enlisted in international brigades to fight with the Loyalists against Gen. Franco. One of these volunteers was Capt. Derek Dickinson, an American pilot who fought an aerial duel with Bruno Mussolini, the son of the Italian dictator.

Bruno Mussolini receives a decoration from his father, the Italian dictator, for his services during the Spanish Civil War.

My Air Duel with Bruno Mussolini

Capt. Derek D. Dickinson

as told to Edwin C. Parsons

For more years than I like to recall I have made war aviation my profession and have naturally been near death many times. But I never came closer than on the day I fought a pre-arranged air duel with Mussolini's oldest son.

For 16 months I was a pilot for the Loyalist forces in Spain, the last ten months as captain in command of the Esquadrilla Alas Rojas (Red Wings) stationed at Castellón de la Plana. Opposing us at Palma de Majorca was a strong detachment of enemy planes under Bruno Mussolini. It was late August, 1937.

One night my superior, Col. de los Reyes, brought me the news that a challenge had come via Insurgent headquarters radio from Bruno himself, offering to meet any five Loyalist planes in single combat. Probably Bruno never expected anything to come of it and was just hoping to build up morale in his own force.

I exploded. "Colonel, he can't get away with that! Get a message back. Tell him he doesn't need to fight five planes. I'll accept his challenge."

The message was sent. Impatiently we waited a week, two weeks, repeating the message frequently. There was only silence from the Insurgent side. We might have given up, but American newspaper men egged us on to continue sending the messages and, I believe, sent goading messages of their own.

Still there was silence, and it was not until 30 days had passed that the answer came, in substance about like this:

I will accept the offer of the American Capt. Dickinson and will meet him in single combat at noon, September 28, midway between our two airfields at an altitude of 15,000 feet. I will bring two observation planes that will remain at least 1,000 feet above us and will under no circumstances take any part in the combat. I shall expect Capt. Dickinson to bring two observers who will follow the same procedure. As soon as we sight each other at the designated point, we will make a complete circle followed by an Immelmann turn which will be the signal to begin combat. Should I become incapacitated and wish to acknowledge defeat, I will throw over my glove attached to my scarf as a signal of surrender. I expect Capt. Dickinson to do the same.

BRUNO MUSSOLINI

(The scarf referred to was of silk, over six feet long and three feet wide. Attached to an object the weight of a

47

gauntlet glove, it would spread out like a parachute, easily visible in the air.)

I made no special preparations for the combat, except to see that I had a full load of ammunition for my four-barreled Vickers guns (synchronized with the propeller) and the two electrically operated wing guns. I was flying a Mosca monoplane, the Russian-built copy of the Boeing P-26 with a 1,050-hp Wright motor.

The two observation planes left the field about 15 minutes before I did. In them were four of my closest comrades from the Esquadrilla. They had strict orders to act merely as witnesses to our combat.

The next quarter hour was the hardest. But finally I shoved off and streaked for the rendezvous.

I had covered nearly half the distance toward Palma de Majorca when I spotted four ships well above me, two by two, making fairly tight circles.

I hit the rendezvous exactly at noon; simultaneously from the direction of the enemy's stronghold a tiny, black speck drew near. It was Bruno Mussolini, flying a Fiat Romeo monoplane with a 1,300-hp Hispano-Suiza motor (which gave him a 250-hp advantage over me).

We both made a wide circle and an Immelmann, as agreed, and then headed directly for each other in a tremendous surge of speed. I saw flames belch from his motor guns and, above the roar of my motor and the hammering of my own guns, I heard the shrill whine of lead past my ears and sensed rather than felt the dull thud as bullets ripped through the wings and spars of my ship. The duel came within inches of finishing then and there. Neither of us would give way, and a collision seemed inevitable.

At the last split second, our wings almost touching, we both pulled into a half loop-and-roll so close that I could distinguish every feature of Mussolini's face. My breath let go with a whoosh at the narrowness of the escape. Then standing on wings tips in the tightness of our banks, we whipped back into the struggle.

The next 15 minutes are still a nightmare. I can hardly recall any single voluntary action — it all happened so fast. Instinctively I pulled every acrobatic maneuver I knew. But for every one I pulled, Mussolini had one as good or better. His additional horsepower gave him just that added surge of speed at the right second that was so important.

My plane was vibrating terribly, for the Russian engineers had failed to provide additional bracing to compensate for the added weight and horsepower on a ship designed for a much lighter engine. It affected my aim. Frequently when I thought I had him at point-blank, I found I was firing into empty space.

Up and down, around and around we zoomed, dived, looped, and rolled, one second on our backs, the next standing on our heads, slicing in and out at a speed that drained the blood

48

The I-16 fighter which the Soviet Union tried out during the Spanish Civil War was the first low-wing monoplane with retractable landing gear to go into combat. It was called *Mosca* (Fly) by the men who flew it in Spain and *Rata* (Rat) by the Insurgents. Captain Derek Dickinson was in an I-16 when he fought his aerial duel with Bruno Mussolini.

from arms and legs. The pounding of air against my body was like a continuous beating from a rubber hose. The roar of the motor and constant hammering of machine guns crashed against my brain till I actually shrank from the sound.

Never again do I expect to be sprayed by so many bullets and escape alive. I was hosing lead at him at every opportunity, for his guns worked unceasingly. Down and down we fought — fourteen, eleven, eight thousand feet.

Meantime, above us, the observation planes circled and spiraled, watching for the climax, at no time making any attempt to take part.

Suddenly, in the middle of a particularly wicked burst from Bruno, I felt a searing pain shoot up my left arm. Blood sprouted from a nasty gash on my hand. Momentarily stunned, I pulled out in a full power dive. It was an almost fatal error. Bruno was on my tail like a flash, pouring lead.

I pulled the old skid trick, leveling off, retarding my motor, at the same time giving full left aileron and full right rudder. Crabbing through the air, I slowed as if I had hydraulic brakes.

Mussolini, at full speed, was on and past me. As he passed, I had a chance to give him a full blast. Some of my bullets must have gone home, for I could swear that I saw his ship quiver from the shock. If I actually wounded him, tearing his leg muscles as we heard afterward (although we were never able to authenticate this), I imagine it was then. But in a second he was back, and we were at it again.

Five thousand, four, three. Eighteen minutes, then twenty, of combat and the devil's tatoo of barking guns continued.

Then my toes curled and my stomach became a vacuum. I felt the blow as a slug crashed through the instrument board, leaving a shambles of dangling springs and tubes. Splintered glass from the shattered instruments struck back into my face. I thought all was over.

I resolved to take a last desperate chance, but I also began to unwrap the white scarf from my neck. If I failed I would have to surrender.

I pulled up as if starting a loop, then went into a hammerhead stall, half rolled, and came out on my back. I expected to get it in the stall, for in that brief instant I was a broadside target almost impossible to miss. I tried to squeeze my body into the smallest possible space, in anticipation of the mushrooming slug that would tear me to shreds. But it failed to arrive.

As I came out on my back, I found my gamble had been successful. Mussolini's ship was full in my guns as big as a house. This time I wouldn't fail to get him. My fingers were just closing down on the trips of my guns when my heart leaped. I saw my enemy's arm go up and a dark object hurtle over the side, followed by a fanlike white tail which blossomed out as it slowly sank. The scarf and glove!

I'm glad he didn't know how close I was to doing the same thing.

As I rolled up into level flight, he waved his arm, dipped the nose of his plane in salute, and sliced off for his field. Completely spent, I pointed my nose for Castellón de la Plana.

We had fought 22 minutes. I had gotten off with only a flesh wound, for which I was thankful, considering the 326 separate bullet holes that my mechanics counted in my ship. I hadn't brought Bruno down, but he was subsequently removed from command of the Palma de Majorca air forces.

PART THREE

GREAT AIR BATTLES OF
WORLD WAR II: EUROPE

Introduction

THE COMBAT PLANE, which was in its infancy during World War I, reached a remarkable state of development during World War II as did the strategic use of air power to attack the enemy far behind the battle lines. In Europe alone, 2,700,000 tons of bombs were dropped by the American and British air forces. Germany's principal cities were reduced to rubble; an estimated 3,600,000 dwelling units were destroyed or damaged; 300,000 people were killed and another 780,000 wounded. The industry that Germany needed to keep her army fighting and her air force in the air was paralyzed making it impossible for her to continue the war. To produce this result Allied bombers flew 1,440,000 sorties and Allied fighters 2,680,000 sorties.

The air action of World War II began with the whine of Stuka dive bombers over Poland on the morning of September 1, 1939, and after that there never was any doubt about the use that would be made of air power. The planes of the Luftwaffe appeared again over Norway, the Lowlands, and France to underline the fact that the side that controlled the air won the

battle on the ground. The English had learned this lesson well as was proved during the Battle of Britain when they refused to give up control of the air over their island. The result was a defeat for Hitler, his first, but it was to be followed by others.

Gradually, as the strength of the Royal Air Force increased and men and planes arrived from the United States, the Allies began to make their bid for control of the skies over continental Europe. Like the air battles that were fought when Germany was on the march, the battles that resulted from the increasingly frequent appearance of British and American planes over German targets were fierce and often deadly. In addition to attacks on Germany itself, allied airmen were able to knock out enemy positions in Italy and in France to prepare the way for invasion. Then they provided the protection necessary to make the invasions successful.

Air power alone could not have defeated Germany, but the men who did their fighting in the skies above North Africa and Europe made Allied victory certain.

Malta is a British colony consisting of three small islands in the Mediterranean Sea about 60 miles south of Sicily. Prior to World War II it was an important British naval base. The Mediterranean Fleet had been shifted to the more easily defended port of Alexandria, but the British hoped to use strategically located Malta as a base for staging, reconnaissance, and repair activities.

When Italy entered the war the future of Malta was in grave doubt. It was only a few minutes' flight from Italy and the British had been unable to build up its defenses. It seemed likely that Malta would have to be sacrificed to the Italian air force.

Three Against an Air Force

Kenneth Poolman

THE DAY STILL had sleep in its eyes when the sirens howled on Malta. The Italians had timed their first raid well. They had picked that hour of the day when people had just come into the streets or were beginning their work, their minds and bodies heavy with half-remembered nightmares of the night before. For this was June 11, 1940 — the morning after Mussolini had declared war on the Allies.

High in the Mediterranean sky the Italian bombers approached their targets. As they came in toward Valetta, they split up into two formations, one making for Hal Far, the airfield in the southeast corner of the island, the other for the naval dockyard. They dropped their bombs, turned, formed up again and headed back toward Sicily. They had seen no trace of any British aircraft; they had not expected

any. Everything had gone according to plan.

A gunner in the starboard rear aircraft sang softly to himself:
"*Vido mare quante bello,*
Spira tantu sentimente . . ."
And that was as far as he got with his serenade. For, just beneath him, a row of bullet holes appeared in the fuselage and his song was drowned by the clatter of machine guns.

There was a fighter on his tail!

So began the epic story of *Faith, Hope,* and *Charity* — the three ancient Gloster Gladiators which held out alone against the wrath of Mussolini's *Regia Aeronautica*. They, and the devoted pilots who manned them, turned defeat into victory, disaster into a glorious and triumphant page of air history.

The Italians had not expected to

55

Malta as it appears from the air. "Faith," "Hope," and "Charity" were based at the airfield at Hal Far in the southeast corner of the largest island.

"Faith," one of the famous trio that saved Malta from the Italian Air Force. All of the Gladiators were eventually damaged or destroyed in combat. "Faith" was salvaged and presented to the people of Malta on September 3, 1943.

meet any RAF planes over Malta. They were right. There were none. *Faith, Hope,* and *Charity,* as they were later to be named, belonged, strictly speaking, to the navy, and had begun their operational life in packing cases en route for the aircraft carrier *Glorious.* It was a pure whim of fate that they came to be on Malta at all. They had missed the carrier when she sailed a few weeks earlier to take part in the Norwegian campaign; then it was planned to divert them to the *Eagle.* Meanwhile they waited on the slipway of Malta's Aircraft Repair Section at Kalafrana.

By the end of March it had become obvious to Air Commodore F. H. M. Maynard, Air Officer Commanding, Mediterranean, that he would not be able to count on any of the fighter squadrons which had been promised him for Malta. Home squadrons would have top priority. If Malta were besieged, it would have to fight on with whatever supplies happened to be on the island. As far as operational fight-

ers were concerned, they were precisely nil!

Maynard was not the type of man to let red tape stand in his way in an emergency. He needed fighters; the navy had them. He asked Rear Adm. Willis, Chief of Naval Staff, if he could have the aircraft, or some of them, to form a fighter force for the defense of Malta. There were eight Gladiators altogether, and the C in C agreed that Maynard could have four of them. There was no time to ask Admiralty permission; they were informed later as a matter of routine.

One day early in April the phone rang on the desk of Flying Officer G. A. V. Collins, Officer-in-Charge of the Aircraft Repair Section, Kalafrana. It was the CO, Wing Comdr. Michie.

"Look, Collins, there are four cased naval Gladiators in our store. Unpack, erect, and get them to Hal Far as fast as you can. We're going to have a Fighter Flight after all, if the AOC can find the pilots and get them trained in time."

So Sea Gladiators N.5520, N.5519, N.5531, and N.5524 were uncrated, assembled, and trundled up the road to Hal Far — and into history.

As soon as the AOC's scheme for a Station Fighter Flight became known, volunteers came forward from the few pilots still left on the island. Seven were finally selected. None of them were fighter pilots.

It was decided that, because there were no spares for the four Gladiators, the obvious policy would be to fly three of them and keep one in immediate reserve. If all three were crippled on a raid, the two most lightly damaged machines could be repaired by as many skilled men as could efficiently be put on the job, and the most heavily damaged aircraft replaced by the immediate reserve machine. Then work would proceed day and night until the badly damaged aircraft was serviceable again.

So it was that on the morning of June 11, 1940, when Mussolini decided to strike, the three fighters stood fueled up and ready out on the flight path. The klaxon screeched. Sirens howled in the distance. A door slammed open and a voice yelled:

"Scramble the fighters!"

In a matter of minutes all three were airborne and climbing flat out. Squadron Leader A. C. Martin, in the leading Gladiator, reported to Control:

"Banjo from Red One, Red Section airborne."

Down below, Control answered him.

"Red One from Banjo. Bandits approaching Grand Harbour from north."

A minute went by, and then Martin's voice, wavering and crackling over the radio: "O.K. chaps, let's get amongst 'em! Tallyho!"

They opened their throttles and drove the Gladiators through the sky above Valetta as fast as their old legs would carry them. The old aircraft quivered and shook as they charged, the early sun glinting on their cockpit hoods. Flt. Lt. George Burges had the best of the three aircraft and began to outstrip the others. He saw a bunch of Italian SM-79 bombers going away to the southwest of the island and circling round to head for home. Climbing hard, he managed to cut off a corner and eventually intercepted the last formation when they were some 30 miles from Malta — about halfway back to Sicily.

Coming in on their starboard quarter, he held his fire to be sure of a hit, then gave the nearest bomber a few quick, sharp bursts. He saw his bullets go home. But as soon as he banked away to come in for another attack, he realized that the Italians were drawing away from him. As he put it later:

"As soon as I opened up, the Italians poured on the coal and the Gladiator just couldn't catch up with them."

It was a bit of an anticlimax, but it was only the opening gambit. One important thing had been accomplished.

58

The Italians and, for that matter, the Maltese too, now knew that Malta had fighters to defend her.

No one really expected the Gladiators to shoot down anything on their first pass at the enemy. Indeed, most people looked on the whole Gladiator effort as a mere token gesture, a thumbing of the nose at Mussolini and a fillip for Maltese morale. The aircraft were the last of the biplane fighters, descendants of the Pups, Camels, and S.E.A.'s used in World War I. They had a maximum speed of 250 mph, four 0.303 machine guns, and a reputation for extreme maneuverability. But the pilots knew that the Italian SM-79's were faster than their own aircraft and they knew they would have to produce extra-special form to overcome the handicap.

"As they're faster than we are," reported Flt. Lt. Burges, "I think our only chance is to scramble and climb as fast as we can and hope that we are four or five thousand feet above them when they arrive over the island. It's no good trying to overhaul them. We shall just have to get into the air quicker and climb faster — somehow."

Tomorrow perhaps some new tactics could be worked out. But the Italians did not wait until tomorrow. They came over eight times in all during that first day. The second time, they paid a tribute to the Gladiators by bringing fighter escorts — CR-42's and Macchi-200's.

The last raiders of the day came over at 7:25 in the evening. What happened when the old Gladiators met modern Macchis, Flying Officer W. J. ("Timber") Woods told in his combat report:

"We sighted a formation of five S-79 enemy aircraft approaching Valetta at a height of approximately 15,000 feet. We climbed until we were slightly above them, and then Red Two delivered an attack from astern. The enemy had turned out to sea. I delivered an attack from astern, and got in a good burst at a range of approximately 200 yards. My fire was returned. I then broke away and returned over the island at approximately 11,000 feet, south of Grand Harbour.

"While still climbing to gain height, I observed another formation of five enemy aircraft approaching. They were at about the same height as myself. I attacked from abeam at about 150 yards and got in one good burst. The enemy started firing at me long before I opened up. This formation broke slightly but left me well behind when I tried to get in an attack from astern.

"Just after that, when again climbing to gain more height, I suddenly heard machine-gun fire behind me. I immediately went into a steep left-hand turn and saw a single-engine fighter diving and firing at me. For quite three minutes I circled as tightly as possible and got the enemy in my sight. I got in a good burst, full deflection shot, and he went down in a steep dive with black smoke pouring

59

from his tail. I could not follow him down, but he appeared to go into the sea."

Woods had proved that a Gladiator could outfly and outfight a more modern opponent, once it could hold the enemy to a definite engagement. He had destroyed a fighter. But the bombers had been able to do their work and get away without loss... "This formation broke slightly but left me well behind"... They would have to do something about that.

Only a bad workman blames his tools, but the pilots of *Faith, Hope,* and *Charity* could legitimately claim that their equipment was outclassed. The men of Aircraft Repair Section got to work. Up to then the Gladiators had the old, constant pitch, wooden airscrews. These were removed, and new propellers, of the three-bladed, two-speed variety, fitted. Then the Mercury engines were tuned to produce every possible ounce of speed.

Scramble procedure was tightened up. Instead of the pilots waiting on the ground, somewhere near their machines, for the alert, they now stayed in their cockpits throughout the whole of their period on duty, strapped in and ready for an immediate takeoff whenever the warning sounded. It was calculated that this innovation gained for them a good 2,000 feet in height, which might make all the difference between catching the Italians and missing them altogether.

As the days lengthened, and the tempo of the enemy attack increased,

both sides got to know the tactics of the other. On June 17, the Italians started making use of one particular tactic to try to trap the Gladiators into their crossfire. One of the Gladiators attacked a formation of five SM-79's above Grand Harbour, and as he came in astern, one of the Italians detached himself from the formation and began straggling behind the others. This was an open invitation to come in and finish him off. When the Gladiator attacked, however, the "straggler" lost height and flew beneath the other four bombers. The Gladiator stuck to his tail and followed him, whereupon the bombers above opened fire with their downward-firing movable guns. It was the "lame dog" trick and by no means a new idea, but on this occasion it nearly put an end to the Gladiator, which was lucky to get away with only superficial damage.

Late on Saturday evening, June 22, the radar reported a bogey approaching from the north. At Hal Far, Burges and Timber Woods were on duty strapped in their cockpits. They scrambled immediately and climbed flat out.

Their target was a single enemy bomber, an SM-79, which approached from the north of Grand Harbour and flew right down the island toward Kalafrana at about 13,000 feet. By the time the enemy machine had reached the center of the island the two Gladiators were high enough to make their attack. They dived toward him. Burges carried out a stern attack from above

60

and later reported tersely: "Port engine and then starboard engine of enemy caught fire and attack was discontinued." Evening promenaders in Valetta were able to watch the whole satisfying spectacle. They saw the Italian bomber fall in flames and watched two of its crew bale out. *Faith, Hope, and Charity* had scored their second victory!

Now they had got their hand in, the men of Fighter Flight threw themselves into the fight with zest and determination renewed. Day after day in the hot June weather, tired machines and weary men took off time and again through the burning air after a nerve-racking wait out on the flight path. Mussolini's *Regia Aeronautica* tried everything they knew to destroy *Faith, Hope, and Charity*. The Three Graces would find themselves engaging, on raid after raid, day after day, formations of 30 or 40 aircraft. CR-42's and Macchi-200's would come hunting for them in packs but somehow the little biplanes outmaneuvered them, slippery and elusive as fishes. As often as not, the Italians would leave one or more of their number crippled or utterly destroyed, behind them.

The Gladiators suffered damage, too, of course, and every damaged cylinder, airscrew, or aileron had to be repaired instantly and, in most cases, out on the open airfield with bombs falling all the time. Some of the damage had to be seen to be believed. On three occasions a Gladiator landed with its tail unit almost shot away and hanging by a couple of spars and a scrap of wire. Another time an aileron was almost cut in two. In all cases, however, the aircraft had remained under control. It was no uncommon thing to find bullet holes all round the cockpit, through the center section of the main plane above the pilot's head and through the instrument panel in front of him.

As the size of the raids was stepped up and the battered Gladiators became more and more patched and battle-scarred, the need for caution increased. The longer their charmed life stretched, the less expendable they became. The pilots were ordered categorically to avoid combat whenever the odds were outrageously heavy. The extent of the odds was left to individual interpretation.

On June 28 help was at hand. A raid had just finished and the two duty aircraft of Fighter Flight had that moment landed. The pilots were walking away from their machines when suddenly there was a roar overhead and four monoplanes came in low over the airfield, waggling their wings. Instinctively the two men ducked for cover. Then, with a look of utter astonishment on their faces, they straightened up and said as one:

"My God! Hurricanes!"

These were the first four of what were later to be sizable reinforcements. With Hurricanes, the pilots would be able to meet the enemy on more equal terms. *Faith, Hope, and Charity* had held the breach.

61

Spitfires on patrol during the Battle of Britain. Spitfire and Hurricane fighters were the Royal Air Force's chief defense against the bombers of the Luftwaffe.

After the fall of France, Great Britain stood alone against the might of Germany and she was next on Hitler's list. His plan for the invasion of England was called Sea Lion. Sea Lion was to begin with an attack on the Royal Air Force. When it had been knocked out of the air, the German army would move across the English Channel in barges collected at ports in France and Belgium. The destruction of the Royal Air Force was to be accomplished in a matter of weeks — between two weeks and a month was one estimate.

Three powerful German air fleets were ready to take part in the action — Luftflotte 2 based in Holland; Luftflotte 3 based in France; and Luftflotte 5 based in Norway and Denmark. Together they could supply at least 250 dive bombers, 1,000 long-range bombers and 1,000 fighters at the beginning of the battle. Against that formidable armada the Royal Air Force Fighter Command could muster 700 aircraft of which only 620 were Hurricane and Spitfire fighters.

The Germans date the Battle of Britain from the afternoon of August 13, 1940. The English say it began on the previous day when the Luftwaffe first shifted its main attack from channel shipping to airfields and radar stations. After September 6, the Luftwaffe's bombs were concentrated on London.

In spite of its superiority in numbers of aircraft, the Luftwaffe's losses were heavy from the beginning. Its JU-87 and HE-111 bombers proved to be too lightly armed making it necessary to use fighters as close support. The Royal Air Force, on the other hand, had the advantage of eight-gun fighters and radar to warn of approaching enemy aircraft. By October it was obvious that the Royal Air Force could not be destroyed and that an invasion of England would not be successful. Hitler had lost the Battle of Britain.

It was an expensive battle on both sides. Between July 10 and October 31, 1940, the Luftwaffe lost 2,698 aircraft to enemy action. The Royal Air Force lost 915. In addition, the tons of bombs dropped by the Luftwaffe on England took many lives and destroyed much property. In spite of the losses and hardships they endured, the British people refused to give in; it was Hitler's first defeat in World War II.

Here is an account of one of the attacks on London by Britain's wartime Prime Minister, Winston Churchill.

The Battle of Britain

Winston Churchill

WE MUST TAKE September 15 as the culminating date. On this day the Luftwaffe, after two heavy attacks on the 14th, made its greatest concentrated effort in a resumed daylight attack on London.

It was one of the decisive battles of the war, and, like the Battle of Waterloo, it was on a Sunday. I was at Chequers. I had already on several occasions visited the headquarters of Number 11 Fighter Group in order to witness the conduct of an air battle, when not much had happened. However, the weather on this day seemed suitable to the enemy, and accordingly I drove over to Uxbridge and arrived at the Group Headquarters. Number 11 Group comprised no fewer than twenty-five squadrons covering the whole of Essex, Kent, Sussex, and Hampshire, and all the approaches across them to London. Air Vice-Marshal Park had for six months commanded this group, on which our fate largely depended. From the beginning of Dunkirk, all the daylight actions in the South of England had already been conducted by him, and all his arrangements and apparatus had been brought to the highest perfection. My wife and I were taken down to the bomb-proof Operations Room, fifty feet below ground. All the ascendancy of the Hurricanes and Spitfires would have been fruitless but for this system of underground control centers and telephone cables, which had been devised and built before the war by the Air Ministry under Dowding's advice and impulse. Lasting credit is due to all concerned. In the South of England there were at this time Number 11 Group H.Q. and six subordinate fighter station centers. All these were, as has been described, under heavy stress. The Supreme Command was exercised from the Fighter Headquarters at Stanmore, but the actual handling of the direction of the squadrons was wisely left to Number 11 Group, which controlled the units through its fighter stations located in each county.

The Group Operations Room was like a small theatre, about sixty feet across, and with two stories. We took our seats in the dress circle. Below us was the large-scale map-table, around which perhaps twenty highly trained young men and women, with their telephone assistants, were assembled. Opposite to us, covering the entire wall, where the theatre curtain would be, was a gigantic blackboard divided into six columns with electric bulbs, for the six fighter stations, each of their squadrons having a sub-column

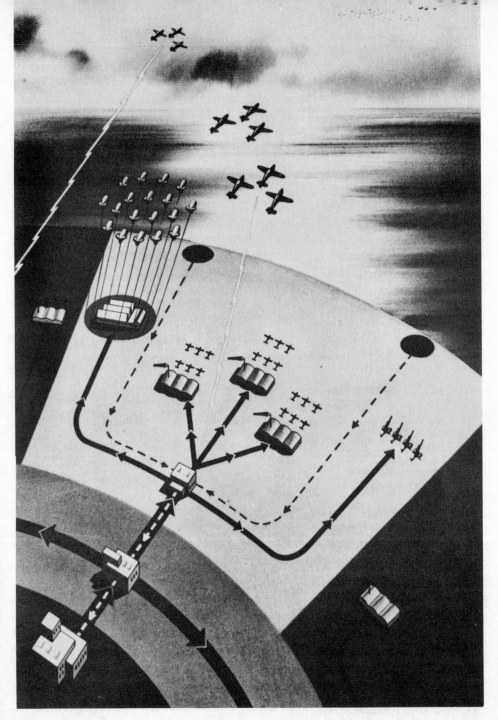

How the defense of Britain was organized. Information on approaching enemy aircraft was transmitted by observers and radar stations to control points which in turn ordered antiaircraft guns, barrage balloons and fighter planes into action as they were needed.

of its own, and also divided by lateral lines. Thus, the lowest row of bulbs showed as they were lighted the squadrons which were "Standing By" at two minutes' notice, the next row those "At Readiness," five minutes, then "At Available," twenty minutes, then those which had taken off, the next row those which had reported having seen the enemy, the next — with red lights — those which were in action, and the top row those which were returning home. On the left-hand side, in a kind of glass stage-box, were the four or five officers whose duty it was to weigh and measure the information received from our Observer Corps, which at this time numbered upwards of fifty thousand men, women, and youths. Radar was still in its infancy, but it gave warning of raids approaching our coast, and the observers, with field-glasses and portable telephones, were our main source of information about raiders flying overland. Thousands of messages were therefore received during an action. Several roomfuls of experienced people in other parts of the underground headquarters sifted them with great rapid-

Plotters in one of the RAF's Operations Rooms following the action during an air battle.

ity, and transmitted the results from minute to minute directly to the plotters seated around the table on the floor and to the officer supervising from the glass stage-box.

On the right hand was another glass stage-box containing Army officers who reported the action of our anti-aircraft batteries, of which at this time in the Command there were two hundred. At night it was of vital importance to stop these batteries firing over certain areas in which our fighters would be closing with the enemy. I was not unacquainted with the general outlines of this system, having had it explained to me a year before the war by Dowding when I visited him at Stanmore. It had been shaped and refined in constant action, and all was now fused together into a most elaborate instrument of war, the like of which existed nowhere in the world.

"I don't know," said Park, as we went down, "whether anything will happen today. At present all is quiet." However, after a quarter of an hour, the raid-plotters began to move about. An attack of "40 plus" was reported to be coming from the German stations in the Dieppe area. The bulbs along the bottom of the wall display panel began to glow as various squadrons came to "Stand By." Then in quick succession "20 plus," "40 plus" signals were received, and in another ten minutes it was evident that a serious battle impended. On both sides the air began to fill.

One after another signals came in, "40 plus," "60 plus"; there was even an "80 plus." On the floor table below us the movement of all the waves of attack was marked by pushing discs forward from minute to minute along different lines of approach, while on the blackboard facing us the rising lights showed our fighter squadrons getting into the air, till there were only four or five left "At Readiness." These air battles, on which so much depended, lasted little more than an hour from the first encounter. The enemy had ample strength to send out new waves of attack, and our squadrons, having gone all out to gain the upper air, would have to refuel after seventy or eighty minutes, or land to rearm after a five-minute engagement. If at this moment of refuelling or rearming, the enemy were able to arrive with fresh unchallenged squadrons, some of our fighters could be destroyed on the ground. It was, therefore, one of our principal objects to direct our squadrons so as not to have too many on the ground refuelling or rearming simultaneously during daylight.

Presently the red bulbs showed that the majority of our squadrons were engaged. A subdued hum arose from the floor, where the busy plotters pushed their discs to and fro in accordance with the swiftly changing situation. Air Vice-Marshal Park gave general directions for the disposition of his fighter force, which were translated into detailed orders to each fighter station by a youngish officer in

67

the center of the dress circle, at whose side I sat. Some years after I asked his name. He was Lord Willoughby de Broke. (I met him next in 1947, when the Jockey Club, of which he was a steward, invited me to see the Derby. He was surprised that I remembered the occasion.) He now gave the orders for the individual squadrons to ascend and patrol as the result of the final information which appeared on the map-table. The Air Marshal himself walked up and down behind, watching with vigilant eye every move in the game, supervising his junior executive hand, and only occasionally intervening with some decisive order, usually to reinforce a threatened area. In a little while all our squadrons were fighting, and some had already begun to return for fuel. All were in the air. The lower line of bulbs was out. There was not one squadron left in reserve. At this moment Park spoke to Dowding at Stanmore, asking for three squadrons from Number 12 Group to be put at his disposal in case of another major attack while his squadrons were rearming and refuelling. This was done. They were specially needed to cover London and our fighter aerodromes, because Number 11 Group had already shot their bolt.

The young officer, to whom this seemed a matter of routine, continued to give his orders, in accordance with the general directions of his Group Commander, in a calm, low monotone, and the three reinforcing squadrons were soon absorbed. I became conscious of the anxiety of the Commander, who now stood still behind his subordinate's chair. Hitherto I had watched in silence. I now asked, "What other reserves have we?" "There are none," said Air Vice-Marshal Park. In an account which he wrote about it afterwards, he said that at this I "looked grave." Well I might. What losses should we not suffer if our refuelling planes were caught on the ground by further raids of "40 plus" or "50 plus"! The odds were great; our margins small; the stakes infinite.

Another five minutes passed, and most of our squadrons had now descended to refuel. In many cases our resources could not give them overhead protection. Then it appeared that the enemy were going home. The shifting of the discs on the table below showed a continuous eastward movement of German bombers and fighters. No new attack appeared. In another ten minutes the action was ended. We climbed again the stairways which led to the surface, and almost as we emerged the "All Clear" sounded.

"We are very glad, sir, you have seen this," said Park. "Of course, during the last twenty minutes we were so choked with information that we couldn't handle it. This shows you the limitation of our present resources. They have been been strained far beyond their limits today." I asked whether any results had come to hand, and remarked that the attack appeared

68

to have been repelled satisfactorily. Park replied that he was not satisfied that we had intercepted as many raiders as he had hoped we should. It was evident that the enemy had everywhere pierced our defences. Many scores of German bombers, with their fighter escort, had been reported over London. About a dozen had been brought down while I was below, but no picture of the results of the battle or of the damage or losses could be obtained.

It was 4:30 P.M. before I got back to Chequers, and I immediately went to bed for my afternoon sleep. I must have been tired by the drama of Number 11 Group, for I did not wake till eight. When I rang, John Martin, my principal private secretary, came in with the evening budget of news from all over the world. It was repellent. This had gone wrong here; that had been delayed there; an unsatisfactory answer had been received from so-and-so; there had been bad sinkings in the Atlantic. "However," said Martin, as he finished this account, "all is re-deemed by the air. We have shot down a hundred and eighty-three for a loss of under forty."

Although post-war information has shown that the enemy's losses on this day were only fifty-six, September 15 was the crux of the Battle of Britain. That same night our Bomber Command attacked in strength the shipping in the ports from Boulogne to Antwerp. At Antwerp particularly heavy losses were inflicted. On September 17, as we now know, the Fuehrer decided to postpone "Sea Lion" indefinitely. It was not till October 12 that the invasion was formally called off till the following spring. In July, 1941, it was postponed again by Hitler till the spring of 1942, "by which time the Russian campaign will be completed." This was a vain but an important imagining. On February 13, 1942, Admiral Raeder had his final interview on "Sea Lion" and got Hitler to agree to a complete "stand-down." Thus perished "Operation Sea Lion." And September 15 may stand as the date of its demise.

On June 13, 1944, seven days after the Normandy invasion, the first V-1 flying bomb landed in England. It was followed by 8,000 others before the Germans switched over to the more advanced V-2 rocket three months later.

The V-1 was a pilotless, jet-propelled plane that carried a ton of explosives. It could be set for any desired target; most of them seem to have been aimed at London where they did considerable damage. Barrage balloons and antiaircraft fire were used to knock down the flying bombs, but fast fighter planes were the first line of defense against the deadly robots.

This series of pictures, taken of models but based on an actual fighter mission, shows how one Spitfire pilot destroyed a flying bomb.

A Spitfire Attacks a Flying Bomb

A Picture Story

Alerted by ground controllers who had picked up the V-1 on their radar screens, the Spitfire pilot closed in on the bomb from the rear.

After trying unsuccessfully to shoot down the V-1, the Spitfire flew alongside and carefully placed his wingtip under the wingtip of the robot.

The pilot then flipped his wing sharply to tip the V-1 over. This upset its guidance system and caused it to crash short of the target.

The historic cathedral at Coventry after the raid on the night of November 14, 1940. The ruins have been incorporated in a new cathedral opened in 1962.

Although the Battle of Britain was over by October, 1940, air attacks on England continued. Heavy losses forced the Luftwaffe to shift from daylight to night bombing and London, which had been a prime target, was abandoned in favor of attacks on British industrial cities. One of the hardest hit was Coventry. In a raid that lasted from dusk until dawn on the night of November 14, 1940, 437 German aircraft dropped 56 tons of incendiaries, 394 tons of high explosives and 127 parachute mines on the city. Twelve aircraft plants and nine other factories were hit. Power, gas and water systems were damaged and Coventry's beautiful fourteenth-century cathedral was completely destroyed.

Among the Royal Air Force fighter pilots who flew to meet the German bombers over Coventry was an American, Byron Kennerly. He was a member of one of the Royal Air Force's Eagle Squadrons.

The Eagle Squadrons (there were three) were made up of Americans who fought with the Royal Air Force before the United States entered the war. Most of the American pilots arrived in Britain by way of Canada where they had enlisted in the Royal Canadian Air Force. After basic training in Canada they were sent to Britain for advanced training. In October, 1940, the Americans were transferred to the 71st Royal Air Force Pursuit Squadron. It was the first of the Eagle Squadrons and still new at the time of the attack on Coventry. Here is Pilot Officer Kennerly's story.

Coventry

Byron Kennerly

as told to Graham Berry

THE CO, Andy, Bud, Luke, and I were playing poker in the hut. We hadn't gone up on patrol. The CO had kept us grounded because, he said, "something important might develop."

He interrupted the game every few minutes to talk over the French field phone to operations. Then he would use the box phone to instruct the mechanics to keep our aircraft warmed up. We occasionally heard a "cough, cough" and "brrrrup" as a crew started up a motor.

Suddenly over the Tannoy loudspeaker came the command:

"Night-flying pilots come to readiness! Come to readiness!"

The CO jumped from his chair and grabbed the field phone. We crowded around him.

"Yes," he was saying, "Coventry.

We're in readiness now. Fifteen minutes. Check."

Big flap meant a big raid! And we were to get a crack at the Nazis. As the four of us reached for our parachutes, the CO warned, "Take it easy, boys. We have to wait in the hut fifteen minutes to get final orders. Let's finish our game."

It was no time for poker, but the CO wanted to keep the four of us from getting nervous. Tenseness resulting from this slows muscular reactions. Fifteen minutes later, right on the nose, we got telephonic confirmation to take off immediately.

Wearing fur-lined Irving suits because it was very cold, we helped each other with our parachutes and ran out into the darkness. Every light on the airdrome was turned off. There were a few scattered clouds, but not enough to completely hide the landscape, which was painted with the bluish light of a full moon.

"Thumbs up, boys. We'll get a crack at 'em tonight," called the CO as he left our running group for his aircraft. All the planes were on the line, ready to take off.

I jumped onto the wing of my Hurricane and climbed into the cockpit, flipping on the dash lights. Fastening the Sutton harness, plugging in the radio and oxygen tubes and snapping the oxygen mask in place across my face, I turned the electric starter switch, yelling, "Contact!" The motor burst into noisy life. Quickly I closed the hatch and pulled on silk gloves and flying mittens as my electrician wheeled away the portable batteries that were plugged into the Hurricane's belly to power the self-starter.

The corporal of the flare path flashed a green light at the CO. Immediately his motor roared and his Hurricane swung out onto the runway. I could see the undulating flash of his exhaust. As he lined up into the wind, the flare-path lights were switched on. Tail up, the CO's Hurricane roared off into the night.

I counted ten seconds on my watch. Then Luke roared out and took off. Ten more seconds. I pushed the throttle and taxied to the starting mark. Two members of my crew shoved the wings at right angles to the wind, then gave me a thumbs up salute. I responded and thundered down the runway. Nearing the last light I pulled her off the turf. I heard Luke informing operations, or Locust Control, he was airborne. Moving the undercarriage lever, I heard a thump as the wheels folded inward and reached their retracted position. The powerful aircraft picked up climbing speed the instant the wheels were up. The flare-path lights must have been on about 30 seconds now and I hoped there were no Nazi bombers lurking about. The lights would make a perfect target.

Flipping the radio key to send, I called: "Hello, Locust Control. Rinzo Two Zero calling. Are you receiving me?"

"Hello, Rinzo Two Zero," came the answer. "Receiving you loud and

74

The Duke of Kent, brother of the King of England, talks with two Eagle Squadron pilots. Note the Eagle Squadron badge on the left shoulder of the Royal Air Force uniform worn by the two Americans.

clear. Over."

"Hello, Locust Control. Rinzo Two Zero airborne. Over."

"Hello, Rinzo Two Zero. Locust Control answering. Understand you are airborne. Listening out."

The radio was quiet for several seconds until operations gave the CO and Luke a vector. As I climbed steadily, waiting for directions, I heard Bud and Andy report they were airborne. My eyes roved over the instruments. I was trying to check them all to keep from feeling a bit nervous. As the altimeter needle touched the 500-foot mark, I changed the prop pitch to 2,600 rpm so the motor wouldn't turn over so fast. At 1,000 feet I banked into a 180-degree, one needle-width level turn. Somewhere ahead in the blue blackness were the CO and Luke. Behind were Bud and Andy. By following prearranged navigation plans precisely we would all reach the same

75

objective and without any danger of a collision.

The radio crackled in the earphones and operations called me; I answered that I was receiving operations "strength nina." "Nina" meant nine but was more easily understood over the RT. Strength nine meant reception was strong. Operations ordered me to "vector two, one, five. Angels twelve." The orders were to set the gyro compass at 215 and to climb to 12,000 feet.

In a gradual climb, I reached 12,000 in about three minutes. Glancing out the hatch, I could see nothing below but the bluish blackness of moonlight reflecting on a slight haze. I hoped we could spot the Jerries in this semi-illumination. It was a strange sensation, I thought as more minutes passed, being on the way to protect an invisible city against an unseen foe. Little did I know I was going to witness one of the most devastating bombing raids in the history of warfare.

My knees got cold above my boots in this high altitude and I slapped them vigorously to stir up circulation. The radio began to give off mutterings. It wasn't static, but some sort of mumbling conversation. I tried to catch it but couldn't. It might be a German controller on nearly the same wavelength as ours talking to his planes.

Finally the mumbling was drowned by the CO's voice:

"Tallyhoooo!"

Somewhere a little more than a mile ahead the CO was attacking a Jerry! Happy hunting, Rinzo Three Nine! Ahead in the darkness was a tiny streak of light, like a dim shooting star, moving across and down in front of me. It must be the CO's tracer bullets as he followed his target. Over the RT came a faint muttering that might be his machine guns. The light blacked out, only to resume again. For an instant, I caught the glint of a wing in the moonlight. A ruddy streak appeared, at first descending in a slant, then falling directly earthward and disappearing. One of the planes in that scrap was downed!

I listened anxiously for the CO's voice on the RT. All I heard was operations telling Luke to climb higher. Had the CO been shot down?

"Hello, Rinzo Two Zero. Locust Control calling," operations' voice crackled. "Are you receiving me?"

"Hello, Locust Control. Rinzo Two Zero answering. Receiving you strength six. Over."

Operations answered by ordering me up another thousand feet. "Ops'" voice was fainter, about strength six. This was natural because I was moving away from the station. If reception dropped to strength two or three, operations would switch me to a closer station. If the nearer station's reception wasn't louder it meant the radio was failing and I'd have to be vectored to an airdrome in a hurry.

I flew for five more minutes in the great, lonely well of night. The only object I could see distinctly was the round moon. Operations called once to vector me still higher. I turned on the oxygen and took several satisfying inhalations of the stuff. Then again the radio crackled to life and operations' voice came over the earphones:

"Rinzo Two Zero. Locust Control calling. Orbit. Objective."

I was over Coventry already! Banking into a wide turn I looked below. Aside from a few light and scattered clouds, reflecting a wraithlike bluish glow of the moon, I could see nothing. To the east searchlight beams moved slowly in the sky.

A welcome sound came over the RT. It was the CO, calling operations for a vector. I was much relieved to know he was still in the sky. I wanted to ask him what had happened, but of course I couldn't. The RT had to be clear for sudden orders.

I'd set a course for a circle of several miles' radius over the objective when I heard Andy and then Bud receive instructions to orbit. Now the five of us must be over the objective, not all flying at the same altitude, however. We weren't the only interceptors aloft; there must be many others from other airdromes. Their radio wavelengths were different from ours, so we didn't interfere with their conversations.

Suddenly far below a tiny orange light appeared. Then another. They were stationary so they must be on the ground. As I looked, several more winked on, a considerable distance from the first ones. They were fires

starting from incendiary bombs. As others became visible, the first one went out. Then the second disappeared. But for every one that was extinguished, five blossomed in the night. They looked innocent enough from this altitude, like fireflies at rest on a lawn. The fire watchers and wardens who were fighting them probably had a far different impression.

A wider and wider area was being sown with the fast-growing seeds of destruction. Several of the spots spread and blended into others and soon in the place of pinpoint fires there were gigantic infernos. The Nazis must be coming over by the score, using the thin cloud wisps below as a cover. The rapidly increasing reddish light from the fires made the clouds glow dully at the edges.

Then, several thousand feet below and silhouetted against the glow of the fires, I spotted a winged object skulking through a cloud. It was a twin-engined Nazi bomber! It had large bat wings, the "bites" or inward curves on the trailing edges of the wings where they joined the fuselage marking it as a Heinkel-III.

Luckily I had set my gunsights for the 75-foot wingspan of a Heinkel. Here was my chance! My right hand trembled as I snapped on the sights and turned the firing button guard to "fire" position. Quick, before the Heinkel disappeared beyond the fire! Sucking in deep breaths of oxygen through dry lips, I put her into a dive.

The Heinkel He 111, one of the German bombers that took part in the attack on Coventry. With 2,200 pounds of bombs, its range was 1,510 miles.

It would be a quarter attack. The Hurricane roared down, then leveled off in the thin mist.

Where was the Heinkel? There! Just ahead. The Hurricane caught up with the racing silhouette. But it was transparent! Holy thunder! I was attacking the shadow of a bomber that was flying somewhere below the cloud! If any of the fellows had heard about this they'd call me Pilot Officer Don Quixote! The only good thing was that, in the excitement of expected battle, I'd forgotten to shout "Tally-ho."

The Hurricane swept under the cloud and began rocking a little. The fires below were creating a strong thermal of rising warm air, making the atmosphere rough. I couldn't see the Heinkel so I took a squint below. Miniature cars, probably ambulances, and fire trucks, brightly lighted by a dozen fires, were crawling through streets that must be furnaces! Almost directly below were four flashes of light, tossing up undulating billows of smoke. The Jerries were beginning to drop explosives.

Looking up I caught sight of three Heinkels skimming in a vic just inside the clouds. They weren't shadows, either. There were crosses on the underside of their wings. I yelled "Tallyho!" as the Hurricane vaulted upstairs to make a belly attack on the bomber to my left. Just before I got within range, the big aircraft dropped a stick of bombs and pulled up into the cloud. I was so anxious to get him I went up into it, too, although I knew I probably couldn't spot him quickly enough among the shadowy cloud mists to get in a long burst. My heart was thumping almost as loudly as the motor.

The mist came down to meet me and I caught sight of something dark that might have been the black belly of a bomber. For the first time in my life I pressed the firing button. The stick vibrated a bit and I heard through my helmet a long "brrrrrrrruuuup" as bullets shot from the eight machine guns. White tracer streaks disappeared into the black object, which slid past me directly overhead.

Had I maneuvered to follow him I would have blacked out, so I went on up through the cloud, the Hurricane's wings emitting a screaming whistle. The protecting flaps over the gunports, put on to lessen air resistance, were shot away and the wind, passing by at about 250 mph, was whistling in the gun barrels. I'd had my first crack at the enemy.

Near the illuminated edge of a cloud the enlarged shadows of four more bombers flashed by, going in the opposite direction from me. The Nazis must be sending them over by the hundreds tonight. Although the fires and moonlight made aircraft plainly visible in certain areas, the small clouds and smoke caused the trickiest shadows. It was a weird sensation, stalking the enemy and his huge reflections.

I returned to my assigned level and resumed patrol. Unfortunately, now it was all too easy to circle the objective. Great fires were raging below. I thought of the many women and children who must be suffering from this inhuman devastation. Another "Tallyho!" over the RT cheered me up a little. I couldn't recognize the voice, but one of the boys in the squadron was making an attack. There was more RT conversation. I didn't pay much attention to it for I was too busy trying to spot another Nazi.

There was a great flash of light somewhere in a cloud beneath me. That meant a bomber had exploded. Perhaps it was the result of the "Tallyho" I'd just heard.

As the Hurricane rounded the east side of the city and headed west I sighted an aircraft, the underside of which was etched in red. It was traveling in the same direction as I, and was about 500 yards in front. The black aircraft ahead appeared to be smaller and looked like a British Blenheim-I There were no Blenheims up here and the only Nazi bomber that looked like them was the Junkers-88. This must be one of them. Since its wingspan was 15 feet less than a Heinkel, I corrected the gunsight.

Slanting down to ride in on his tail, the Hurricane began closing in a bit too fast. Not wanting to overshoot him, I lowered the flaps a little and eased off the throttle. My thumb was tense against the trigger button and I

79

had to concentrate to keep from firing too soon. If the Jerry saw me, he could dive for a cloud. The oxygen felt cold against my face where it slipped out the side of the mask. Steady! I squinted into the sights, which glowed dull red, and kept a bead on the Jerry. Apparently I hadn't been spotted yet as the Junkers streaked straight ahead at about 280 mph, rising and falling in the heat-roughened air. Once the Hurricane jumped around as it got in his propeller blast. I climbed above it.

"Tallyho!" I yelled throatily into the mike, hoping the radio key was on send. It was too late to find out now. I had to keep one hand on the firing button and the other on the throttle.

His wing tips touched each side of the sight ring. He was within range! My thumb pressed the firing button. The Hurricane slowed from the recoil and I gave her a little throttle. Snaky streaks of white from the tracers reached from my wing into the tail of the Junkers.

The Jerry banked slightly and I glanced through the windscreen to see that he didn't try to get away. Suddenly blackness enveloped the windscreen. I could see nothing! I blinked and stopped firing. It wasn't my eyesight that was failing because the instrument panel still glowed brightly. I glanced around and saw light coming through the rear part of the glass sliding hatch.

Then I realized what had happened. The Nazis had a trick of throwing out black oil to blind a chasing enemy.

Dirty oil was plastered on my windscreen. Had I been an experienced pilot, I wouldn't have sailed calmly up on the tail but would have stayed several feet above.

Pulling up the flaps I gunned her again. The rushing air blew off part of the fuel oil, at least enough so I could see out dimly. The bomber had disappeared.

Climbing to my patrol level, I noticed the windscreen was still badly streaking with oil. I snapped off the gunsight and turned the firing button to "safe," hoping to get one more crack at a Jerry tonight!

The fires below had become so great that I could easily have read a newspaper in the cockpit from the glare. The air was quite bumpy and warm. Visibility actually was cut by the light, which glanced glaringly off the windscreen. Enormous smoke clouds billowed up from below. Occasionally I passed through one. As I glanced down at this dirty work of the Nazis, there were two huge explosions on the ground, shooting up enormous umbrellas of smoke that gradually stretched upward in great treelike masses. Many seconds later I heard two dull booms over the roar of the motor and shriek of the gun mouths.

Still more explosions dotted the fiery mass below. It must be an enormous raid. The Nazis evidently were coming over in small formations, keeping within the clouds for the most part. I saw three bombers downed, one in flames, one with a wing torn off and a third blown up. The night patrol planes were taking a toll.

The smoke began to thicken and obliterate the fires. Visibility dimmed. It seemed an age since I had come aloft. Smoke crept into the cabin and smarted my eyes as I kept hunting, hunting for the Nazi bomber fleets that were sneaking in to drop their explosives.

The RT crackled a vector to the CO. Then an order came for Luke, Bud, Andy, and me. The patrol was being recalled. Either we were to be replaced or all British aircraft were to be removed so the antiaircraft guns could open up.

I had to cross over the heart of the fire to get to the base. The Hurricane pitched and bucked in the turbulent air. Suddenly the aircraft rose so quickly I was nearly shoved through the armored seat. Then it banked on its port wing and I had to move fast to keep her from turning over. What was happening?

Just below, black puffs of antiaircraft shells exploded around a Nazi bomber that had popped out of a smoke cloud. Before I could turn and dive on it, a shell exploded under his starboard motor, wrenching it from its nacelle. The Nazi went into a shallow glide. Just before it disappeared into some more smoke its starboard wing buckled upward. That guy wasn't going to do any more bombing in a hurry. It had been concussion from the exploding antiaircraft shells that had nearly upset my Hurricane. The

Archie gunners below hadn't seen me.

I got out of that fire and smoke as quickly as possible. The petrol was getting low and the oil streaks on the windscreen still interfered with my vision. When I left the red glow of Coventry behind, the moonlight atmosphere seemed unusually peaceful and quiet. The sky was clear and the round moon looked down peacefully. It was an almost unbelievable contrast to the ugly night over Coventry, where a Nazi warlord was trying to blast a city off the face of this moonlit land.

After many minutes I got radio instructions: "Pancake! You are over base."

The flare path was turned on and I settled her down for the landing. At this instant a strong crosswind eased the plane dangerously close to the flare-path lights. The lines of oil on the windscreen had caused me to misjudge the distances and land too close to the lights. The Hurricane was coming in a little too hot — 120 mph — and I saw the corporal of the flare path duck when my starboard wing nearly smacked him on the back. As the wheels hit the ground hard, the Hurricane bounced up about 50 feet. I gave her the throttle a bit and mushed her down. The next time she hit she stayed down and taxied along at 100 mph, barely missing the portable chance light or field searchlight.

I eased on the brakes and she slowed to a stop near the end of the field. Perspiration was oozing out of me as I turned her and taxied to the dispersal bay. My ground crew cheered wildly as the aircraft stopped. They'd heard the wind whistle in the gunports and knew I'd gotten a crack at a Jerry.

I told them I'd had my first shots at the Nazis but hadn't bagged any aircraft. Inspection of the Hurricane showed a mess of dirty oil over the motor cowling, but no damage. I was glad of that.

Andy and Bud already were back and had asked the CO if we couldn't refuel and go up again. He'd shaken his head. The boys said he felt very blue, even though he had knocked down two Heinkels.

Luke came in and landed. None of us could claim victories, although three of us had used our guns. We walked over to the CO, who had waited on the field until Luke had climbed from his Hurricane. Several other boys from our squadron joined us as we congratulated the CO and tried to buck him up.

"Coventry took a hell of a pasting, boys," was all he said as he turned, parachute under his arm, and walked wearily into the office to make out his combat report.

Although they were reluctant to kill friendly civilians, the Allies were forced to attack German industrial capacity in occupied countries as well as in Germany itself. One such target, a large powerhouse in Amsterdam, was the objective of an attack by the Royal Air Force on May 3, 1943.

Under the command of Squadron Leader Leonard Trent, 12 Ventura light bombers set out for Amsterdam. Due to an unforeseen circumstance, 90 enemy fighters were waiting for them over Holland. Trent alone was able to reach the target and bomb it. For this accomplishment he was later awarded the Victoria Cross. Here is his story.

Target: Amsterdam

Leonard Trent

"FLUSHING DOCKS today, Len. I'll lead your flight and the squadron." Such was the greeting I got on a sunny May morning in 1943 when Wing Commander Grindell popped his head into my office shortly after 9 A.M.

"Oh, no, you don't sir!" I said. "I didn't cross the egg line yesterday, and I have still got a load of bombs hanging on my airplane." The egg line was an imaginary line a few miles out from the enemy coast, and if this line was not crossed, the crews were not entitled to the prized egg and bacon on return.

Anyway, a long argument ensued, which I won, or lost, according to one's point of view. I had the usual attack of butterflies as we sat in the briefing room and went through the usual gambit of weather, fighter escort, timing, bombing height, and so on.

We left the briefing room with an hour to spare, so I returned to my office, wrote the usual note for my wife, emptied my pockets, and joined the boys in the nervous queue. A visit to all aircraft killed a bit more time, and then we collected our gear and moved toward the bus which was waiting to take us to the various dispersal points. We were just clambering aboard, when there was a shout: "Everyone back to the briefing room!" When we were seated, the wing commander announced an early lunch and a new target.

The butterflies were fairly successful in spoiling my lunch, and finally we were all seated back in the briefing room to hear the worst. "Well, today it's to be a target which hasn't been bombed before: Amsterdam. Here is your target, the powerhouse on the northwestern edge of the city. It is

83

a very important target, and our Intelligence has information that the Dutchmen working in powerhouses throughout Holland are awaiting a lead from Amsterdam to go on strike because of our bombing. You are also tied up with a low-level attack by Bostons on Ijmuiden steelworks. They will be on target just as you are approaching Ijmuiden on the way out. We expect that all eyes and guns will be turned inland as the Bostons approach their target from the sea." And with that jolly little speech and a rude sign to me, the wing commander sat down, grinning fit to burst. Amsterdam was a vastly different kettle of fish from Flushing; and, as I looked at the map with the distance inland, plus the defenses around Amsterdam, I realized my brave speech of the morning had boomeranged somewhat.

However, "you're not to worry," I told the butterflies; we had looked at worse prospects and come through with no more than a dry mouth. The butterflies weren't to be fooled, until at last we clambered aboard, and started to taxi out for the formation takeoff of 12 Venturas. It was a peculiar thing, how all signs of nervous tension departed once the airplane started to move.

We were all lined up in two lots of six, and three minutes later roared away low level across Norfolk to pick up our close escort of fighters from Coltishall. Three miles from the airdrome we could see the Spitfires taking off and skimming the trees in a left-hand turn, to station themselves 100 yards on both sides of our formations. Right on time and all well, we set course for the Dutch coast.

We continued flying at 100 feet to avoid detection by the enemy radar. We hoped to get within ten minutes of the Dutch coast before being plotted, and, when at this point, we did a full-power climb to bombing height. In this way, we usually were able to complete the bombing run, and be homeward bound before the German fighters were in a position to attack.

The enemy was not usually "scrambled" until the bomber formations appeared on the radar screens. They then had to get off and climb to a position to attack, keeping in mind our high and medium cover, which meanwhile had come from north or south into our area. Only rarely did we catch a glimpse of this support, but it was a great comfort to know it was there, for the Ventura was cold meat for a fighter. A top turret with two .3's, plus .3's (two) in a prone position under the tail, was hardly a deterrent for a determined pilot in a cannon-firing fighter. It is true the Ventura pilot had two .5's and .3's under his thumb, but flying in formation and unable to maneuver quickly, no one but Pilot Officer Von Prune-Cluck was likely to get in the way of that lot. However, I had heard a friend of mine, flying Bostons, relate how a Focke-Wulf had hung on its prop in front of him, firing at a box of six Bostons less than 100 yards in front.

84

By the time he had knocked the safety catch off his four .3's, the fighter was away, and the chance never came again. Big tears would splash in his beer as he told the story, for we all wanted to be fighter boys, anyway! As a morale booster, once over the sea, I always placed my front guns on "Fire."

As we skimmed along the water and tested all guns and fused the bombs, one of the Venturas turned away and feathered a propeller. If it had happened a few minutes earlier, the reserve aircraft which had accompanied us to the coast could have taken his place. Little did they know what they were about to miss, for the stage was already being set.

The German governor of Holland had decided to pay a state visit to Haarlem that particular afternoon, and fighter reinforcement had been brought from as far as Norway and France. Unfortunately, Haarlem was only five miles left of my track to Amsterdam, and midway from the coast. Even more unfortunate, a fighter diversionary wing made some mistake and got 20 minutes ahead of schedule. Instead of drawing any enemy fighters which felt hostile down toward Flushing, this wing flew into our area and succeeded in bringing up over 90 Focke-Wulfs and Messerschmitts. This formidable array was therefore high in the sky when our puny force appeared on the radar.

Of course, the Germans thought our Intelligence had got wind of the state visit and imagined our target was Haarlem! The enemy refused battle with the diversionary wing, who soon had to return to refuel, and were unable to stay to help our top cover and close escort.

Meanwhile, I was approaching the climbing point still low on the water, which looked very unfriendly, for the seas were mountainous. There was a 25-knot wind on the surface that day, so I didn't relish the idea of ditching.

"Climb in 30 seconds, sir," said my navigator, so up we went, as steeply as the 2,000 hp engines would take us. From 1,000 feet we could see the gleam of white sand from the coast, and this unfriendly sight encouraged us to push the engines to the limit.

At 5,000 feet a jubilant shout from my navigator: "We're dead on track, sir!" The coast from this height looked very close indeed, and so we started a gentle weave every ten seconds, just in case some AA (antiaircraft) guns were where they were not supposed to be. I picked up my tin hat and placed it over my flying helmet. This idea of mine was quite a squadron joke. Some of the boys laughed at me. But a few decided to wear tin hats when I described scalp wounds caused by explosive cannon shells hitting the canopy. I had visited a friend in hospital during the Battle of France, and on the way home had got to thinking!

And so we climbed, onward and upward, until we were 12,000 feet over the coast, and still not a shot fired, and we were still unaware of the enemy fighters jockeying for position. Of

85

course, the escort knew all about the situation, but I was not informed. Although I had recently been fitted with a VHF (very high frequency) set to be in contact with the escort, the Venturas around me had not had their magnetos and plugs properly screened, and so my set was still virtually useless. However, I was not bothered, for we had an arranged signal that if for any reason the escort couldn't cope, one Spitfire would fly across my bow, waggling his wings. I had never seen this signal, and didn't even expect to see it!

From a cloudless sky and in good visibility, we could see Haarlem, and just make out Amsterdam, ten minutes' flying from our position over the coast. We leveled off, and using the extra 2,000 feet to gain speed, I thought it was just a case of "Look out, powerhouse, here we come!"

My wireless operator had taken up his usual position in the astrodome. He was responsible for reporting the range and bearing of fighters attacking from beam to rear. The formations were reported in good order, and I got a "thumbs up" from my Nos. 2 and 3 — the only Venturas I could see. The Spitfire close escort had moved out to a position 500 feet above and 500 yards on either quarter. This was quite usual, for there was no point in keeping too close, thus making a large target for the AA, and also restricting movement.

Suddenly, things began to happen: Thomas, from the astrodome, shouted:

"Here's a whole shower of fighters coming down out of the sun; they may be Spits, 20, 30, 40. Hell's teeth, they're 109's and 190's. Watch 'em. Tren!" This is to my gunner. Then he continued . . . "The 190's are engaging the close escort, get ready to turn starboard, sir, the 109's are heading for us, 1,000 yards, 800, turn now, 600 yards; they're firing, give 'em hell, Tren!" and I could hear Tren's guns rattling away and smell the cordite. As I turned, I could see them coming in one after the other — about a dozen had attached themselves to my box and the same number were attending to Flt. Lt. Duffield and his box.

Duffield was hit in the first attack and went down with smoke pouring from his tail. Two of his crew were badly injured, but he regained control near the ground and limped off home unnoticed by the enemy. My No. 5 was set on fire and fell away. As the last of the attackers whipped by just underneath us, I straightened up and turned back on course, searching the sky for signs of the top cover. I had caught a glimpse of a glorious dogfight going on miles back — obviously, the close escort was more than busy. Our attackers could be seen pulling around underneath, with the obvious intent of attacking from the starboard again. By this time we were approaching Haarlem, and, as I realized later, they were trying to make me turn away to the south, and to keep turning. This, to a certain extent, they were successful in achieving, but I wasn't going to

Haarlem, anyway! About this time I had a horrible idea where I was going if that top cover didn't arrive PDQ.

The next attack came from the starboard beam, and as they came in I turned slightly to the right to get the wings out of the way, thus giving our gunners a clear field of fire to the last moment as the fighters ducked under the formation. It also gave the fighters a full deflection shot. As they came in this time, I didn't need the range, I could see only too well. At about 400 yards the leading edges suddenly burst into flames, and this ugly sight continued until it appeared a collision was inevitable. Down underneath and around to the right again, and still we hadn't knocked one down. But my No. 4 had gone the way of No. 5.

This had all happened in something like two minutes, which seemed like two years. I suppose the thought process gets speeded up a bit in such situations, but I now realized something had gone seriously wrong, and the top cover could not help. What to do? We were on our own in a hopeless situation, obviously in for the "chop" in a matter of minutes. Might as well be shot down over the land as come down in that rough sea — even supposing we got back that far. If the idea of turning for home occurred to anyone, they certainly didn't voice it. My navigator still had his eyes on Amsterdam, and was urging me to turn back left toward it whenever I could.

But here they came again, from starboard bow and beam. From half up and 1,500 yards, we could see them wing over in loose pairs and come darting in. Once again at 400-yards the twinkling flames from the leading edges; then I pulled up slightly to put them off aim and give them room to get underneath. And then an encouraging thing happened. P.O. von Prune-Cluck himself! Instead of diving down, this merry goon pulled around level in front of our formation. I am sure he misjudged our speed, and obviously he had been studying anything but the armament of the Ventura. There he was, banked toward us, the range about 150 yards. He appeared very close. I scarcely had to move the aircraft. He was flying straight toward the center of my old ring and bead sight. There was a terrible vibration as I pressed the button — one — two — three, got him! His wings suddenly rocked, and he slowly turned upside down, and was last seen going down out on the starboard side, vertically and very fast. There were yells of glee from everyone on board, but we didn't have time to follow his progress to the ground — another pair were already shooting at us. Since the war, a Dutch boy, who was then eighteen, has written an account of what it all looked like from the ground. In his account, he reports a ME-109 diving into the ground at this point. From then on it was just a succession of attacks, and I was amazed that we had lasted so long. Eight minutes had gone by, and we were approaching the target. My No. 3 had pulled out with the port in flames.

And so my No. 2, who was flying as if it was a practice over Norfolk, was the only one left as the first of the built-up area appeared in the bombing sights. Suddenly, about a dozen or more black puffs appeared just ahead and slightly right. Good, I thought, at least the fighters will stand back a bit now. The black puffs started to appear all over the place. Sometimes we could feel the bumps and hear the bangs. But, most surprising of all, the fighters took no notice of the AA and appeared to redouble their efforts to get us before the AA batteries.

My navigator now started to direct me on to the target; and at the same time my fire controller was shouting the range and bearing of the attacking fighters and imploring me to turn right as my navigator was saying: "Left, left steady, ten seconds to go." I had to tell my poor controller to shut up, and I never heard him say another word.

My mouth was dry as a bone, for the AA appeared everywhere and I wasn't able to take proper evasive action. "Left, left, five seconds to go," as I concentrated on keeping the correct height and airspeed. That bombing run lasted a lifetime . . . then a jubilant "Bombs gone." I looked up from the instrument panel and discovered my No. 2 had gone. We were on our own.

As I reached for the lever to close the bomb doors, I thought: "Down on the deck's the only chance." But even as my hand came away from the lever

there was a fearful bang, and, horror of horrors, all the flying controls had been shot away. The engines were going perfectly, and I waggled the stick and rudder again to convince myself it was true.

"We've had it, chaps, no controls, bale out, abandon aircraft, quick," and my navigator dashed past me from the nose and disappeared into the main fuselage. I struggled with the controls for perhaps another five seconds, and then suddenly the airplane reared right up, and although I throttled back, the nose wouldn't drop. The Ventura fell off the top of the loop and promptly whipped into a spin.

It's me for out! I jettisoned the hatch above my head and ripped off my harness and helmet. But in these few seconds the old airplane had really got wound up. The forces of the spin kept throwing me back into my seat, and I started to fight like a madman to get out of that top hatch. I remember getting my head in the breeze and my left foot on the throttle quadrant. Then there was a bang and I was outside. The airplane had broken up.

A glance at the ground was sufficient to show that I was at about 7,000 feet. As I reached for the rip cord, I suddenly thought of the enemy fighters. I had always had a nightmare of being shot in my parachute, and this fear was still uppermost in my mind, even in my present situation. I had seen a fellow do a delayed drop in New Zealand, and it didn't look too bad, so I hung on to the rip cord and kept an eye on the ground. I fell surprisingly slowly. "I'll pull the cord at 3,000 feet," I thought, but just before that height I turned on my back and slightly headfirst. As I couldn't right myself quickly, I didn't like this position, so gave the cord a good smart jerk. The shroud lines came whipping out, and one lot shot around my right leg, which I just succeeded in kicking free as I was pulled up with a jerk.

I appeared suspended in space at about 3,000 feet. Then, to my consternation, several large hunks of airplane went fluttering by like large autumn leaves. But my luck held and nothing hit my canopy. I found myself clutching the silver rip-cord handle like grim death, so I dropped it and watched it fall away at high speed toward a huge area of water, acres in extent, and into which it would appear I was about to follow. I thought about pulling on one side of the shroud lines, but decided to leave well enough alone! A glance in the target area revealed a large column of black smoke, and I thought: "Good, that's the bombs." But, thinking it over afterward, it was probably the aircraft burning. There was something wet on the back of my head, and an investigation brought forward a handful of blood. Frightened me to death, but it was only a small scalp wound received after I had taken off my tin hat, I think. And then I realized my left leg appeared broken just above the knee. Hell! I thought, this is going to be jolly. A strong wind and a heavy land-

ing. By this time I was less than 100 feet, and could see I was traveling at a fine old rate of knots and was going to miss the lake by a couple of hundred yards. It was going to be a plowed field right on the edge of the built-up area. The ground suddenly rushed at me. Bang! I went end over end over end, and finally came to rest stunned and spitting out earth. Suddenly the parachute pulled me flat on my back and dragged me off at high speed. But I soon stopped that by ganging the release box, and the parachute went off with a Dutchman in pursuit.

Several people soon gathered. As I dusted myself off I looked ruefully at my left trouser leg, which was my "No. 1 blue," now torn from top to bottom. I realized my leg was not broken, only badly bent, so I thought: "Escape is the thing!" Looking at the dozen or so Dutch people standing back a few paces watching my antics, I said: "Do any of you people speak English?" No response. Then I heard a shout. Looking over my shoulder, I saw a German with a gun, running and waving frantically. I knew I was finished, so I took my escape kit from my pocket and dropped it behind me so that the Dutch people could see, kicked some earth over it, and walked to meet my captor with my hands high. He advanced with his gun in a businesslike way and carefully frisked me. *"Kom mit,"* and I limped off in the direction indicated. A quarter of a mile away was an AA post of heavy guns, and as we drew near, lots of

Germans gathered to see their prize.

A corporal dressed the wound on my head, and, as he finished, a captain drew up in an open car. He spoke English, and promptly started to question me, but, of course, got nowhere. He seemed very interested to know what my target had been.

We were about to drive away when I heard a shout: "Hiya, Len." It was the first time my navigator had taken the liberty of using my Christian name. I was so glad to see him, he could have called me anything. And what a sight he looked! Hair and blood all down his face and everything covered with black slime. It appeared that the release box of his parachute had stopped a bullet, leaving a twisted piece of metal, which he was unable to turn. He had been dragged by his parachute through two dykes and across several fields. He had finally got his arms around a post and had hung on till help arrived.

His head wound was dressed also, and from the inch-wide cut on his brow, which was on the hairline, only white hair has grown ever since. This looks very peculiar in an otherwise jet-black thatch, but he assures me it has been worth many a pint in the local pub.

We were taken together to an Officers' Mess in the middle of Amsterdam, given coffee and cigarettes and a further unsuccessful interrogation. Later, we were taken to a military hospital for a further dressing and a stitch or two, then on to a huge military barracks, where the cell doors of solitary confinement clanged behind us.

I sat on a narrow, hard bed and stared into space for hours, wondering what had gone wrong. Had I made the right decisions? What a shock it was going to be for my poor wife. These disturbing thoughts accompanied me to the interrogation center of Dulag Luft, about ten days later. Another fortnight of solitary confinement with no books, then the interrogation. A few days later, about 50 new prisoners who had been gathered from all points of the compass were entrained for Stalag Luft III, the main Air Force Officers' Prison Camp. I was to have many adventures in this camp, but that is another story.

In the spring of 1943 the Royal Air Force Bomber Command launched an all-out attack on the important industrial area located in Germany's Ruhr River valley. The region was a center of coal mining and heavy industry; manufacturing in all parts of Germany depended on its products.

In its attack on the Ruhr the Royal Air Force planned to use water as well as high explosives. A series of dams had been constructed in the area to control water levels and supply electric power. Destruction of the dams would cause serious flooding and a shortage of electricity. Three of them, the Möhne, Eder, and Sorpe dams, were selected as targets.

A picked squadron under the leadership of Wing Comdr. Guy Gibson was formed and given several weeks of intensive training. The assignment was a dangerous and difficult one. They were to carry a specially designed bomb and drop it from the extremely low level of 60 feet. To help them find and maintain that altitude each Lancaster bomber had two small searchlights attached to its wing tips. The lights were set so that the two beams intersected exactly 60 feet below the aircraft. If the pilot flew so that they met at the surface of the water, he would know that he was at exactly 60 feet.

The crews flew hundreds of practice flights and dropped 2,500 practice bombs. They studied models of the dams and detailed maps of the route.

The weather was right on the night of May 15 and 19 heavily loaded Lancasters took off at dusk and headed for Germany. They were to attack in three waves. The first wave, led by Gibson, was to attack the Möhne dam and then the Eder dam. The target for the second wave was the Sorpe dam. The third group was to act as a reserve.

Here is an account of the successful attack on the Möhne dam. It resulted in extensive water damage to the surrounding area and, even more important, it greatly reduced the power supply of the Ruhr. The dam was not completely repaired until August, 1944.

The Dam Busters

Paul Brickhill

GIBSON slid over the Wash at 100 feet. The cockpit was hot and he was flying in his shirtsleeves with Mae West over the top. The sun astern on the quarter threw long shadows on fields peaceful and fresh with spring crops; dead ahead the moon was swimming out of the ground haze like a bull's-eye. Gibson flew automatically, eyes flicking from the horizon to the airspeed indicator,

Wing Commander Gibson (standing on ladder) and his crew about to enter their Lancaster bomber.

to the repeater compass in its rubber suspension.

The haze of Norfolk passed a few miles to port. In the nose, Spafford said, "There's the sea," and a minute later they were low over the water, flat and gray in the evening light. England faded behind. *G George* dropped down to 50 feet, and on each side Martin and Hopgood came down too, putting off the evil moment when German radar would pick them up.

You couldn't put it off indefinitely; about 20 miles from the Dutch coast the blips would be flicking on the radar screens and the orders would be going out to the flak batteries and fighter fields.

Martin ranged up alongside and there was a light winking as he flashed his Aldis lamp at them.

"What's he saying, Hutch?" Gibson asked.

"We're going to get plastered tomorrow night." The radio operator picked up his own Aldis and winked back, "You're damn right. Biggest binge of all time." Hutchison didn't drink.

Taerum spoke: "Our ground speed is exactly 203½ mph. We will be there in exactly one hour, ten minutes, and thirty seconds. We ought to cross the coast dead on track. Incidentally, you're one degree off course." The last part was the standing joke. The pilot who can fly without sometimes yawing a degree or so off course has yet to be born.

In the operations room of 5 Group Headquarters at Grantham, Cochrane was walking Barnes Wallis up and down, trying to comfort him. Wallis was like an expectant father, fidgety and jittery, and Cochrane was talking of anything but the bomb, trying to get Wallis' mind off it, but Wallis could think of nothing else.

"Just think what a wonderful job you made of the Wellington," Cochrane said encouragingly. "It's a magnificent machine; been our mainstay for over three years."

"Oh, dear, no," lamented the disconcerted scientist. "Do you know, every time I pass one I wonder how I could ever have designed anything so crude."

A black Bentley rushed up the graveled drive outside, pulled up by the door and the sentries snapped rigidly to attention as Harris himself jumped briskly out. He came into the room. "How's it going, Cocky?"

"All right so far, sir," Cochrane said. "Nothing to report yet." They walked up and down the long room between the wall where the aircraft blackboards were and the long desk that ran down the other side, where men were sitting. Satterly was there, "The Gremlin," the intelligence man, and Dunn, chief signals officer, sitting by a telephone plugged into the radio in the signals cabin outside. He would get all the Morse from the aircraft there; it was too far for low-flying planes to get through by ordinary speech.

Harris and Cochrane talked quietly, and Wallis, looking miserable, was walking with them but not talking, breaking away every now and then to look at the big operations map on the end wall. The track lines had been penciled in and he was counting off the miles they should be traveling. It was 10:35 when Cochrane looked at his watch and said, "They ought to be coming up the Dutch coast now."

The sun had gone and the moon was inching higher into the dusk, lighting a road ahead across the water; outside the dancing road the water was hardly visible, a dark mass with a couple of little flecks.

Taerum said, "Five minutes to the Dutch coast," and the crew snapped out of the wordless lull of the past half-hour. "Good," Gibson said. Martin and Hopgood eased their aircraft forward till the black snouts nosed alongside Gibson and veered out to make a wider target, their engines snarling thinly in gusts above the monotonous roar in *G George*. Flying so low, just off the water, they seemed to be sliding very fast along the moonpath toward the waiting flak.

Spafford said, "There's the coast." It was a black line lying dim and low on the water, and then from a couple of miles out on the port side a chain of glowing little balls was climbing into the sky. "Flak ship," said Martin laconically. The shells were way off and he ignored them. The sparkling moonpath ended abruptly; they tore across the white line of surf and were over enemy territory. "New course 105 magnetic," Taerum called, and the three aircraft swung gently to the left as they started the game of threading their way through the flak.

The northern wave made landfall about the same time, sighting Vlieland and turning southeast to cut across the narrow part and down over the Zuyder Zee. Munro led them across the dark spit; it was so narrow they would see the water again in about 30 seconds and have another 70 miles of comparatively safe water; but without warning there were flashes below and up came the fiery little balls. Munro felt the shock as they hit the aircraft, and then they were past and over the water again. Munro called on the intercom, to see if the crew were all right, but the earphones were dead.

Pigeon, the radio operator, was standing by his shoulder shouting into his ear, "No radio. No intercom. Flak's smashed it. I think everyone's O.K." Munro flew on several miles, trying

to fool himself they could still carry on, but it was no good and he knew it. Without radio he could not direct the attack on the Sorpe; could not even direct his own crew or get bombing instructions. Swearing, he turned for home.

Inside the Zuyder the water was dark and quite flat, treacherously deceptive for judging height. Geoff Rice slipped down a little to level at 60 feet by his belly lights, but the lights were not working properly and lured him lower as he tried to get a fix. A hammer seemed to hit the aircraft like a bolt and there was a tearing roar above the engines. Rice dragged her off the water, but the belly was torn out of her and the bomb had gone with it. The gutted fuselage had scooped up a couple of tons of water; it was pouring out of her and the rear gunner was nearly drowning in his turret. Marvelously, she still flew but was dropping back, and when they found the bomb was gone Rice turned back toward England.

The remaining two, Barlow and Byers, skirted their pinpoint on the cape at Stavoren and ten minutes later crossed to the enemy land again at Harderwijk. No one knows exactly how soon it was that the flak came curling up at them again, but there is a report that as Barlow's aircraft hit the ground the bomb went off with a blinding flash, lighting the countryside like a rising sun for ten seconds before it died and left nothing. It was either then or soon after that Byers

94

Möhne Dam as it appeared in a picture taken before the attack.

and his crew died too. Nothing more was heard from him. Only McCarthy was left on the Scorpe team, flying 60 miles behind, and perhaps that is what saved him.

Over Holland, Gibson, Martin, and Hopgood were down as low as 40 feet, playing hide-and-seek with the ground, the bomb aimers calling terse warnings as houses and trees loomed up, and the aircraft skimmed over them. They were cruising fast and under the cowlings the exhaust manifolds were glowing. Once the three pulled up fast as the pylons of a power line rushed at them, and they just cleared the wires.

Four miles to port they saw the flare path of Gilze-Rijen, German night fighter field, and a few miles farther on they passed just to the left of the night fighter airfield at Eindhoven. They could expect night fighters now; the operations rooms for miles around must be buzzing. Martin and Hopgood closed in on each side of Gibson for mutual protection. They should be able to see any fighter coming in because he would be higher, while they, low against the dark ground, would be hard to see, and that was their strength. Also their weakness where the flak was concerned. Their aircraft were higher, outlined. Just past Eindhoven, Gibson led them in a gentle turn to the northeast on the new course that would take them round the bristling guns of the Ruhr.

A few miles back the other two V's

of three were on course too. Dinghy Young pinpointed over the canal at Rosendaal and turned delicately to take them between the fighter fields, but Bill Astell did not seem sure this was the exact turning point. He bore off a little to the south for a minute and then turned back, but had fallen half a mile behind and was a fraction off track. They did not see him again, and it must have been quite soon after that the flak or fighter, whatever it was, got him.

Fourteen left.

The leading three slid across the border into Germany and saw no light or movement anywhere, only darkness filled with the beat of engines. Taerum thought they were south of track, so they edged to the north, a little nervily because this was the treacherous leg; they were coming up to the Rhine to sneak between the forewarned guns of Hüls and the Ruhr. Just short of the river some 12 light flak guns opened up without warning; the aircraft gunners squirted back at the roots of the tracer and then they were out of range. No one badly hit. The Rhine was rushing at them and up from a barge spat a thin line of tracer, but they were past before the bullets found them.

Two minutes later more guns opened up, and this time three searchlights lit on Gibson. Foxlee and Deering were shooting at the searchlights. One of them popped out but the two others held, and the air was full of tracer. The rear gunners came into ac-

96

tion, the searchlights switched to Martin, blinding him, and Gibson could read the big P on the side of the Lancaster. Every gun was firing, the aircraft shuddering with the recoil, and then they were through with throttles wide.

Ahead and just to the left another searchlight sprang to life and caught Gibson. Foxlee was firing instantly, holding his triggers in a long burst, his tracer whipping into the light. It flicked out, and as they went over in the dying glow they saw the gunners scattering. Tammy Simpson opened up from the rear turret till they were out of range.

They were past and shook themselves back into formation. Hutchison tapped out a flak warning, giving the exact position, and way back in Grantham Dunn picked it up and the powerful group radio rebroadcast it at full strength to all other aircraft.

Gibson swung them north around Hamm, whose marshaling yards will for years be notorious. Taerum said, "New course, skipper, 165 magnetic," and then they were hugging the ground on the last leg, slicing between Soest and Werl. Now the moon was high enough to light the ground and ahead loomed the dark hills that cradled the water. They climbed to the ridge that rimmed the horizon, crossed into the valley, and down below lay the flat sheet of Möhne Lake.

It was like looking down on the model; the same saucer of water, the same dim fields and across the neck of the lake the squat rampart hugging the water, crowned by the towers. In the half-light it looked like a battleship, but more impregnable. Reinforced concrete 100 feet thick.

"God," Bob Hay said, "can we break that?"

The dam came suddenly to life, prickling with sharp flashes, and the lines of angry red meteors were streaming into the sky and moving about blindly as the gunners hosed the area.

"Bit aggressive, aren't they?" asked Trevor-Roper. The pilots swung the aircraft away and headed in wide circles round the lake, keeping out of range and waiting for the others. There seemed to be about ten guns, some in the fields on each side of the lake near the dam, and some — a lot — in the towers on the dam.

Gibson started calling the other planes, and one by one they reported, except Astell. He called Astell again at the end, but Astell had been dead for an hour. After a while, Gibson gave up and said soberly over the intercom, "Well, boys, I suppose we'd better start the ball rolling." It was the end of the waiting and the start of action, when thought is submerged. He flicked his transmitter switch:

"Hello all Cooler aircraft, I am going in to attack. Stand by to come in in your order when I tell you. Hello *M Mother*. Stand by to take over if anything happens."

"O.K. Leader. Good luck." Hopgood's voice was a careful monotone.

Gibson turned wide, hugging the

hills at the eastern end of the lake. Pulford had eased the throttles on and she was roaring harshly, picking up speed and quivering, the nose slowly coming round till three miles ahead they saw the towers and the rampart of the dam, and in between, the flat dark water. Spafford said, "Good show. This is wizard. I can see everything." They came out of the hills and slammed across the water, touching 240 now, and Gibson rattled off the last orders:

"Check height, Terry! Speed control, Pulford! Gunners ready! Coming up, Spam!" Taerum flicked the belly lights on and, peering down from the blister, started droning: "Down . . . down . . . down . . . up a bit . . . steady, stead-y-y." The lights were touching each other, *G George* was exactly at 60 feet, and the flak gunners had seen the lights. The streams of glowing shells were swiveling and lowering, and then the shells were whipping toward them, slowly at first like all flak, and then rushing madly at their eyes as the aircraft plunged into them.

Gibson held her steady, pointing between the towers. Taerum was watching out of the blister, Pulford had a hand on the throttles and his eyes on the airspeed indicator, Spafford held the plywood sight to his eye and the towers were closing in on the nails; Gibson shouted to Pulford, "Stand by to pull me out of the seat if I get hit!" There was a sudden snarling clatter up in the nose; Deering had opened up, his tracer spitting at the towers.

The dam was a rushing giant, darkness split with flashes, the cockpit stank of cordite and thought was nothing but a cold alarm shouting, "In another minute we shall be dead," and they rocketed over the dam between the towers. A red Very light soared up as Hutchison pulled the trigger to let the others know, and then the deeper snarling chatter as Trevor-Roper opened up on the towers from the rear.

It was over and memory was confusion as they corkscrewed down the valley, hugging the dark earth sightless to the flak. They were out of range and Gibson lifted her out of the hills, turning steeply, and looked back. A voice in his earphones said, "Good show, Leader; nice work."

The black water between the towers suddenly rose and split and a huge white core erupted through the middle and climbed toward the sky. The lake was writhing, and as the whole column reached its peak and hung 1,000 feet high, like a ghost against the moon, the heavy explosion reached the aircraft. They looked in awe as they flew back to one side and saw sheets of water spilling over the dam and thought for a wild moment it had burst. The fury of the water passed and the dam was still there, the white column slowly dying.

Round the lake they flew while Hutchison tapped out in code to base. In a few minutes Gibson thought the lake was calm enough for the next bomb and called:

"Hello *M Mother*. You may attack now. Good luck."

"O.K. Leader; attacking." Hopgood was still carefully laconic. He was lost in the darkness over the hills at the end of the lake while the others waited. They saw his belly lights flick on and the two little yellow pools sliding over the water closing and joining as he found his height. He was straight and level on his run; the flak saw him and the venomous fireflies were darting at him. He plunged on; the gap was closing fast when the shells found him and someone shouted "He's been hit!"

A red glow was blossoming round the inner port wing tank, and then a long, long ribbon of flame trailed behind *M Mother*. The bomb aimer must have been hit, because the bomb overshot the parapet on to the power-house below.

M Mother was past the dam, nose up, straining for height so the crew could bail out, when the tanks blew up with an orange flame, a wing ripped away, and the bomber spun to the ground in burning, bouncing pieces. The bomb went off near the powerhouse like a brilliant sun. It was all over in seconds.

A voice said over the radio, "Poor old Hoppy."

Gibson called up: "Hello *P Popsie*. Are you ready?"

"O.K. Leader; going in."

"I'll fly across the dam as you make your run and try and draw the flak off you."

"O.K. Thanks, Leader."

Martin was turning in from the hills and Gibson headed across the lake, parallel to the dams and just out of effective range of the guns. As Martin's spotlights merged and sped across the water Gibson backtracked and Deering and Trevor-Roper opened up; six lines of tracer converged on the towers, drawing their attention. For some seconds most of the guns did not notice Martin rocketing over the water. He held his height, tracking straight for the middle of the dam between the moon-bathed towers, when the gunners spotted him and threw a curtain of fire between the towers, spreading like a fan so he would have to fly through it. Martin dove straight ahead. Two guns swung at them, and as the shells whipped across the water sharp-eyed little Foxlee was yelling as he squirted back, his tracer lacing and tangling with the flak.

A sharp "Bomb gone!" from Bob Hay, and in the same instant a shudder as two shells smacked into the starboard wing, one of them exploding in the inner petrol tank. A split second of flashes as they shot through the barrage. Tammy Simpson opened up from the rear turret, Chambers shot the Very light out and they were down the valley. Whittaker was looking fearfully at the hole in the starboard wing, but no fire was coming. He suddenly realized why — the starboard tank was empty!

Martin shouted, "Bomb gone, Leader."

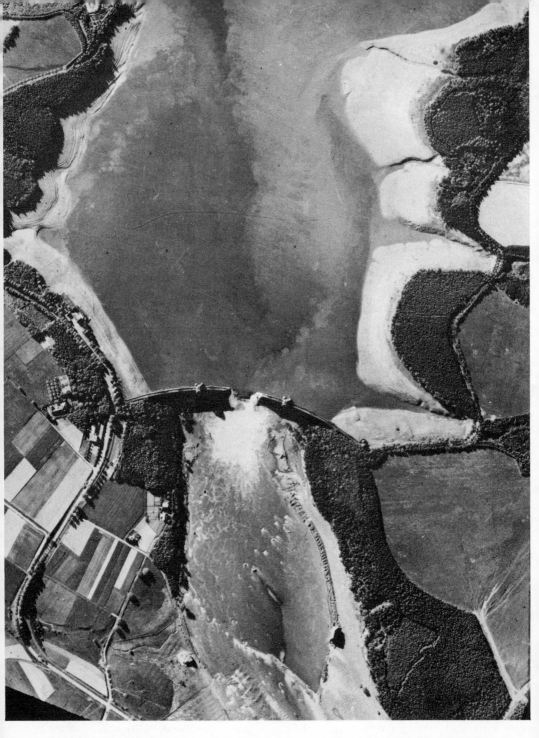

Möhne Dam after the attack by Royal Air Force Lancasters on the night of May 15, 1943. Water is pouring from the lake on the left through a 200-foot breach in the dam.

"O.K. *P Popsie.* Let me know when you're out of the flak. Hello *A Apple.* Are you ready?"

"O.K. Leader."

"Right. Go ahead. Let me know when you're in position and I'll draw flak for you."

Martin called again, "*P Popsie.* Clear now, Leader."

"O.K. Are you hit?"

"Yeah. Starboard wing, but we're all right. We can make it."

The lake suddenly boiled by the dam and the great white column climbed again to 1,000 feet. More water was cascading over the dam, but it cleared soon and the dam was still there.

Dinghy Young was on the air again. "*A Apple* making bombing run."

Gibson headed back over the lake, and this time Martin did the same. As Young came plunging across the lake Gibson and Martin came in on each side, higher up, and the flak did not know where to shoot. Young swept past the dam and reported he was all right. The great explosion was up against the dam wall, beautifully accurate, but the dam was still there. Again Gibson waited till the plume of spray had cleared and the water was calm.

He called Maltby and ordered him in, and as Maltby came across the water Gibson and Martin came in with him, firing with every gun that could bear and flicking their navigation lights on this time to help the flak gunners shoot at the wrong target. The red cartridge soared up from

Maltby's aircraft to signal "Attack successful."

In a few moments the mountain of water erupted skyward again under the dam wall. It was uncanny how accurate the bomb was. The spray from the explosions was misting up the whole valley now and it was hard to see what was happening by the dam. Gibson called Shannon to make his attack, and the words were barely out of his mouth when a sharp voice filled his earphones:

"It's gone! It's gone!"

Wheeling round the valley side Martin had seen the concrete face abruptly split and crumble under the weight of water. Gibson swung in close and was staggered. A ragged hole 100 yards across and 100 feet deep split the dam and the lake was pouring out of it, 134 million tons of water crashing into the valley in a jet 200 feet long, smooth on top, foaming at the sides where it tore at the rough edges of the breach and boiling over the scarred earth where the power-house had been.

Gibson told Shannon to "skip it."

The others flew over and were awed into silence. In the moonglow they watched a wall of water rolling down the valley, 25 feet high, moving 20 feet a second. A gunner still on his feet in one of the towers opened up at them until lines of tracer converged on the root of the flak and it stopped abruptly. The awed silence was broken by a babble of intercom chatter as they went mad with excitement; the only man not looking was Hutchison, sitting at his keyboard tapping out the single word "Sambo."

Soon the hissing steam and spray blurred the valley. Gibson called Martin and Maltby to set course for home, and told Young, Shannon, Maudslay, and Knight to follow him east to the Eder. Young was to control if Gibson was shot down.

This picture was taken during one of the air attacks on Pantelleria. Medium and heavy bombers and fighter-bombers dropped a total of 6,200 tons of bombs on the island. The first targets were the port and airfield areas. Then coastal batteries and gun emplacements were hit to prepare the way for the invasion planned for June 11. When the landing was made at noon on D-day, there was no resistance. Pantelleria had already been conquered from the air.

*One of the decisions made by Allied leaders at the January, 1943, confer-
ence in Casablanca was to follow up their success in Tunisia with the con-
quest of Sicily. Control of Sicily would open the Mediterranean to Allied
shipping and provide a steppingstone to the Italian mainland. Halfway
between Africa and Sicily was the fortified island of Pantelleria. Because
Sicily itself was beyond the range of fighter planes based in Tunisia, Pantelleria had to be taken first. This posed something of a problem because
rocky Pantelleria had only one area where a landing could be made and
that was heavily guarded. In addition, its airfield could accommodate
enough fighters to make an invasion very costly. In the face of these difficulties, General Dwight D. Eisenhower decided to reduce Pantelleria by
heavy bombardment. The offensive began on May 18, 1943, and continued
for almost a month.*

The Battle for Pantelleria

A Picture Story

Wrecked Axis aircraft littered Pantelleria's Marghana airfield after the air attack on the island
began. By June 1, there were no more serviceable planes left. The airfield's buildings and supply
dumps were also destroyed. When the invasion of Sicily got underway on July 10, the airfield had
been repaired and Marghana served as a valuable Allied air base.

Gunners manning the 50-caliber machine guns in the waist section of a B-17 bomber.

The Allied invasion of Sicily began in the early morning hours of July 10, 1943. For eight days prior to D-Day the airfields of the island fortress were subjected to an all-out attack by Allied air forces. Its purpose was to eliminate effective air opposition to the invasion forces. There were 19 large airdromes in Sicily; of these the ones located around Gerbini were the most important. The biggest attack against Gerbini took place on July 5 when an estimated 100 enemy planes were destroyed. Here is the story of the B-17 gunner who accounted for seven of them.

The Wild Waist Gunner

Jack Pearl

AT DAWN on July 5, 1943, Staff Sgt. Benjamin F. Warmer hoisted himself into one of the 30 B-17's squatting on the runway of a U.S. airfield in North Africa. Along with the other airmen boarding their planes, Warmer knew what their target for the day was: the complex of Axis air bases around Gerbini on the Nazi fortress island of Sicily.

It wasn't the kind of mission that allowed for much preflight levity. Even the stock jibes about Warmer's breathtaking 6 feet 6 inches, 275-pound bulk weren't forthcoming this morning. Usually he was greeted by shouts of "Somebody weigh down that other wing with a light tank before this plane tips over!" or "What this outfit needs is an airplane with six engines!" It was a fact that when Sgt. Warmer levered himself onto the deck of a B-17, the big plane heeled over noticeably to starboard.

Like the others, Warmer embarked on his preflight tasks soberly and efficiently. Even to a bystander, unfamiliar with the "Top Secret" orders carried by the ship commanders, the serious nature of the mission could be read in the tense, impassive faces of the airmen. Gerbini, at the base of Mt. Etna, was the nerve center of all the air defenses on Sicily. Nowhere, with the possible exception of Berlin, had the Nazis amassed greater fighter and antiaircraft defenses.

Unlike many men of great size and power, Sgt. Ben Warmer was even tempered, good natured, and tolerant of less endowed companions, whom he could have snapped in two without much sweat. It was a kind of lazy, supercilious Olympian manner that sometimes infuriated more mortal men. For the most part, though, Ben inspired awe and admiration from his air mates, and he was one of the most

105

popular personalities in the 12th Air Force.

With smoothness resulting from long teamwork, the crewmen of the big four-engined Fortress took their posts. A B-17 bomber sprouts ten .50-caliber machine guns, situated to cover the sky around it in a three-dimensional sphere of 360 degrees. Designed as an "entity," the ship could defend itself against enemy fighter attack on long-range missions beyond the range of fighter cover. In both the European and Pacific theaters of war it won the grudging admiration of Nazi and Jap aces as a worthy foe.

Sgt. Warmer took his place by the right waist gun and went through his checklist: oxygen mask, radio earphones, the electric leads of his heated flight suit. Bulging with fleece from collar to toes, the gargantuan gunner resembled a monster grizzly bear. Clothing and paraphernalia placed all kinds of prohibitions on movement and comfort. But without them men couldn't live on high-altitude bombing runs where lack of oxygen caused permanent blackouts in seconds and the temperature hovered at 72 degrees below zero. On more than one occasion a careless B-17 crewman had touched the aluminum skin of the plane with a bare hand and watched his flesh turn into a white, dead chunk of ice before his horrified eyes.

Warmer folded his ammo belts neatly in the wooden box alongside his gun. He peered out through the plexiglass window in the side of the plane and waggled the snout of the protruding .50-caliber. It swiveled easily in the accordion-type "skirt" which fixed it in the fuselage of the B-17.

The great leviathan rumbled slowly down the desert runway, picked up speed and rose into the air like a giant condor. The Mediterranean Sea spread out beneath her like an enormous glossy mirror in the sunrise. It was a long, slow climb to the assigned altitude, and the gunners spent the time in relaxing small talk.

Directly across from Warmer, on the port waist gun, Sgt. E. R. Worthy sat crosslegged like a Buddha, his back propped against the side of the plane.

"You're gonna get a real chance to add to your score in this show, Ben," he drawled. In their last mission over Naples, Warmer had shot down two German ME-109 fighters. It was a rare thing for a gunner to get two confirmed kills in one day, and the feat had added to Warmer's celebrity status in the squadron.

Warmer grinned. "I gotta do better than last time, that's for sure. This is a very special day."

"How's that?"

"My wedding anniversary. Married seven years today."

Worthy was impressed. "No kidding? Bet you never figured then you'd be jockeying a waist gun in a Flying Fortress 10,000 feet above the Mediterranean on your seventh anniversary did you?"

The big man shrugged. "I wasn't

wasting my time worrying about what I'd be doing seven years ahead — or one year for that matter."

"You got the right idea, Ben," called the belly gunner from his plexiglass bubble, suspended from the underside of the B-17, where it hung out in sheer space.

Worthy giggled. "Don't he sort of remind you of a goldfish in a bowl out there? Man, those Nazi pilots must water at the mouth when they see a fat target like that."

The belly gunner snorted. "Nuts! I'd rather be all balled up tight in my little cocoon than standing broadside like you guys when we go into battle. You don't think that aluminum skin is gonna stop any slugs do you?"

"Guess not," Worthy admitted wryly. Then giving up on the bubble gunner, he slid the needle into Warmer. "I'm sure glad I ain't as big as Ben though."

The belly gunner whistled. "God, yes! What a target. Like aiming at a barn door. Any slug hits the ship is almost bound to hit Ben too."

Warmer laughed easily and flexed a huge bicep. "I got thick skin. Slugs just ricochet off me like peas off a boulder."

Another gunner aft yelled up the well of the long fuselage. "You guys hear about the special mission we got? After all the bombs are dumped, we're gonna drop Ben through the bomb bay. When he hits, the whole Gerbini complex will be finished."

The other crewmen really enjoyed that one. Ben laughed the hardest of all.

Horseplay ceased abruptly as the pilot's voice crackled over the intercom: "O.K. you guys, break it up. Let's get on the ball now."

The clouds lay far below now as the big planes strained into the clear upper reaches of the atmosphere. The air was too thin for comfortable breathing and each exhalation sent forth a spout of vapor as thick as steam. Oxygen masks were adjusted; electric leads plugged into sockets from boots and clothing.

"Test-fire your guns," came the command from up front.

Sgt. Warmer tilted the nose of his .50-caliber toward the Mediterranean and squeezed off a short burst. The dully gleaming cylinders, lying in neat endless ranks in their belt, fed into the breech with cosmolined smoothness.

The other nine guns on the ship cleared their throats too. Peering out through the plexiglass rectangle, Warmer could see the other bombers in the formation following suit. Muzzle flashes, tracers arcing seaward, the dim cacaphony of simulated battle filled the air.

The only medium of communication now was over the intercom radio. Conversation fell off self-consciously. As they closed in on the target, the desire for small talk was absent. No time for thought really. All the senses were subservient to the sense of sight, keen eyes probing the clear blue all around them for suspicious specks that could be enemy fighters.

Then, as the formation cleared the coast of Sicily, the awaited announcement came.

"Bandits 12 o'clock high!"

And immediately:

"Bandits at three o'clock!"

"And low!"

The sky was black with specks, growing ever bigger, materializing into the vicious needle-nosed silhouettes that every Allied airman knew so well. Messerschmitts, pride of the Luftwaffe — the best fighter planes in the world in 1943.

"God," Warmer thought to himself, "there must be a million of them!"

It was a slight exaggeration. There were, in fact, 100 German fighter planes in the air that day. One hundred Messerschmitts against 30 lumbering bomb-laden B-17 Fortresses. If the bombers had been anything but B-17's the odds might just as well have been a million to one.

"Bandits coming in at two o'clock!" the radio earphones crackled.

Ben peered through the plexiglass and saw them, at least 20, too many to count — Messerschmitt-110's swooping down out of the sun just off the Fortress' right wing. He swiveled his gun to meet the threat. The lead plane seemed to be rushing straight at him, spitting fire from the front edges of its wings. The tracers reached out for him and he tensed for the shatter of plexiglass and the rending of lead at his flesh. But the tracers fell short, drop-ping beneath the B-17's belly.

He waited until the German plane filled up his sight, then hit the trigger hard. The .50-caliber bucked and its own tracers arched out toward the ME, felt for it and found it. The enemy ship broke sharply to the left and down, trailing flame and smoke.

Ben Warmer did not let up on the trigger. The Germans were swarming like darning needles before the plexiglass window. A second ME spouted fire from its engine and maintained a grim collision course with the B-17. Warmer recoiled, almost slipping on the empty shell casings that clattered to the deck continuously from the bomber's .50-calibers. Rolling around like marbles, they presented a serious hazard to any gunner who tried to shift his footing. Ben caught himself with both hands, gripping his gun, and watched the oncoming ME. At the last instant it flipped over on its back and skidded away.

"That's two for Ben!" an excited voice shouted over the intercom.

The Flying Fortress was under attack from all sides now, the voices on the intercom blurred and confusing.

"Watch that baby at nine high!"

"Two bandits at six o'clock. What the hell's the matter with that tail gun!"

The violent action had loosened the pliable skirt around the barrel of Ben's gun, admitting a stream of sub-zero air into the plane. It hit his face like a frosted fist. Instantly a shield of ice formed on the exhaust valve of his

Staff Sergeant Benjamin F. Warmer who shot down seven Nazi planes during a single mission.

oxygen mask, blocking the flow. Ben brushed it away easily with one hand and it clattered to the deck like broken glass. Behind him one of the other crewmen hadn't fared as well, however. Clawing at his mask he staggered up the deck, struggling for breath. He collapsed beside Ben. The big waist gunner quickly knelt and readjusted the man's oxygen valve. A moment later he was back in action, with a grateful nod to Ben.

"I got me one!" Sgt. Worthy crowed delightedly as the fury of the German attack increased.

An ME-109 dove in at the ship in a banking turn from two o'clock. Ben gave it a short burst and with some surprise watched it roll out of sight beneath the Fortress' right wing smoking furiously. No. 3 of the day for Warmer!

"Nice shooting" — the rest of the words faded in an explosion underneath the B-17's belly, hurling it 20 feet higher in the sky.

There was a small fire forward, but it was quickly extinguished by the crew in the cockpit. The Fortress was reeling under the pasting it was taking from the fighters' guns, but it did not falter. The B-17 was the hardiest ship the Allies had ever put aloft.

German fighters whirled around them on all sides, trying to break up the solid formation of the Flying Fortresses, like Indians circling a wagon train in a cowboy movie. And with comforting regularity first one, and then another of the ME-109's and 110's would "bite the dust," flipping over on its back with an agonized whine before it plummeted to destruction. And less frequently one of the big bombers, too, would quiver, flounder, shake itself, stagger on with coughing engines as flames licked at its vitals, then sink away from its companions in a fatal dive. Each time it happened Ben would watch anxiously for the blossoming parachutes, the cold clutch of dread at his heart. There were good friends aboard most of these ships . . .

"Watch it Ben! Three o'clock high!"

The ME bored in like lightning, guns flashing. The steep angle of its dive caused the pilot to undershoot his target, the tracers dropping off beneath the belly of the B-17. He jerked the nose up and the tracers lifted toward Warmer. But before they climbed high enough, the waist gunner caught the ME head on with a burst of 20 fifties. The German plane disintegrated in a ball of fire. No. 4 for Ben!

Time and time again the fearsome tracers bracketed the B-17 like fiery tentacles but never touched her. The fiery darts seemed so close at times that the gunners felt they could reach out and catch the glowing balls. But there was no time for fear. The Fortress' ten guns worked continuously, swiveling back and forth, up and down, pumping like the pistons in a V-8 engine. They took a terrible toll of the attacking Germans.

"Nine o'clock! Two bandits!"

Sgt. Worthy's gun swung on the planes, found the bead and blazed. The tracers from the opposing planes mingled; for a moment there was the insane illusion that they could collide head on. However, the Germans were shy a few yards.

Worthy's guns blasted the lead plane, and it twisted out of sight in an agony of fire and smoke. "I got me

No. 2!" he exulted.

"Rack one up for me!" said the belly gunner as he plastered a 109 trying to sneak up from below.

The voices heard over the intercom were fewer in number now, and to Ben's trained ears the clamor of the B-17's guns was not as robust as it had been. Maybe six — no more than seven — were still operating. There was no time to ponder on the "who" and the "why" of it.

An ME curved in from four o'clock, tracers from the B-17's tail gun snapping at its heels. As it broke toward him, Ben gave it a long burst that chewed the German's left wing to pieces where it fitted against the fuselage. The pilot tried to roll away from the deadly 50's but the strain was too much for the crippled wing. It snapped off cleanly from the body, and the ship plummeted wildly out of control.

Ben snapped off a burst at another Messerschmitt. Six shots sounded, then the bolt slammed hollowly on an empty chamber. The ammo box was empty. Cursing, he dropped the gun and looked around for spare ammo belts. They were stacked a few feet away. The deck of the cabin was littered with empty casings now, thousands of them skittering back and forth, fore and aft, with the motion of the ship. They made a discordant swishing sound, like the rush of the sea across a sandy beach. Ben Warmer stepped, flatfooted and cautious, across the tops of a mass of them toward the ammunition belts.

"Damn!" his feet shot out from under him and he crashed to his knees. Impatiently he reached for the belts and slung several around his broad shoulders. Then came the short, precarious trip back across the rolling casings.

There was no time to stack the belts in neat fashion in the ammo box. Ben draped a belt across his right shoulder so that it could slide freely and loaded one end of it into his gun. Though the method was unorthodox, the .50-caliber worked smoothly with the ammo belt playing out unhampered across the fabric of Ben's jacket.

Sgt. Worthy proclaimed his third kill of the day. "Only two more to catch you, Ben!"

"I hope you do," Ben called back.

They were over the target now. Below the cloud cover lay the airfields of Gerbini. The red and black plumes of antiaircraft fire appeared in their midst. Strangely enough the Americans welcomed them since ack-ack posed as much of a threat to the ME fighters as it did to the bombers in this tangled, air-to-air close combat. In the first few minutes two of the Germans were disabled by their own friendly ground fire.

The B-17's unloaded their eggs, sticks of six and eight and ten high-explosive bombs, falling in neat precision. The air above Gerbini was thick with them. Within minutes, the installations below would be saturated with fire and devastation.

Free of their burden the B-17's

soared high and light on the updrafts pushing at their broad wings. Speed and maneuverability improved twofold.

Despite the cold, Ben was perspiring freely inside his clothing. The ammo belts slid across his shoulder with a gentle whirring sound, the friction imparting a definite warmth to the leather.

The words of a popular song of the day ran through his brain crazily:

"Praise the Lord and pass the ammunition . . .

"Praise the Lord and pass the ammunition . . ."

"Bandits 12 o'clock high!" the earphones crackled.

The guns up forward were out of commission so the German pilot encountered no resistance as he poured lead into the top of the Fortress. A long line of holes appeared in the roof and the deck as slugs stitched the ship from fore to aft.

Then the ME veered off and sailed in clear silhouette across Warmer's line of vision. Ben worked the 50's into the flashing target, leading her the way a hunter leads a flying duck, his teeth bared in malicious glee. Bull's-eye on the cockpit! A second burst of deflection shots ripped into the twisted cross of the black swastika on the fighter's fuselage. The pilotless plane flipped and dove with smoke in her wake. No. 6 for Sgt. Ben Warmer!

The German force was less than half of what it had been when the battle began. Dozens had died under the bombers' volatile guns. Others had given up the fight when the formation headed back to Africa. The diehards that remained made one final furious assault on the bombers.

Two planes cut under the belly of Warmer's ship, then climbed straight up at her. The tail gunner flamed one, but the other eluded his fire and climbed at the Fortress from five o'clock, tracers reaching for the emergency fuel tanks. Warmer swung his gun back and down, as far as it would go, squeezing off bursts at the German. One burst caught the ME squarely in the engine, killing it instantly. The fighter floundered like a wounded bird, then her nose dipped and she fell into a vertical spin. No. 7 of the day for Ben Warmer! No. 13 for his crew! An exceedingly unlucky number — for the Germans.

It was a weary, battered — but happy and victorious — bunch of U.S. airmen who stumbled or were carried out of their aircraft back at the Algerian bases. Some would not return to share in the celebrations that lasted all through the night, but their share of the glory was none the less. Forty-one Nazi fighter planes had been knocked out of the Sicilian skies that morning.

More significantly, the raid on Gerbini had been a success. What's more, the air raids on the enemy nerve centers in Sicily would continue unabated for four more days. On July 9, when Patton's Seventh Army and Montgomery's Eighth Army stormed ashore from invasion barges on the beaches of Licata, Gela, Scoglitti, Noto, and Syracuse, they would encounter only slight resistance from the air. For the first time since the beginning of World War II, Allied planes would hold uncontested control of the skies.

For his particular feat on July 5, 1943, shooting down seven Nazi fighters in a single engagement, Staff Sgt. Benjamin Warmer received a unique honor. Within the massive records of USAF for World War II there is one list that is select above all others. It includes the names of men who have achieved the status of "ace" (five or more enemy planes shot down in air-to-air combat) — men like Maj. Dick Bong, Maj. Gregory "Pappy" Boyington, Capt. Bob Johnson, Capt. Joe Foss, and many other revered pilots. It is made up exclusively of pilots and officers — except for one entry:

Staff Sgt. Benjamin F. Warmer ... 12th AF ... nine planes.

Mobbed by reporters after the mission, Ben Warmer seemed embarrassed.

"I didn't do anything so great," he said modestly. "They just kept flying into my sight, and I kept pulling the trigger and bagging them as fast as they came. Any fair duck hunter could have done it."

Bombs away! A Lancaster bomber of the RAF Bomber Command over the target.

President Franklin D. Roosevelt of the United States, Prime Minister Winston Churchill of Great Britain, and their military leaders, meeting at Casablanca, Morocco, in January, 1943, decided the time had come to use Allied air strength for the "destruction and dislocation of the German military, industrial and economic system and the undermining of the morale of the German people." Bombs were to be dropped on Germany around the clock with the Americans carrying out precision daylight attacks and the Royal Air Force bombing at night.

One of the cities chosen as a target was Hamburg. Its population of a million and a half made it the second largest city in Germany. Hamburg was an important seaport and contained many industries. Its location on the coast made it easy to reach. This was important because a sustained attack was planned. Four great raids were to make Hamburg one of the most heavily bombed cities in Germany.

The "Battle of Hamburg" opened on the night of July 24, 1943. Seven hundred and forty Royal Air Force bombers dropped 2,396 tons of high explosive and incendiary bombs in two and one-half hours. The British also dropped strips of foil called Window to confuse German radar and only 12 bombers were lost.

The second Royal Air Force raid took place three nights later. This time 739 bombers dropped 2,417 tons of bombs, many of them incendiaries. The combination of the new attack and the fires still burning from the first bombing produced the phenomenon known as fire storms — currents of rapidly moving, superheated air that spread fire and destruction over large areas.

Here is the story of one of the Royal Air Force's Lancaster pilots who took part in that attack as he told it to author Martin Caidin.

Flak Burst

Martin Caidin

ON THE SECOND big raid into Hamburg — I missed the attack against the Krupp works in Essen that was sandwiched in between — I never had the chance to see the fire storm in full strength. Many of the other fellows did, and their stories were almost be-yond belief. A few of the Lancs got caught in the flue of superheated air as they passed over the city at 16,000 feet, and it was as if they were nothing more than wood chips in a storm at sea.

The pilots told me they had no control of their aircraft any longer. They were thrown about by the heat and even flipped over on their backs. Everything sort of went to hell until the Lancs managed to get free of the severe turbulence.

I didn't see the fire storm, and I nearly never saw another morning, either. This was the last raid I flew for a long time.

We were at 16,000 feet. Everybody was still tossing Window out of their airplanes, and we howled in glee as we listened in on the Jerry wireless and heard them going crazy. The flak and the searchlights were like the first raid; they waved about aimlessly, and if you caught a packet of flak, it was by the sheer odds of so many aircraft being in the same air space with so much of the stuff.

We caught it, all right, and there was no warning; nothing. I was flying along, heading for the city, when suddenly there was a brilliant flash. The bomber lunged wildly; it could have been any kind of motion, a violent lurch, a jerk, but it certainly was wicked. Everything disappeared in a second of blinding light, and the next moment, when the shock of the impact left me, I felt a gush of cold air streaming in from under the instrument panel.

Things really came apart in those moments, to say the least. The blast of wind, and perhaps the uncontrolled motions of the airplane, pushed the oxygen mask over my eyes. I fumbled at it frantically and finally managed to tear it down so that I could see.

Just a glance at the instruments stopped my heart cold, for the bomber — with all that heavy stuff in its belly — was in a steep right spiral, almost hung up on her wing and gaining speed with every second. It took me a good 6,000 feet to come out of the spiral, to roll into a dive, and pull her out. I kept shouting for the copilot to help, but when he didn't respond I concentrated on just saving our lives.

At 10,000 I had her fairly straight and level, although the wind was no bargain. I yelled at the copilot again, but still he didn't answer. When I felt I could trust the ship for a moment, I turned to look at him. His head was well over; he was limp, his head on his chest, and obviously either unconscious or dead. But I didn't know what had happened. Another flak burst that shook us up gave me a bit of light and I saw that the window on the copilot's side was blacking out.

I reached for the flashlight in my flying boot — and almost cried with the pain. That was the first moment that I realized I'd been hit myself. It was a heavy, sharp pain that seemed to be all over my body. Whenever I moved my arms and legs, I felt I'd simply pass out. But there was nothing else to do but fly, and so I did.

I played the light on the copilot, and right then and there I knew that he'd never talk to me or to anyone else again. The window was blacking out from a heavy spray of blood whipping away from the side of the

116

Making Window in a British factory. The strips of metallic paper were dropped from planes during bombing attacks to confuse the German radar system.

copilot's head and his neck; he'd been killed instantly.

They say that real trouble waits to fall on you like a ton of bricks, and my time seemed to be up. The flight engineer came forward and reported that we had one engine completely gone. Not just knocked out, you see; he meant his words literally. The flak burst tore it right off the wing and threw it away somewhere over Germany. Another engine was losing oil

pressure with frightening speed; the oil sprayed back and it looked like we would have fire on our hands in a moment. I feathered this one, and that left me with two engines on one side.

The flight engineer did the best he could to work with me, then shouted something about an emergency, and he disappeared. I increased the manifold boost to about 54 inches, holding the left wing low.

We were losing altitude steadily,

and Hamburg was almost below us. Funny, never for a moment during all this did we even think of abandoning the bomb run. Just as long as the old girl would fly, we kept right on course. We were real low now, and this actually worked in our favor, as the flak whanged away at the bomber stream well over our heads.

But the bombs wouldn't let go; the mechanism was all shot up. The engineer went to the bomb bay and fiddled with the gear. He finally ended up stomping on two of the bombs to get them free of their shackles.

Thank the Lord for all that weight falling away. The moment the bombs let loose the ship reared up her nose, and then settled down in a fairly steady attitude. We were losing height at about 150 feet a minute, but that isn't really too bad, considering that we'd come down this far like a rock. I rolled her into a wide turn and set for home. Even that wasn't any guarantee — for after we left the target and I had the chance to look around, I wasn't at all sure we would make it.

The first thing I learned was where that draft came from. We had no nose left. The flak burst had ripped away the entire nose section — it was just a big hole up front. As for the navigator — he had been acting as bombardier — he was blown out into space, dead or alive. I've never learned which. It was this mess up front that kept forcing us down. Normally the old bird would fly like an angel on only two engines, but with that fearsome drag she just

didn't have it.

That made a navigator-bombardier lost and most likely dead, and the co-pilot dead as well. The flight engineer came back to report that steel splinters had torn the radio navigator's hand right off his arm. He'd managed to get a tourniquet on, and it looked as if the boy would live.

The top-turret gunner, however, had less than a fifty-fifty chance, for his right leg was gone. They'd put a tourniquet on his leg, and used the first-aid kit as best they could, but it was touch and go because of all the blood he'd lost.

On top of this, most of the instruments were knocked out. The radio was shot to pieces, and that meant all our navigation gear was gone. I had some flight instruments, and that was all. I turned for England almost by instinct, and thank heaven for those fires already flaring up in Hamburg. We — the tail gunner, that is — could see them for more than 90 miles going away, and that gave me the reference I needed for direction. It was a clear night as well, or else we would never have made it home.

The pain kept getting worse, but there was nothing I could do. Things weren't so bad if I simply sat, but whenever I moved my arms and legs any distance at all, someone slammed a red-hot poker right into my back. There wasn't much use in making any noise about it, though, for if I didn't fly the airplane, who would? And the radio navigator and the turret gunner

BEFORE CAMOUFLAGE.

BINNEN
ALSTER

STATION

RAILWAY
LINES

In an unsuccessful attempt to protect Hamburg from attack, the Nazis camouflaged some of its landmarks and target areas. The Binnen Alster (a river dammed up to form a lake in the city's center) was covered to resemble a built-up area and "roads" were painted on top of the main railroad station.

AFTER CAMOUFLAGE

BINNEN
ALSTER

STATION

RAILWAY
LINES

couldn't bail out in their condition. Besides, no one likes to call it quits when the machine is still flying.

Over France we were down to 3,000 feet, and still giving up our precious height. We made the Channel at just above 1,000 feet, and it was a touch-and-go struggle to make it across the water. But make it we did, and I dropped her down at the first field that came into sight, while the flight engineer fired off all the flares he could find.

When the aircraft rolled to a stop, I couldn't believe we were really back and safe on the ground. I undid the belt and started to get out of my seat; or perhaps I should say that I tried to do all this.

That was the last I remembered for quite a while. I didn't see any colored lights or a red haze or anything. I just blacked out. When I came to I was in a hospital bed, wrapped almost from head to toe in plaster. It seems I took not only the full force of the flak burst, but got quite a few of its pieces as well.

The doctors told me I had 23 fractures, including three in my spine. No one could explain — least of all myself — how I got that crate home.

One of the outstanding air operations of World War II was the low-level B-24 attack on the Ploesti oil refineries in Romania. The attack was launched from Ninth Air Force bases at Bengazi in North Africa on August 1, 1943. Never before had bombers traveled so far to their target. The purpose of the daring mission was to deprive Germany of badly needed aviation and diesel fuels and thus to shorten the war.

Preparations for the Ploesti raid were extensive. Five units, the 376th, the 93rd, the 389th, the 98th, and the 44th Bombardment Groups were assembled at Bengazi where they flew numerous low-level practice missions which included bombing from low altitudes. A reproduction of the Ploesti area was laid out on the desert to familiarize the crews with the appearance of the target and the location of enemy defenses.

One hundred and seventy-seven planes carrying 1,726 men took off for Ploesti on that fateful morning. Their carefully planned route took them across the Mediterranean and over Albania, Yugoslavia, and the Danubian plain. They were to attack the target from the northwest. It was hoped that the combination of a circuitous route with low-level flying would enable the bombers to escape detection by the enemy.

As it turned out, the five groups became scattered in clouds over the mountains. Radio silence made it difficult for them to reorganize. Valuable time was lost and the formidable ground and air defenses of Ploesti were alerted. An already bad situation was made considerably worse when the lead plane mistook the IP (Initial Point) where the final turn to the target was to be made. Instead of proceeding to Ploesti the leading 376th Group headed for Bucharest.

We pick up the story of the Ploesti raid with the 376th Group under Col. Keith K. Compton after it had made the wrong turn toward Bucharest. The experiences of the 93rd, 389th, 98th, and 44th groups over the target area follow.

Fifty-four bombers were lost in the course of the attack on the Ploesti refineries — forty-one of them in the battles that raged between the bombers and defending fighters and antiaircraft installations on the ground. Five hundred and thirty-two American airmen were listed as dead, imprisoned, missing or interned.

Due to the problems encountered by the attacking force, damage to Ploesti was less than had been anticipated. An estimated 42 per cent of its refining capacity was destroyed. The production of lubricating oils was reduced and 40 per cent of Ploesti's cracking capacity was knocked out for several months.

It was roughly 1,150 miles from Bengazi to Ploesti. One hundred and sixty-four planes reached the heavily defended target where the bombing was done under the worst possible conditions. No less than five Medals of Honor were awarded to men who took part in the mission — an indication of the feats of flying and fighting that were accomplished.

Ploesti

Leon Wolff

BANTERINGLY and otherwise there had been a good deal of conversation back in Libya about Romana Americana, the only plant in Ploesti which had been seized by Germany from an American interest: Standard Oil of New Jersey. Briefing officers had emphasized that for political and diplomatic reasons it was essential that no favorites were to be played and that this particular target be smashed for certain. It had been assigned to the most experienced group of the entire task force — Col. Compton's 376th — which was to bomb the Romana Americana installation and none other, in

A Liberator over the Astra Romano refinery, one of the eight refineries in the Ploesti area. After the August 1, 1943, attack it was estimated that enough damage was done to Astra Romano to keep it immobilized for six months.

contrast to three of the remaining groups which were given two refineries each to locate and attack. Nonetheless Col. Compton's aircraft never did touch Romana Americana that day, nor did anyone else.

After the run-up through the valley (referred to as "difficult by Gen. Brereton in his memoirs) and the wrong turn toward Bucharest instead of Ploesti, Compton found his formation in an uncomfortable predicament. To go back toward the IP and start all over again seemed impossible. Pandemonium had already broken loose. On the other hand, to run through the strongest sector of antiaircraft guns in a dubious effort to locate the target from an unfamiliar direction would, in effect, base the entire 376th operation on pure guesswork. After discovering the mistake he had, at most, one minute in which to make up his mind. All 30 planes were now flying over the suburbs of Bucharest itself.

Following a hurried conversation with Gen. Ent, Compton decided to head straight for Ploesti from the southwest. Thereupon, the 376th, still followed by Addison Baker's group, executed the tightest possible turn toward the target 25 miles away. The closer Compton's men approached Ploesti, the more intense became the flak, fired by German gunners at remarkably oblique angles directly into the path of the oncoming planes; 88-mm. cannon fired point-blank over open sights, like so many shotguns. Machine-gun bullets came up in sheets. Three

bombers apparently crashed during this phase.

In desperation Compton then led his remaining aircraft in a great 20-mile semicircle around Ploesti, hoping to get at it from a northerly direction. While this would be a roundabout route, at least the final approach would be more or less as planned, and the planes would be coming in from the direction where Intelligence had forecast the least number of defending guns.

So the 376th drove in from the new angle, northeast of Ploesti. Though obscured by smoke, their target, Romana Americana, could be dimly seen in the distance. However, the volume of AA fire seemed as great as it had been previously to the south. At this point Gen. Ent himself got on the interplane radio and directed the 376th Group to attack "targets of opportunity." This was, in effect, an admission that the individual attack of this group had misfired. The five squadron commanders, each leading six planes, were now on their own.

Most of these planes ranged over the general Ploesti target area and unloaded on anything that looked good. It was in this action that the volunteer, Maj. Jerstad, and most of his crew were killed. When a burst of flak caught his plane it began to burn. He continued to fly toward the refinery that he had selected, and stayed on course for three miles while the flames sheathed both wings and began to envelop the body of the plane as far back

123

as the top turret. After bombing the plant, his plane plummeted into the target area.

Maj. Norman C. Appold, a tall, thin youth with a large Adam's apple, decided to make a try for the Concordia Vega installation. He led his squadron straight in, and all aircraft unloaded practically at once. An inferno of fire and smoke burst skyward. The six planes plunged through it and emerged on the other side, miraculously unharmed but covered with soot. While the target was in this fashion well plastered, it had been intended for Addison Baker's target force.

And, finally, a few planes from the now thoroughly dispersed lead group set out for Campina, where they bombed the Steaua Romana refinery, which had already been smashed by Jack Wood's outfit.

Bitter and frustrated over the turn of events, Col. Baker and his 93rd had been dragged willy-nilly into this imbroglio from the south, behind Compton's formation. Compton, as noted, had turned right (east) at the outskirts of Ploesti. It was the second time his group had turned unaccountably right, and perhaps Baker was becoming annoyed, for he ignored the leading group and the AA fire and plunged directly into the target from the south, followed by his intact group of 35 aircraft. Prior to the mission Baker had emphasized the stringent necessity of keeping a tight formation so as to hit their small targets with the greatest number of bombs. He had warned:

"If anything happens to the lead ship pay no attention. Don't swerve. No matter what happens, keep straight . . ."

Baker's Target Force No. 2 Liberators had been assigned Concordia Vega, but they could not locate it from their reverse approach. However, as noted, Maj. Appold's squadron had been kind enough to bomb it by mistake, and with excellent results.

Meanwhile, Target Force No. 3, also under Col. Baker and commanded by Maj. Potts, was doing its best to find something resembling its assigned targets. As related by the major, "Several of the planes in my formation had dropped by this time . . . we went ahead and bombed what we thought was the right target, but probably not more than five planes in my formation bombed the right target. The others were dropping their bombs on what they thought was the target, but they were confused. As we went over . . . coming in, as I say, from the south, the wrong direction, the planes on my right and left went down . . ."

Meanwhile a shell had struck the right side of the cockpit of Col. Baker's Liberator, killing the copilot and injuring the colonel. The forward section of the ship began to burn. Almost immediately it was hit again, by a heavier-caliber shell. A wavering mass of flames, the bomber stayed on course long enough for Baker's bombardier to dump his entire bombload into a single refinery a few dozen yards below. Baker tried to pull up so that his crew could bail out, but the plane would not respond. It began to somersault end over end lightning-fast, like a boy's toy, and then crashed heavily on the edge of the refinery it had just bombed, with all men still aboard.

Enemy fighters, portents of things to come, had already begun to appear in small units. In spite of them and the flak, the 93rd accurately bombed its improvised targets from heights as low as 100 feet. These later turned out to be Astra Romana, Phoenix Orion, and Columbia Aquila, refineries which had been intended for the attentions of Kane and Johnson and their respective men. Eleven B-24's from the 93rd Group were lost over these targets alone. One plane crashed into a women's prison, allegedly killing about 100 inmates.

The easiest objective had been given to Jack Wood and his somewhat less experienced collection of 30 crews, the 389th Bombardment Group. They were to fly to the suburb of Campina and bomb only the Steaua Romana refinery, giving Ploesti and the other squadrons a wide berth coming and going. But here again things did not work out quite as planned.

"We had been warned," said Col. Wood, "to avoid drifting left after we crossed the Danube because of a GCI (ground-controlled interception) station in that direction, and to stay strictly on our northeast course. But what do the two groups in front of us do but veer left at exactly that point.

"I was checking my navigator to the fraction of an inch — I wasn't at the controls — I had a pilot and copilot flying the plane and I was squeezed in almost between them with a map on my knees. As soon as I saw Kane and Johnson swing left I turned to my pilot and said, 'I don't know where the hell those fellows are going, but from now on we're on our own.' We kept straight on for Ploesti."

Wood could afford to be more independent than the other commanders, for his group was the only one with a single, separate target not in Ploesti proper. After reaching their IP they banked slightly northward and at 4,000 feet headed laterally across the mountain ranges which temporarily prevented them from coming down to zero altitude. Their task was to pick out a particular valley about three miles wide, and then to follow it straight into Campina. They then proceeded to descend into the wrong valley. When this mistake was discovered, Wood calmly led his outfit up to 4,000 feet again, and over into the next valley, which turned out to be the right one. The bombers coasted down to minimum altitude once more, and raced toward their target. At this stage machine-gun nests on the sides of the hills were firing down on them — a novelty, certainly, in antiaircraft annals. Some of the planes ripped their wings through the treetop branches. As they approached the target many gun duels ("like a wild-West movie") took place between the bombers and

B-24 Liberators over the target at Ploesti.

the flak and machine-gun batteries concealed below in haystacks, in railway flatcars, and in farmhouses. Over four hundred .50-caliber American machine guns, including the new nose armament, which was used to good advantage, poured a flood of millions of bullets from all directions at anything that moved. This sweeping mass of fire killed, wounded, and scattered great numbers of the defenders during the earsplitting sweep toward the town.

Youthful Second Lt. Lloyd Hughes was among those killed at Steaua Ro-

mana. His plane was hit by machine-gun bullets during the run-in through the valley, and sheets of gasoline poured out of the left wing and bomb bay. But since the plane was not yet afire, Hughes decided to make his run to the target. In doing so he passed through a tongue of flame which touched off the left wing. After releasing his load of explosives and incendiaries he tried to land in a dry creek bed, found a bridge in the way, pulled up and tried again; but it was too late, and his B-24 spun into the ground. (From another plane, moving pictures were taken of the entire sequence of this tragedy, from the moment when gasoline started pouring out of the tanks until the flaming machine crashed — a remarkable film still on secret Air Force file.)

Lt. John Fino, bombardier of the 389th lead plane, dropped a 1,000-pound bomb directly through the large double doors of one power plant which apparently had not had time to reduce its steam pressure. As a result this single bomb created innumerable explosions within the plant by tearing out high-pressure steam conduits.

Another plane from a later wave was destroyed like a moth in a flame when a boilerhouse hit by a previous bomber blew up just in time to catch it in the explosion. But the 389th hit Campina accurately and as briefed. In ten narrow waves of three planes each the group passed over the target exactly as planned and practiced over the mock-up in Libya. At this point one stray squadron from Compton's 376th began to show up, for, it will be recalled, some of them had decided to go to Campina after Gen. Ent's order to attack "targets of opportunity."

"We could see these aircraft about three or four miles to our right coming in at right angles to our line of approach, and we couldn't figure out what they were doing around here, especially since they were bound to arrive after we were all finished." And several minutes after the 389th made its turn back to home base the bombers from Compton's group reached the holocaust that had once been the Campina refineries, and inflicted further damage on the roaring, blackened remnants of this installation.

"We had expected to take losses," Col. John Kane said, "but I never will forget those big Libs going down like flies." His radio operator, Ray Hubbard, added, "I looked through the open bomb-bay doors and could see flames from exploding gas tanks shooting right up into us. The fire wrapped us up. I looked out the side windows and saw the others flying through smoke and flames. It was flying through hell . . . I guess we'll go straight to heaven when we die. We've had our purgatory." Official AAF historians admit that the 98th and 44th Bombardment Groups would have been morally justified in turning back from the target under the circumstances.

Kane's 98th was after Phoenix Orion and Astra Romana, but Baker's squadrons had been there first. So for Killer's aircraft to bomb them, which they proceeded to do, they were forced to fly directly into the fires and explosions left behind by their own people. In addition, the delayed-action bombs were now beginning to detonate. This, in fact, was the most insidious hazard of all, not only for Kane's group but later for Johnson's as well. A sheet of flame and a billow of smoke could often be avoided by an oncoming plane, but nothing could be done about sudden explosions from delayed-action fuses dropped previously by planes which had attacked refineries not assigned to them. Possibly a total of six aircraft were cremated in midair by these gigantic and unexpected blasts.

Kane's plane itself was hit in one engine just as it came over one of the targets. He feathered the propeller and added power to the other three engines. "From below, ack-ack batteries were firing at us point-blank . . . like a skeet shoot."

Wringing wet with perspiration from the roaring fires on the ground and from the emotional tension of the mission, Kane's men severely damaged Phoenix Orion, left it behind, and drove on doggedly for the great Astra Romana plant. It was unbearably hot in the planes from the wall of flames and explosions rising over 300 feet, the August heat of the day, and the machine guns, which had been firing steadily until the gun barrels were blistering to the touch. The colonel reported, "we could see reservoir tanks exploding, with fire shooting up like ruddy tongues in the middle of the smoke. It was so hot the hair on my arms was singed. I thought I could smell it burn . . ." The smoke was a constant worry, for it obscured chimneys and balloon cables lurking within it.

An unexpected factor over the target area was the violent turbulence caused by flames and explosions. At best a B-24 is not easy (like a B-17) to fly steadily; even in routine formation it tends to wander and slide when not on automatic pilot. Over Ploesti this defect was dangerously magnified. Only with difficulty could the planes be kept under control near the heart of the inferno. They rolled and pitched like sheets of paper in a breeze. Many a bomber could be seen hanging crazily on a wing tip; others sagged and then were wafted upward by a hot billow of uprushing air. Crew members had to strap themselves down. Pilots and copilots flew their ships simultaneously; the job was too much for one man. There is little doubt that several planes went into the ground purely through accidental dives and sideslips. Sometimes pilots were forced to change course right in the middle of a bomb run; off they veered to attack another refinery instead, in split-second switches caused by the simple necessity of avoiding collisions with other bombers off course or out of formation.

The ships swept on, weaving in and out of the smokestacks, through several miles of storage areas and small farms. "We [had] many airplanes come back with cornstalks hung in their bomb bays," remarked Maj. Shingler. "In a B-24 the bomb bays open up like a clamshell, and of course we were right down on the deck. When they shut the bomb-bay doors . . . they just gathered up a little corn with it." The remnants of the 98th hit Target White 4 in four waves at a speed over the objective of about 185 mph. The smudge pots, fortunately, turned out to be no great nuisance.

Enemy fighters began to hover over

the wild scene, waiting for the bombers to leave the area and come up from the floor. A few of them tried to attack the heavy planes hugging the ground, but the majority of the ME-109's and other interceptors grimly bided their time. The bombers stuck to their assignment, manifold and prop settings as low as possible, and mixtures lean, to save gasoline.

"Our pinpoint was a smokestack," said Capt. William Banks. ". . . all we needed was a split second to sight it. And we had to get it with the first try; there would be no time to turn around for another run this trip. Somebody ahead of us had bombed our target by mistake. We all felt sick when we saw the oil tanks exploding and great swirls of smoke pouring up from the ground. There was nothing to do but try to hit it again . . .

"Oil tanks were still going off right under us, and on both sides German ack-ack batteries were firing in unison. We were so low that they were actually trained down on us.

"We kept straining our eyes for that stack. We couldn't see it yet, and I began to worry. It looked as if we weren't going to get the damned thing after all . . . We just plowed on, sweating blood and not saying a word. The *Sad Sack* was bristling with guns for this mission and we were firing every one of them as we roared in. The whole plane shuddered with fire.

". . . Finally I decided to pull away. We had finished our run and hadn't even seen our pinpoint. At that mo-

ment Joe Souza yelled. He had spotted our smokestack and power plant through an opening in the smoke. I held her steady for a split second while Joe sighted and let his bombs go, and then I almost jumped out of my seat. Carl shouted, 'Jesus!' and I pulled back with all the strength I had. Right in front of us, square in the middle of the windshield and looming up almost out of sight was the tallest . . . smokestack I have ever seen.

". . . Shaking all over with the racing of her motors, the *Sad Sack* leaped up and climbed for the top of it. I prayed as she lost speed and the stack rushed at us. We cleared it as if we were pole-vaulting . . ."

Some contact bombs failed to explode, but few of the crewmen noticed this in the confusion around them. Banks continued: "There were B-24's going down all around us now. We saw two fall right in front of us that had apparently climbed up out of formation and had been hit by pursuit planes. The ground was spotted with them, including some that had managed to land safely. The crews of these last were beside them, watching the planes burn and waving to us as we went by . . . We ducked even closer to the ground and scooted for home."

The squadron in which Capt. John Palm was flying had been ordered to climb to 100 feet when they arrived 30 seconds from their assigned target. This he did, but when he reached it his plane was the only one of the six left. And as he was nearing the refinery, his own forlorn Liberator was finally hit. An antiaircraft shell knocked out three engines. The plane went into a shallow dive. Two men in the nose were killed outright. Capt. Palm's right leg was blown off. He glanced down and noted, almost absently, that it was hanging by a few strands. At the moment he had other problems. The plane was going in fast, just above the refinery that was to have been bombed. He yanked the emergency release.

As the action increased in intensity, a pall of dense black smoke added to the difficulties and caused several near-collisions. B-24's were crisscrossing the area. Much of the confusion was caused by Compton's earlier aircraft, which were roaming haphazardly over the entire target area seeking targets of opportunity, as instructed by Gen. Ent. This meandering, plus the maneuvers of Baker's aircraft in bombing installations not under their brief jurisdiction, and from a reverse direction, created a particular hazard that no one had dreamed would take place during this meticulously planned operation. Yet all but eight of Kane's element got over the target, one having cracked up in the takeoff, and seven others having turned back with mechanical troubles. This group suffered the worst losses of all; twenty-one of Kane's 38 American heavies that arrived at Ploesti were knocked down.

The last was the most unfortunate group of all, for it perforce arrived at a scene of unparalleled confusion left by the previous three groups assigned to Ploesti proper. This was the 44th, originally from England, led by Col. Leon Johnson.

"It was more like an artist's conception of an air battle than anything I had experienced," Johnson said. "We flew through sheets of flame, and airplanes were everywhere, some of them on fire and others exploding. It's indescribable to anyone who wasn't there." Eng. James E. Cailliar added, "As we passed over [Brazi] our ship filled up with smoke and it was quite a while before it all cleared out."

Two of the planes from this group (and possibly others from other groups) ran into balloon cables and crashed. However the British briefing officers were partially vindicated, for other planes had in fact snapped the cables, as predicted, though their wings were slashed back to the main spar in the process.

The 44th experienced the same keen disappointment as Kane's formation before them: their Ploesti target (though not the one in Brazi) was burning before they arrived. So they would have to bomb it all over again, or go home empty-handed, or find something else to bomb. The decision is described by Col. Johnson: ". . . We had all agreed ahead of time that we weren't going that far without trying to get our targets, so even though they had been fired on . . . we made our runs . . . and we'll point out for the interest of the people that weren't there that the fires were so close together that some of the planes had the paint on their wings burned and scorched . . . I remember the cracking plant loomed up and we let our bombs go.

". . . We found that we could weave around the fires like we weaved over the trees and over the high-tension wires, because the fires were not a continuous line across. There would be a tank burning on your right, and maybe one staggered back — well, it seemed like only the width of an airplane, but it must have been more than that. You could weave through with a formation, although it looked . . . too narrow to get three airplanes through."

Thus Columbia Aquila was tagged again for good measure, and the first blows were delivered to Creditual Minier at nearby Brazi. Each time one of the incendiaries struck home there would follow a hoarse roar, a sheet of flame, and a billow of black smoke. In the course of these actions 11 of the big planes were shot down by machine guns and heavier AA fire, or burned to a crisp in gigantic explosions beneath them.

Johnson later remarked: "We saw the 93rd and 376th groups swinging below us . . . or even with us, and some of us had to pull up to let the others go by. It was a sight that was hard to forget, because you see planes going in on fire, and I remember seeing one pull straight up, and two chutes come out of the window of this big bomber, and I saw it pull straight

up and then fall to the ground.

". . . Then the antiaircraft opened up on us. We were headed almost parallel to it . . . We decided that the only thing to do was to head over it — we didn't think they would traverse 180 degrees overhead . . . If we went parallel we knew they'd knock us all down. As a result we flew immediately over them. And we shot and fired at all the gunners as we went by . . . I distinctly remember seeing a number of them leaving their guns and running for cover . . ."

If the two early groups (Compton and Baker) had been even earlier, or if the two later groups (Kane and Johnson) had been later, affairs would not have been so bad. As it was, the time spent by the formations that had gone to Bucharest and then belatedly swung around toward Ploesti and Campina brought them there, by an unfortunate coincidence, at almost the same moment that the other formations arrived, and from an opposite axis of attack. Thus, according to Johnson, "We had airplanes going in at just all the directions we could think of . . . We'd have to pull up and find airplanes below us and other airplanes above and around us. I mean, it was just a general confusion around the target area — of squadrons and groups, not individual flyers." But part of Compton's lead outfit had arrived several minutes earlier — for example, Appold's squadron. When later aircraft came in, they saw what had happened. The timing was all wrong.

The delayed-action bombs of the first wave were going off ahead of them and under them. They barreled through nonetheless and unloaded. Twelve of one outfit went into the smoke and only nine broke through on the other side.

There is a saying among bomber crews that while en route and over the target they were employed by Uncle Sam, but after "Bombs away!" they were out of work. The Ploesti raid of August 1, 1943, was over to the extent that the explosives had been laid on the target to the best of the ability of the participants. Their problem now was to save their skins. From this standpoint the raid was less than half-finished.

All the ground fire that had been traversed on the way in would now have to be met on the way back. Also, there had been no fighters worth mentioning on the way to the target and over the target, but now they were wheeling overhead in swarms, and they would hang on all the way out into the sea "like snails on a log." Many bombers had already been lost. Therefore the concentrated firepower of the rest was reduced. And all planes were damaged now to some degree. Some were limping on three and even two engines. These could not possibly keep up and had to be more or less discounted from defensive calculations. Many crewmen were dead or wounded, reducing the gun strength of their aircraft that much more. The Odyssey of the Ploesti warriors was many hundreds of miles, many hours, many deaths from done.

The first Allied landings on the Italian mainland took place early in September, 1943, when the British Eighth Army crossed the Strait of Messina and the American Fifth Army came ashore at Salerno. On the 16th of that month the two armies made contact and began their long, slow drive toward Rome. North of Naples they were stopped by the formidable German fortifications known as the Gustav Line. The town of Cassino was located at the center of the Gustav Line where the Allies attempted a break-through; on a hill overlooking the town was the ancient Abbey of Monte Cassino.

The Bombing of Monte Cassino

A Picture Story

After attempts to break through the Gustav Line at Cassino by direct assault failed, the Allies reluctantly called in the bombers of the Mediterranean Allied Air Forces to attack German fortifications on Hill 516 where the abbey was located. This photo, taken at the beginning of the air attack on February 15, 1944, shows ammunition stored by the Germans in the east wing of the abbey exploding in huge clouds of flame and smoke.

133

A reconnaissance photo of the abbey taken after the February 15 bombing shows thirty-five direct hits on the building and its inner courtyard. A total of 142 heavy and 112 medium bombers dropped 576 tons of high explosives on the target. Although the abbey was destroyed, the Gustav Line still held.

A month later, on March 15, 1944, 475 bombers dropped 1,000 tons of bombs on the town of Cassino in a 3½-hour attack. Cassino was flattened but bad weather, rubble and the huge craters left by the bombing held up the advancing Allied troops. The attempt to break through the Gustav Line at Cassino had to be called off until conditions were more favorable. It was May 19 before all of Cassino was in Allied hands and the Gustav Line was finally broken.

The ruins of the Abbey of Monte Cassino were surrendered to the Allies on May 12, 1944. Two weeks later the Germans were in full retreat from Italy.

NORTH SEA

ENGLAND

DEPARTED
LOWESTOFT
0935

DEPARTED ORFORDNESS 1314

ARRIVED FELIXSTOWE 1731

DEPARTED
CLACTON
1313

DIVERSIONARY
SORTIES BY
FIGHTERS AND
MEDIUM BOMBERS

FRANCE

EVREUX

LAON

LILLE-
VITRY

FLORENNES

ST. TROND

METZ

JEVER

LEEUWARDEN

OLM

BERGEN

SCHIPHOL

DEELEN

ENSCHEDE

VENLO

MUNSTER

GILZE

WOENSDRECHT

GLADBACH

KOBLENZ

MANNH

SWITZERLAN

136

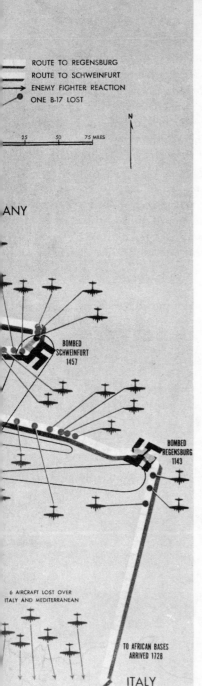

ROUTE TO REGENSBURG
ROUTE TO SCHWEINFURT
ENEMY FIGHTER REACTION
ONE B-17 LOST

N

25   50   75 MILES

ANY

BOMBED
SCHWEINFURT
1457

BOMBED
REGENSBURG
1143

6 AIRCRAFT LOST OVER
ITALY AND MEDITERRANEAN

TO AFRICAN BASES
ARRIVED 1728

ITALY

One of the roughest missions flown by U.S. bomber forces during World War II — and one of the fiercest air battles of that war — took place on August 17, 1943. The B-17s of the Eighth Air Force had two targets that day, both critical and both located deep inside Germany. They were the anti-friction bearing industry at Schweinfurt and the Messerschmitt aircraft complex at Regensburg.

A force of 376 B-17s was dispatched from Eighth Air Force bases in England; 146 of them were to bomb Regensburg and land at bases in North Africa. The rest of the force was to hit Schweinfurt and return to England.

Trouble dogged the double mission from the start. The Regensburg bombers took off first and met unexpectedly heavy fighter opposition over Germany. Twenty-four bombers were lost in the aerial fighting that resulted. Meanwhile the Schweinfurt mission was delayed in England for 3½ hours by bad weather. This gave the German fighter force time to land and refuel before meeting the second group of bombers. Thirty-six of the Schweinfurt B-17s were shot down by the fighters who attacked them all the way to the target and as far as the English Channel on the return journey.

The loss of sixty bombers made the Regensburg-Schweinfurt mission a costly one for the Eighth Air Force. However, bombing results were good. Every important building at the Messerschmitt works was hit and at Schweinfurt the two largest ball-bearing plants received 80 direct hits.

The Regensburg-Schweinfurt Mission

A Picture Story

137

The war was going badly for Benito Mussolini in 1943. The Italian army had been defeated in North Africa and in Sicily; Italian cities were being reduced to rubble by Allied air power in preparation for an invasion. Then, on July 20, Rome was bombed for the first time. Five days later a worried Fascist Grand Council met. Control of the armed forces was taken away from Mussolini and returned to the king. The former dictator was interned on the island of Ponza and Marshal Badoglio was given the job of organizing a new government.

After a short stay at Ponza Mussolini was moved to La Maddalena off the coast of Sardinia. At the end of August he was secretly moved a second time — to a small resort hotel in Abruzzi in the mountains of central Italy. From this isolated and inaccessible hideaway he was rescued by German paratroopers led by the daring SS colonel, Otto Skorzeny. Here is how it was done.

Mussolini walks toward the small Fieseler Storch airplane which carried him off the mountain. A German soldier walks behind him.

Kidnap By Air

Charles Foley

"I HAVE A MISSION of the highest importance for you." Adolf Hitler looked intently at the person who stood with him in a private room at his secret hideout, the "Wolf's Lair." A man of towering proportions was with the Fuehrer. Well over six feet tall, the man's physique was enough to terrorize any antagonist. His forbidding appearance was heightened by the chalk-white, thin scar which ran from the left temple to the corner of his mouth and across a massive chin — a memento of a duel with swords fought in Austria before the war.

The man was "Scarface" Skorzeny, then newly appointed as chief of Germany's Special Troops — a man who was destined to become one of the Allies' toughest opponents in the years to come and one of the world's greatest experts in unorthodox warfare.

In tones of rising anger, Hitler told Skorzeny how his partner, Mussolini, had just been betrayed and arrested. The invasion of Italy by Britain and her allies seemed imminent and now, in July, 1943, came the news that the king of Italy and others planned to go over to the Allies' side — and take Mussolini with them as a prisoner. The Duce would be a useful pawn when bargaining with the Allied Powers.

"I cannot and will not leave Mussolini to this fate," exclaimed Hitler loudly. "He has got to be rescued before these traitors can surrender him to the enemy."

Then, in quieter tones, came the words: "You, Skorzeny, are going to save my friend."

This was the order which set Skorzeny off on a career in which he alone was to cause the Allies more worries than a whole division of the German army. The task was formidable.

Complete secrecy had to be maintained. Neither the General Staff of the Italian army, nor the Rome Embassy could be trusted to know about the operation. No one knew where the Duce had been taken. Skorzeny had to find out where the prisoner was before he could rescue him.

With 50 of his best men, including those who spoke Italian, Skorzeny flew to Italy to begin his quest. He flew with Gen. Student, chief of airborne troops, in the general's own Fieseler Storch spotting aircraft flown by his personal pilot, the ace flyer Capt. Gerlach.

There followed weeks of frustrating search. Rumors were rife and every one had to be investigated. No help could be expected from the Italians.

Once the prisoner was located for

certain and an attack was planned. On the eve of the assault, Skorzeny learned that only that morning had Mussolini been moved yet again by his wily captors.

At last, the vital clue came — an intercepted message reading: "SECURITY MEASURES AROUND GRAN SASSO COMPLETED." The message was signed CUELI — Gen. Cueli, the official responsible for Mussolini's safety as a prisoner!

The Gran Sasso was the loftiest peak in the Apennines, 100 miles from Rome as the crow flies, and the peaks soared up to over 10,000 feet. The only habitable place in the region was the Hotel Campo Imperatore, 6,000 feet up. This could only be reached by cable railway — an easily broken link with the outside world. The captors had chosen the ideal spot.

How to assault the hotel and carry off Mussolini was Skorzeny's problem. Paratroops plummeting through the thin air would be dashed to pieces; there was no place for an airplane to land; gliders — gliders!

Skorzeny looked again at the air reconnaissance pictures he had taken of the place — that triangular patch by the hotel. If it were really flat and smooth a few gliders might land there . . .

On a bright and windless September morning in 1943, a force of gliders left an airfield in Italy and were towed toward Gran Sasso. Soon the hotel came into view and Skorzeny could see again the dizzy perch on which he was to land his gliders.

"Let's go!" he told his pilot. The towrope parted and they were swooping freely, with no sound but the rush of the wind on their wings. As they went lower they saw the landing field they had chosen more clearly. It was a sloping shelf, for all the world like a ski jump; and, as they lost more height, they saw it to be studded with outcrop rock.

The pilot turned his goggled face toward Skorzeny. No words were needed for the leader to understand the question on the flyer's lips. "Dive — crash-land! As near the hotel as you can," Skorzeny ordered the hapless pilot.

They hurtled toward the mountain, the parachute brake whipping out from their tail. In another instant the glider was jolting and pitching over the boulders like a dinghy flung upon a reef. A shuddering crash, then it was still.

Skorzeny's bulk burst from the wrecked glider: before him, like a cliff face 20 yards ahead, was the wall of the hotel. An Italian carabiniere was standing there rooted to the spot, stupefied by the apparition which had fallen almost at his feet from out of the silent sky.

Skorzeny plunged past him to the first doorway: inside was a signalman tapping at a transmitter. A kick sent the chair from under him: Skorzeny's gun smashed the radio. But the room led nowhere.

Out again and full tilt around a

corner; he heard his men pounding behind him. A ten-foot-high terrace — they hoisted him up to it. From there, at an upper window, he spotted an unmistakable shorn head. "Get back!" he yelled to Mussolini. "Get back from the window." And dashed off round the terrace.

At last; the main entrance, flanked by two sentry posts. The guards wore a look of wild amazement. Before they could get their breath, Skorzeny's men had booted their machine guns off the supports and scrambled through the door.

Skorzeny butted his way through a press of soldiers in the lobby; they were at too close quarters to fire, even if they had known what had come on them. He took a flight of stairs, turned a corner and flung open a door. The first thing he saw — Mussolini with two Italian officers.

One of Skorzeny's brawniest subalterns, Lt. Schwerdt, panted into the room after his leader. A couple more men swarmed up the lightning conductor and climbed through the window. They overcame the Italian officers and dragged them from the room. Schwerdt took over as Mussolini's bodyguard.

Three more gliders crash-landed outside and troops poured out. A fourth, landing some distance away, was smashed to pieces — no one moved from the wreckage. Skorzeny could not hope for more strength so he turned back across the room, threw open the door, and shouted in his bad Italian,

"I want the commander, he must come at once." Some bewildered shouting — an Italian colonel appeared.

"I ask your immediate surrender," Skorzeny said. "Mussolini is already in our hands. You have 60 seconds to go and reflect." Before the anxious minute was up the colonel came back. This time he carried a goblet brimming with red wine. "To a gallant victory," he bowed. Skorzeny thanked him and drained the goblet — he was thirsty. Cheers arose from the Germans below as a white sheet was flown from the window.

Now Skorzeny had time for Mussolini. The Duce came forward: a stocky man, looking older than his portraits showed him, in a blue suit that was too large. He wore a stubble of beard; his pate sprouted gray bristle. His eyes were black, ardent and excited.

Skorzeny spoke to him in German: "Duce, I have been sent by the Fuehrer to set you free." Mussolini replied: "I knew my friend Adolf Hitler would not abandon me. I embrace my liberator."

Skorzeny went to see to the disarming of the Italian garrison and discovered that he had captured an important personage from Rome — none other than the Gen. Cueli who was responsible for keeping Mussolini sealed up and shut away. Having, through his intercepted code message, unwittingly put Skorzeny on the scent leading to the Gran Sasso he was further unfortunate in choosing this day for a visit to

Count Otto Skorzeny, the S.S. colonel who rescued Mussolini from the mountain hotel where he was being held as a prisoner. This picture was taken in May, 1945, after Skorzeny's capture by Allied forces. He was tried on a charge of war crimes but was acquitted.

his charge. Skorzeny was delighted to see him.

But now a more urgent matter occupied Skorzeny's mind — the getaway. Paratroops had been landed in the valley below to take charge of the lower end of the cable railway and had carried out their job well. The plan was to take Mussolini to the nearby airfield of Aquila, which would be held briefly by German troops, while Mussolini was flown to Germany. But no radio contact could be made with the airfield. An alternative plan, worked out in advance, was to fly Mussolini out by a light aircraft which had landed in the valley. But on coming in to land, this plane had wrecked its undercarriage and could not fly off.

There remained a third, desperate

choice. **Capt. Gerlach, Gen. Student's** personal pilot, might try and land his tiny Storch alongside the hotel itself and pick up Mussolini from the mountain's edge — an operation so hair-raising that Skorzeny had only put it to Student as a theoretical possibility. Now it was their only hope.

Skorzeny glanced heavenward, and there, sure enough was the Storch circling as arranged. It had been said that Gerlach could perform miracles in the air — let him perform one now.

The German troops, helped by Italian prisoners, cleared some of the biggest boulders from the landing ledge and, at a signal, Gerlach came delicately down on it. Gerlach was ready for anything until he heard what was actually wanted. To weigh down his frail aircraft with the united loads, each in its own right substantial, of Mussolini and Skorzeny! It was mad: he refused point-blank to consider it.

Skorzeny insisted. At last Gerlach gave in. "Have it your own way," he said. "If it's neck or nothing anyway we'd better be on the move." Squads hurriedly set to work again clearing rocks and even Mussolini gave a hand.

They squashed into the plane; Mussolini behind the pilot, Skorzeny behind Mussolini. While Gerlach revved the engine, 12 men clung to the Storch, digging their heels in for the tug of war. Gerlach held a hand aloft until the engine's pitch rose in a crescendo; as he dropped his hand the men let go and the plane catapulted across the scree.

Skorzeny grasped the metal spars on either side of him, throwing his weight from side to side against the swaying motion as one wheel or another was lifted by a rock. Suddenly a crevasse yawned before them; the plane shot over it and continued its career beyond with the port wheel buckled. Then it went hurtling over the edge of the ravine.

Gerlach brought off his miracle. With consummate skill he lifted the Storch from its nose dive to flatten out a few feet above the valley floor.

The rest seemed smooth sailing; even the glissade at Rome and the landing on starboard and tail wheel only.

Within a few hours, Skorzeny and his valuable charge were back in Vienna. Skorzeny, in his hotel, was soon answering the congratulatory telephone calls from Himmler, Goering, and Hitler, himself. Then a full colonel, wearing the regalia of the Knights Cross, was ushered into his room.

He clicked his heels, bowed, took off his decoration and hung it around Skorzeny's neck. "Orders of the Fuehrer," he explained. For the first time this high award had been conferred on the very day that it was earned.

The Mosquito Mark VI, a fighter-bomber, went into service with the Royal Air Force in the late spring of 1943. It proved to be an outstanding plane for low-level attacks. When the RAF received a request from the French underground for help in releasing prisoners held by the Germans in the jail at Amiens, the assignment was given to the Mosquito Mark VI.

Amiens prison was built in the form of a cross. Its walls were 20 feet high and three feet thick. In order to open the prison, bombs had to be dropped on precise targets from a very low altitude. This is the story of how it was done.

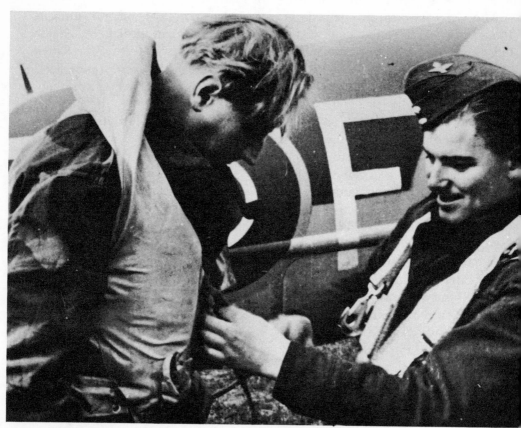

Group Captain P.C. Pickard (left) has his Mae West adjusted by F/Lt. J.A. Broadley just before the take-off for Amiens. Both men were killed when their plane was attacked by FW 190's after the successful raid.

They Blasted Amiens Jail

Pat Pointon

ON A BITTER February day in 1944, a small force of Mosquitoes roared at treetop height across France to carry out one of the most daring raids of the war. Their task was to make a low-level, precision attack on the jail at Amiens to effect the release of over 100 patriots who were imprisoned within its grim walls.

Boldly planned, and bravely carried out, the operation was an audacious challenge to fortune by a band of gallant men. Their courage fired the imagination of the free world in the dark days of the war, and added an epic chapter to the chronicle of heroism in the air.

Over 700 prisoners languished inside Amiens jail. Some had defied the Gestapo by carrying out acts of sabotage with the French underground Resistance movement. Others were key links in the British espionage network. Still more had hidden and helped Allied airmen to escape after their planes had been shot down over France. As each patriot was trapped he faced the travesty of a trial and each in turn heard the same sentence pronounced: "Guilty. Condemned to death." From prisons throughout France, the Germans began to move their captives to Amiens — to await execution.

The Maquis resolved that some attempt, however desperate, must at all costs be made to release the prisoners, and they appealed for help from across the Channel. This plea received a prompt pledge of full and speedy assistance.

Unhesitating and unequivocal as the promise of aid was, it nevertheless placed its guarantors in something of a dilemma. What plan was most likely to prove successful?

Obviously, the operation was bound to be a gamble. The risks that had to be considered were great, but not so overwhelming that they completely daunted all hope of success. A low-level, precision bombardment, coupled with a simultaneous attempt at a breakout by the prisoners, was the only possible solution. Carefully, the plan was drawn up, but few people were allowed to have any inkling of its exact nature. Everything hinged on the closest secrecy — coupled with speed.

From intelligence reports and stereoscopic photographs, an exact scale model of Amiens jail was made out of plaster of Paris as it would appear to the pilot from an aircraft flying at 1,500 feet from a distance of four miles.

Each phase of the operation was carefully worked out and timed down to the last second. Perfect synchronization was the prime factor of importance and every facet of the plan had to be meticulously dovetailed into the major scheme with precise continuity and a minimum of overlap. It was obvious that the prison walls would have to be breached in at least two places to enable any escape to be made. At the same time, both ends of the building itself had to be opened up to release the prisoners from their confinement, while the wing that housed the German guards had to be ruthlessly pulverized.

All this had to be achieved as rapidly as possible. There had, besides, to be close liaison with the French underground. Local Resistance groups were responsible for smuggling small quantities of explosive into the jail so that the patriots could blow the locks off the internal doors. It was their task, too, to assist the prisoners once they had managed to win clear of the outer walls, and hide them from the swift retribution that was certain to follow.

Noon on February 18, when the German guards would be eating their midday meal, was fixed as zero hour.

Under the code name of "Operation Renovate" the job of blasting open Amiens jail was assigned to the Mosquito wing — 140 Wing — of the Second Tactical Air Force, which had made a speciality of exacting, pinpoint attacks.

In command of the wing was 28-year-old, Sheffield born, Group Capt. P. C. Pickard, a triple DSO and DFC

who had notched up more than 100 operational sorties against the enemy. Tall, blond-haired and good-looking, his features and his fame were widely known in Britain. "Pick," as he was called, had been chosen to play the part of the pilot in the wartime film of Bomber Command, *Target For Tonight*. Commissioned in the RAF in 1937, his logbook recorded raids on all the major targets in the mounting and not unimpressive list at Air Ministry. He had fought through the Dunkirk evacuation, through the frustrating campaigns in France and Norway, and in 1940, when he was a flight lieutenant, he won his first DFC. In 1941, when he was a squadron leader, he led No. 311 Czech Squadron with such dashing skill and élan that the Czechs awarded him their Military Medal.

After four years on ops, the Powers-That-Be decided that Pick had earned a rest. He was switched to a desk job at Fighter Command Headquarters. He hated it. He itched to be back in the air. He pestered and complained until, at last, he got his wish. He was appointed to command the crack Mosquito wing of Second TAF.

Pick decided to lead the raid on Amiens himself. With him, as navigator, was to fly Flt. Lt. J. A. Broadley, DSO, DCM, DFM. They were a perfect partnership, almost inseparable in the air ever since they first crewed-up together in the early days of the war. Together, they had braved common dangers and shared in common

146

triumphs.

From the most experienced pilots and navigators in three squadrons, Pick chose his team. Six crews from each squadron were needed for the operation. From the wing headquarters at Sculthorpe, he went to the Mosquito base, RAF Station, Hunsdon, to prepare the final arrangements.

Dawn on February 18, 1944. Heavy storms of sleet and snow whipped in an icy fury over the Hunsdon airfield. The route to the target was blanketed with low clouds. As the aircrews sleepily pulled on their clothes and gulped down scalding cups of tea, the whole operation was on the verge of being postponed for 24 hours until the weather improved. Over the underground radio link a faint crackle of Morse carried the despairing appeal from the French Resistance: "Strike now or never. The executions are imminent." That decided the issue. Come what may . . . Ops were on.

The hubbub of chitchat and repartee died away. An Intelligence officer stood up and motioned to an orderly who removed the covering shroud from the model of Amiens jail. Interested eyes followed his movements. Heads craned forward to study the exhibit. Clearing his throat, the briefing officer started to outline the plan.

Each of the three squadrons was so keen for the honor of being the first into the attack, that Pick decided to let them toss for it. A spin of the coin gave the New Zealanders the first place, and then the Australians beat the British squadron for second place. The part each man was to play was now described in detail.

The initial assault by the New

The plaster of Paris model of the Amiens prison that was used by the Royal Air Force for crew briefing.

Zealanders had to be made precisely at noon. At that hour exactly, the leading formation of the three aircraft from No. 487 Squadron had to blast a hole in the eastern wall of the prison. On the run-in, the second box of three planes from the same squadron had to break away at a distance of ten miles from the target, wheel in a circle, and follow on the heels of the first wave, attacking the northern wall at noon plus three minutes, immediately after the leading section were climbing away. Then it was the turn of the Australian squadron, making the second main attack. They had to bomb the ends of the jail building. Like the New Zealanders, the six Mosquitoes from the Australian squadron were to split into two sections of three a short distance from the target. One group had to bomb the southeastern end of the jail, while the other trio dealt with the opposite wing to the northwest.

The third and remaining squadron — No. 21 Squadron, RAF — was to remain in reserve, ready to carry out any part of the plan in the previous attacks which might have failed.

As the briefing ended a hush fell over the Ops Room. In the silence Pick stood up and said simply:

"It's a death or glory job, boys. You have to break that prison wide open. Good luck."

The three squadrons took off from Hunsdon in a blinding snowstorm at 11 A.M. Each plane carried two 500-lb. bombs — including some semiarmor piercing type — all fused for a time delay of 11 seconds. For each formation of Mosquitoes, there was a squadron of Typhoons acting as a close fighter escort, while an extra Mosquito accompanied the party for photographic reconnaissance duties. Pick himself flew with the Australians in the second wave.

From their base, the Mosquitoes headed first for Littlehampton where they made a rendezvous with their escorts. Then, after crossing the Channel and northern France at "naught feet," they swept around to the north of Amiens and approached their target down the straight, poplar-fringed Albert-Amiens road alongside which the prison stood.

The attack went precisely according to schedule. Most of the German guards were peaceably eating their dinner when the Australians' bombs splintered and shattered their wing. As the planes roared overhead, the prisoners condemned to solitary confinement blew out the locks on their cell doors with explosive smuggled to them by the French underground, and speedily made their way through the gaping holes torn in the ends of the building to the yard where other patriots, who had been at exercise in the yard, had already begun to stream through the breaches in the outer wall.

The first squadron of New Zealanders had roared into the fray from a height of a mere 50 feet, and the leader's bombs were seen to hit the eastern wall five feet from the ground. Other bursts were adjacent to the wall, and

Amiens prison after the attack.

some overshot into the surrounding fields. The Australians were equally successful in scoring direct hits on their specific parts of the prison.

Here is part of the account given by the Australian pilot who led a section of the second wave at the debriefing when he landed after returning to Hunsdon:

"From about four miles away I saw the prison and the first three aircraft nipping over the top. I knew then it was O.K. for me to go in. My squadron was to divide into two sections — one to open each end of the prison, and it was now that one-half broke off and swept to attack the far end from the right. The rest of us carried on in tight formation. Four hundred yards before

we got there, delayed-action bombs went off and I saw they'd breached the wall. Clouds of smoke and dust came up, but over the top I could still see the triangular gable of the prison — my aiming point for the end we were to open.

"I released my bombs from ten feet and pulled up slap through the smoke over the prison roof. I looked around to the right and felt mighty relieved to see the other boys still 200 yards short of the target and coming in dead on line. They bombed and we all got away O.K., re-formed as a section, and made straight for base."

Over the target, Pick had detached himself from the Australians to act as "Master Bomber" and direct the op-

149

eration. It was left to him to decide whether or not the objects of the raid had been achieved by the first two waves of aircraft — the New Zealand and Australian squadrons — and to order the reserve force — the Mosquitoes of 21 Squadron — either to attack or withdraw accordingly. Calmly and efficiently, in his unflurried fashion, Pick skillfully took his plane right over the jail, through the smoke and crash of the exploding bombs. Only when he was fully satisfied that each phase of the plan had been efficiently carried out did he announce his decision. Over the radio-telephone the other pilots heard his encouraging tones saying the code word: "Daddy, Daddy, Red, Red, Red."

"Daddy" was a nickname, and Pick had arranged at the briefing that he should say "Red" if the attacks had been successful, and he wanted the planes of No. 21 Squadron to turn for home, or "Green" if any part of the operation had misfired, and he wanted them to go in and drop their bombs.

That short sentence of simple, prosaic and even homely words which signaled complete success was a prelude to personal tragedy. Just as he ordered the last wave to head for base, Pick saw one of his Mosquitoes brought down by the fierce light flak put up by the German defenses. The aircraft piloted by Squadron Leader I. R. McRitchie, who was leading a formation of the Australian squadron, was hit near Albert as it swung away from attacking the target. Losing height, Mc-

Ritchie gamely kept on his course, but near Freneuville his starboard wing tipped ominously and a few seconds later his plane spiraled earthward.

Noticing the incident, Pick wheeled his plane in a tight turn and then pushed the stick down to make a low run over the spot in the hope of determining the fate of the crew. Caught preoccupied and detached from the British fighter escort which was then covering the withdrawal of the main formations, Pick was bounced by a couple of FW-190's rushed to the scene to intercept the Mosquitoes. A vicious stream of bullets tore through the fabric of *F for Freddy*. Smoke streamed from an engine. Next minute the Mosquito flicked on to its back and plunged into a field a few miles from Amiens.

McRitchie lived to fight another day, but for Pick and Broadley the attack was lethal. Villagers who had seen the whole attack on the prison hurried to the spot, but the plane's gallant occupants were beyond all help. They removed the bodies to the local church. Later the Germans forced them to hand over the remains, but not even the local Gauleiter's sternest decree could prevent them from attending the funerals in the cemetery alongside Amiens prison.

After the liberation, when Pick and Broadley's comrades went to seek news of their fate, the villagers presented them with photographs of the flower-heaped graves, and the few personal belongings of the two men which they had secreted from the Germans.

Their deaths had not been in vain. Out of a total of more than 700 prisoners in Amiens jail, over 200 — including nearly all the men facing death for helping the Allies — were able to escape.

True, some were later recaptured, but apart from the immediate results of the operation, the raid on Amiens jail struck a shattering blow at German morale and helped to hasten the rout which only ended with the complete eclipse of the Third Reich.

An enlarged view of a hole that was opened in the prison wall.

Berlin was an important target for Allied bombers for several reasons. It was the capital of Germany and any attack on it would damage German morale; several highly important industries were located in the area around Berlin; and perhaps most important of all, the Luftwaffe was bound to send up every available fighter to protect the capital. This gave Allied air forces a chance to reduce German fighter strength at a time when replacement would be slow because of the bombing of aircraft factories.

The Royal Air Force had bombed Berlin on the night of August 25, 1940, and had returned several times since then. In March, 1944, the United States Eighth Air Force was ready to join in the attack. It sent its bombers to Berlin for the first time on March 4. Two days later they went back and the result was a fierce battle during which 69 of the bombers and 11 of the escorting fighters were lost. On the other hand, the American bomber and fighter crews claimed a total of 179 German planes shot down.

This account tells of the part played by a group of P-47 fighters in that great air battle.

The P-47; 15,485 of them were produced during World War II, more than any other fighter. The P-47 was especially successful as a fighter-bomber, a role that developed from the on-the-deck strafing of ground targets by Eighth Air Force pilots returning from escort missions over enemy territory.

First Strike at Berlin

Edward H. Sims

EVERY AMERICAN PILOT in the Eighth Air Force knew that sooner or later the Eighth would join in the attack on Germany's capital. Therefore, after 14 months of raids on other targets inside Germany, when U.S. bombers and fighters were ordered to fly to Berlin on March 3, 1944, pilots had been anticipating the event. On that day, however, the bombers were forced to turn back because of the weather.

A small force of bombers blazed the way the very next day, March 4, without encountering unusual difficulties. Late on March 5 orders were prepared directing 800 heavy bombers to attack Berlin next day. Naturally, receipt of the orders at bomber and fighter bases around England caused a ripple of excitement and anticipation. The United States had been at war with Hitler's Germany for two years and three months. The Eighth had been operating from England for more than a year and a half. It was time Hitler's capital felt the weight of the Eighth's bombs, and looked up at the awesome sight of four-engined American bombers unloading lethal cargoes over Germany's greatest city in broad daylight — the city Luftwaffe Chief Hermann Goering had said would never suffer such an ordeal.

But in March, 1944, the task of pro- viding fighter escort for heavy bomb- ers on such a long mission was formid- able. Not many of the new long-range fighters, which made the Berlin attacks possible, were yet available. There were P-38's and P-47's, for the most part, which were not able to fly in and out, all the way, and do battle with the enemy also. Thus a schedule had to be worked out for some of the fighters to escort the bombers a certain distance, then be relieved by other fighters, a partial relay process.

The 56th Group, which emerged from the war the second highest scor- ing outfit in the Eighth Air Force, had flown P-47 Thunderbolts through- out the war and were so equipped in March, 1944. The 4th Group — 56th's greatest rival — which finally came out with top honors by a hair (in the victories race), had just been equipped with P-51's. Both 56th and 4th were among the many fighter groups assigned escort duties for the Berlin attack. The Thunderbolts of 56th would split into two groups for the mission, 35 fighters making up each group. The understrength groups would rendezvous with the bombers as they approached Germany, and pro- vide penetration support.

At this time the Nazis occupied the Low Countries and France. Every pilot knew, when he took off on an escort mission and crossed into enemy-occupied territory, that an hour or two later he would have to fly back across the North Sea to England. If he was forced down in France, Holland, or Belgium, short on fuel, it meant capture by the Germans. The enemy, then, was not the only worry of fighter pilots. Each sweated out his fuel supply on the longer missions, especially pilots in P-38's and P-47's.

On the night of March 5 pilots of the 56th were alerted and told a major mission would be flown next morning. Since the number of pilots in the group was not what it was later in the war, 56th flyers knew most of them would participate. With that knowledge, and the forecast that tomorrow's weather would be good, the group's fighter pilots hit their sacks at Halesworth early. Unlike bomber pilots, and crewmen, many did not learn they were going to Berlin until next day.

At 4:30 A.M. next day, the drone of heavy bombers in the winter darkness above roused Lt. Bob Johnson from his slumber. Dressing in OD pants and shirt, silk scarf and leather jacket, and carefully checking the knife he carried in his right boot, Johnson made off into the blackness for a Nissen hut mess hall. There he grabbed a few slices of bread, toasted them against the side of the iron stove in the center of the hut, and drank his coffee. In a few minutes he departed for the Operations Room of 61st Squadron, where pilots checked the position they would

fly, and also their flying equipment. They still did not know their destination for the day.

A jeep carried 61st Squadron to group briefing — where the answers to a lot of questions awaited pilots. A curtain hid the big wall map from view. After pilots from all three squadrons had taken their seats, the group intelligence officer stepped up on the platform at the front of the room and pulled the curtain string.

Pilots let out a howl. The ribbon marking the route stretched from England to . . . Berlin. Amid whispers and excitement, the IO briefed the group on flak, expected enemy resistance, and escape procedures. The weather officer followed — explaining conditions pilots would encounter on the way into Germany and back.

The three squadrons of the 56th were 61st, 62nd, and 63rd. Commanding officer of the 61st, Johnson's squadron, was one of the war's great aces, Francis S. Gabreski. Johnson was one of 61st's flight leaders, destined to emerge from the war in Europe second to Gabreski in the number of confirmed aerial victories. The 61st, then, was an outstanding squadron.

The group commander, Col. Hubert Zemke — one of the greatest of the war — completed the briefing. He announced that 56th would divide into two groups. He would lead A Group and Johnson would lead B. The group's executive officer, Lt. Col. Dave Schilling — who was to become the fourth-ranking American ace in the

Lt. Bob Johnson (second from left, standing) with a group of P-47 pilots from the famed 56th Fighter Group.

ETO (European Theater of Operations) — was not scheduled to fly, nor was Gabreski.

Johnson, then, was to have charge of 35 P-47's, half the group's total effort. Take off was set for 10:32 A.M. If the group encountered no opposition from the Luftwaffe during escort duty, it was to descend to low altitude on the way home and strafe targets of opportunity. After a few last words from Zemke, gripes that the mission was either too short or too long, and exclamations — as pilots eyed the long route-marker ribbon stretching to Berlin and back — group briefing ended.

Pilots and officers of the 61st climbed on their jeep and headed back to the squadron building. After a short ride the jeep arrived and the daily race for the six-holer was on. Pilots leaped from the still-rolling jeep. The driver won last honors in this morning ritual, since he had to park the jeep. Fighter pilots on combat duty were never bothered by irregularity.

At squadron briefing Johnson made his talk brief. He merely confirmed the order of flight, outlined a few general rules for close-in and combat formation, and warned his men to be on the alert. Pilots then went to their lockers and pulled out parachutes, Mae Wests, helmets, etc. Johnson took with him one glove — for his left hand, which would rest on the metal throttle handle much of the time in flight. In March over England and Germany temperatures above 20,000 feet were below zero, and while the cockpit was partially heated, it nevertheless became quite cold at higher altitudes. Pilots lounged around and the morning grew late.

It was a few minutes after ten. Johnson wished his men luck and they walked out to their aircraft. In a couple of minutes he stepped up on the wing of a blunt, red-nosed Thunderbolt, the words *All Hell* painted on its side. Before the day was over Keyworth Red Leader — that was Johnson's code identification — and *All Hell* would weather an experience approximating the aircraft's name.

The fat fighter kicked over a few minutes before 10:32, and after Johnson listened to a few words of encouragement from his crew chief, the radial-engined Thunderbolt, a 150-gallon extra tank slung beneath its belly, rolled away toward the end of a black-surfaced runway on which 61st would take off. Without a hitch, the other fighters of B Group fell in behind Keyworth Red Leader and followed him toward the runway.

Half the fighters lined up on the end of one of Halesworth's two runways and the other half on the other. At 10:32 A.M. Keyworth Red Leader and his wingman roared off toward the far end of one runway. As soon as they passed the intersection where the runways crossed, two fighters on the other runway began to roll. In a few minutes the 35 P-47's were all safely off, turning in a wide left turn, and rolling out on course, almost due

156

east. Col. Zemke's 35 fighters — the rest of 56th — were only a short distance away.

The few clouds which covered England were easily topped in a shallow climb. To conserve fuel, power was set at 1,800 rpm and 29 inches of mercury. Johnson looked behind and around; his P-47's were in perfect formation, closed in properly behind. He was leading three understrength squadrons, totaling 35 fighters in all. Normally, a squadron sent out 16 planes on a mission.

Making better than 150 mph in the gradual climb, the group rapidly left the English countryside behind. The Thunderbolts roared on upward . . . out over the North Sea and toward the coast of Holland. Altimeters registered steady gains . . . 6,000, 7,000, 8,000 feet. Now superchargers were cut in and pilots switched to belly tanks, to use up that gasoline first, since the extra tanks would have to be jettisoned quickly in case of imminent action.

Altitude registers 10,000, 11,000, 12,000 feet. Below nothing can be seen but a vast expanse of water. The width of the North Sea at this latitude is over 100 miles. It is a cold dip for the pilot who is forced down, either going or coming. The blunt-nosed fighters slice upward into the sky . . . pilots check their gun switches . . . begin to look for the outline ahead which will reveal landfall — the Dutch coast. The altimeter needle reads 15,000,

16,000, 17,000 feet. The coast of Holland can't be far away. Johnson orders the three squadrons to spread out into combat formation.

The Thunderbolts wing out wide, come into almost line-abreast formation, continue slanting upward. Altitude reaches 23,000, 24,000, 25,000 feet. Now the coast of Holland is visible ahead. Each pilot flips on his gunsight switch. The yellow circle on the sighting glass appears. Altitude 27,000 feet.

The group crosses landfall. The landscape below is blurred by a general haze, but the sky is cloudless. The group passes over Walcheren Island . . . and then in above the Zuyder Zee. Up ahead the lead boxes of bombers come into view, clusters of small outlines, more than 30 bombers to a box — B-17 Flying Fortresses. Johnson points the group toward the big friends. Of the three squadrons, the 63rd leads the way, Johnson's 61st is slightly back, and Lt. Mike Quirk's P-47's are next — the 62nd.

The dots ahead grow larger. As the fighters approach the bomber boxes, the squadrons split and curve into position around the heavies. One squadron leader takes his eight P-47's directly above the bombers, Johnson banks left and eases up on that side, and Quirk guards the right flank. They stay several thousand feet out from their big friends — begin to S-turn, to keep from running away from the slower bombers.

The spearhead of the aerial armada

157

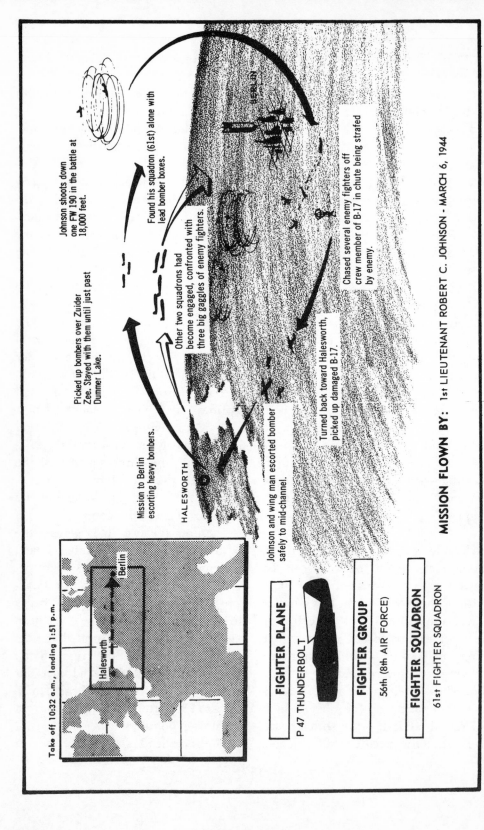

Take off 10:32 a.m., landing 1:51 p.m.

Berlin

Halesworth

Johnson shoots down one FW 190 in the battle at 18,000 feet.

Found his squadron (61st) alone with lead bomber boxes.

Other two squadrons had become engaged, confronted with three big gaggles of enemy fighters.

Chased several enemy fighters off crew member of B-17 in chute being strafed by enemy.

BERLIN

Picked up bombers over Zuider Zee. Stayed with them until just past Dummer Lake.

Mission to Berlin escorting heavy bombers.

HALESWORTH

Johnson and wing man escorted bomber safely to mid-channel.

Turned back toward Halesworth, picked up damaged B-17.

MISSION FLOWN BY: 1st LIEUTENANT ROBERT C. JOHNSON - MARCH 6, 1944

FIGHTER PLANE

P 47 THUNDERBOLT

FIGHTER GROUP

56th (8th AIR FORCE)

FIGHTER SQUADRON

61st FIGHTER SQUADRON

treaks on through the Dutch sky at 24,000-25,000 feet — one squadron of ighters above. For a short time the ilent procession drones on inland. Then it reaches the vicinity of Zwolle. Heavy flak bursts dot the sky. The ighters maneuver radically to be on he safe side — but the guns below are aiming at the bombers, where the bombload on its way to Berlin is arried.

A group of unidentified specks ahead . . . pilots tense. The bogeys are mall-fighters. The 56th readies for a ight. On come the bogeys . . . at the 6th's altitude. As they approach nearer, Johnson leans closer . . . now heir blunt noses are identifiable . . . They are coming right through the 6th's formation! At the last moment, with pilots' fingers itching near trigger buttons, someone calls in identification — the bogeys are P-47's! They ly right through the 56th. It is a new group. It is a dangerous situation . . . but the inexperienced pilots get away with it . . . they flash on by and back . . no one slips and fires at his comrades.

For a few minutes the flight continues uneventfully . . . then bogeys re spotted off the side. Once again scorting fighter pilots tighten up . . . he bogeys come on, closer . . . blunt noses! FW-190's or P-47's? On and on ome the fighters . . . now they are almost on 56th. "Those same boys," someone yells over the radio . . . and once again the wolf pack holds its ire, and curses. The orderly flight

continues. The sky is clear. The bombers leave no vapor trails.

Then, ahead, lies the German border. At this moment Lt. Quirk's eight P-47's break hard right. They go into a dive . . . Johnson looks hard but can see nothing. Johnson maintains position. Quirk's fighters rapidly disappear below. Then, on the radio, Johnson hears shouts from Quirk's men . . . they are in a fight! They spotted a gaggle of ME-109's climbing up for an attack. They jumped the enemy fighters and are having quite a battle. Quirk estimates the gaggle at about 30 fighters.

Johnson calls and asks the location of the dogfight. No answer. He calls again, hoping to get into the fight. Quirk is too busy . . . and maybe the 62nd wants the bandits for themselves. Pilots in the two squadrons with the bombers envy 62nd. Johnson pulls wide, to the left, to search a little wider. The other squadron curves right — to the south — for the same purpose. But neither finds the enemy fighters. Johnson curves back in toward the bombers as the stream is approaching Dummer Lake — an unmistakable landmark on the route to Berlin. The other squadron is still to the south, so Johnson comes in close to the bombers and flies over the boxes. As he reaches the front box, he leans into a left turn. The three boxes of bombers 56th is protecting fly silently and majestically on — dozens of Forts in each closely packed box.

The blunt nose of *All Hell* heels

around toward the north ... and up ahead Johnson spots suspicious specks. It's 11:40 A.M. They're closing on a southerly course. Johnson watches as they come closer. They must be the same P-47's that have already flown through the 56th twice. He speaks over the radio to seven 47's behind him: "Watch these monkeys ahead." At the same time he realizes the oncoming gaggle isn't P-47's. Bandits! Into the mike he yells: "Hell, they're Focke-Wulfs!" Thunderbolts drop tanks, spread out further and wheel out into position to turn in on the enemy fighters as they come through. The Germans are heading for the leading box of bombers. Johnson is so close to the bombers there's no chance to stop the enemy fighters before they reach their objective.

The gaggle now is fast approaching — FW-190's and ME-109's clearly identifiable. Johnson times his maneuver to the second. As the Germans reach his vicinity he swings into a sharp right turn to pull in behind ... throttle wide open. The fighters flash together at 600 mph. In a second they are past the Thunderbolts and boring in on the lead box of bombers. Johnson pulls a tight right turn and is on the tail of the bandits almost immediately. The bandits ignore the U.S. fighters and go for the bombers. Now the big friends get set for the shock of attack ... guns of each Fortress train on the German fighters as the March air is filled with cries of warning and the excitement of combat.

Distance is so close between the German and American fighters it's impossible for Fortress gunners to distinguish between friend and foe. Johnson watches the enemy ahead draw into range ... he's overtaking them. To his left he catches sight of another gaggle, slightly east. In a split second, his eyes pick out a third gaggle above. Each enemy formation contains 30 to 40 fighters.

Johnson's eight Thunderbolts, all that are available at the moment to protect the bombers, close the range behind the gaggle in front. But the Germans are already on the bombers. The sky lights up. Enemy 20-mm shells throw white bursts into the bomber formation. Rockets leave a zigzag smoke trail as they streak into the heavies. The B-17's ten .50-calibers to a bomber open up with all guns. The Germans fly right in. The Thunderbolts follow ... too late to turn off now. The bombers shoot at friend and foe. The P-47's open up on the Germans ahead and German .30-caliber machine guns and cannon and rockets clutter up the air. The fighters flash through the formation, under and over and by the sides of the bombers.

Parachutes begin to dot the sky. The action is so fast, so deadly, it's hard to comprehend. The other two gaggles of German fighters have picked the second and third boxes of bombers and bore in ... splashing fire and shell through the formations, unhindered by defending fighters. The 61st Squadron, right behind the enemy

A burning B-17 drops its bombs on Berlin.

;aggle, passes through and by the lead
)omber box and down and out, hang-
ng on and firing away. Johnson sees
cores of parachutes. One B-17 is cut
n half . . . the tail assembly glides off
n one direction . . . the rest of the
uselage and wing in another. Ten
nen were safe and sound in the Fort-
·ess seconds ago. Other B-17's drop
)ack out of the lead box, trailing
·moke, crippled. Several plunge earth-
vard, trailing a black column of smoke.
Now a hundred parachutes fill the sky!

Several enemy fighters smash into
the big bombers. A huge flash of fire
follows and both planes go down. It is
a savage encounter. A number of enemy fighters are burning. The Americans are taking a heavy toll. Johnson
closes four FW-190's at about 18,000
feet. He slams throttle the rest of the
way forward, approaching from five
o'clock. So far he hasn't scored a kill
and planes are falling all around him.

The FW-190's draw closer into
range, Johnson at full throttle. He

watches the four 190's closely — they're making good speed, in two elements — ahead, slightly left. He looks through his sight ring — one of the bandits is now almost filling it.

Just as *All Hell* flashes into range behind the Germans see the danger to their rear. The four FW-190's break sharply up, in pairs. But Johnson is opening fire. The Thunderbolt roars and shakes . . . and the 190 directly ahead takes hits.

Johnson pulls stick back and hangs on behind the climbing enemy. *All Hell* spits tracers and shells, which converge on the gray-black, radial-engined fighter. Johnson's fire is accurate and inflicts fatal damage.

The enemy's engine is hit . . . his propeller seems to spin slower. Pieces of the FW-190 fly backward. Something moves on top . . . suddenly the enemy pilot leaves the cockpit. He jumps at good speed and falls rapidly. Then, a chute opens below. The FW-190 plunges earthward.

Enemy fighters are scattered all over the area, in singles, in pairs, and larger groups. Johnson, flushed with victory, spots a lone bandit and banks sharply to come in on his tail. He looks back to check his wingman — a new pilot — is shocked to see a German squarely on his tail. He racks around and turns into the enemy as fast as he can, breaking up the attack. Now some 30 falling planes fill the sky.

Again he sees a target ahead. He maneuvers for position, but remembers to check his wingman. Right

behind him is another German fighter. For the second time Johnson breaks off his attack and turns sharply to make a pass at the enemy fighter. In all his combat he has never lost a wingman. The bandit breaks away a Johnson threatens to close his tail.

The scene up above is bedlam Burning aircraft and hundreds of para chutes dot every corner of the sky Johnson has never seen so many burning aircraft and chutes. He notice another fighter curving in behind hi wingman, and almost by habit now stands on a wing and turns into the enemy. He succeeds, for the third time, in driving him off. It's a strange battle. By now he could have scored several victories had he not bothered about protecting his wingman.

Up above Johnson sees two FW 190's firing away. Four men in para chutes dangle in front of the enemy fighters' guns. He yanks the stick back and *All Hell* climbs toward the enemy fighters. As they prepare to make another pass at the parachutists, Johnson — still out of range — opens distracting fire. The tracers catch the attention of the enemy planes . . . they drop their noses down toward the climbing P 47's to converge. Only Johnson and his wingman are left together. The other six P-47's of 61st Squadron are scattered in every direction.

The two enemy fighters grow larger and larger as they approach at great speed. Johnson sees the light flashes from their wing guns. He, too, open fire, but observes no hits. As they close the Germans break to Johnson's right and continue to dive. Johnson shoves stick forward and hits right rudder and plunges after them, burning inside at the thought of enemy fighters machine-gunning airmen in parachutes. For a moment the Germans, with their greater diving speed, pull away, but then the two heavier P-47's come on strong and Johnson can see the FW-190's are no longer gaining.

By now all four fighters are just a few thousand feet above the ground. They continue their steep dive . . . in the direction of Hannover, not far away. The distance begins to close. Airspeed climbs at a rapid clip . . . 325, 350, 375, 400, 425, 450. The two Thunderbolts are gaining. The German pilots realize they're being caught from behind. Without warning, they suddenly part . . . the enemy element leader's wingman turns sharply to the right. Two targets. Johnson must choose. He and his wingman stay with the enemy leader, the other German fighter gets away.

The distance is closing . . . and Johnson is almost in range. The FW-190, now leveling out, tries an old trick. Suddenly the thin dark exhaust smoke from his stacks disappears. Johnson's left hand races for the throttle, jerks it back. The enemy is cutting his engine to make the Thunderbolts overshoot, and zoom out in front of his guns. *All Hell* slows up . . . but still eases up on the German fighter . . . just about right. Now the 190 pilot stands on his left wing in a vertical

turn. Johnson cuts tight behind him, cutting him off in the turn, not going too fast to stay in there on the enemy's tail, as the German pilot had planned. The cutoff turn brings Johnson into range. He presses the firing button. Eight fifties roar and shake *All Hell*. Tracers mark an aerial path to the German fighter. Johnson pulls the stick into his stomach and sees the silhouette of the low-winged enemy fighter pass through his gunsight ring from tail to nose . . . proof he's out-turning his foe. His shells rake over the top of the enemy fighter, from tail to engine nacelle. For a second or two *All Hell* spits shells at the German at close range. Johnson is on top of his victim now and banks to the right, pulls up to come around for another pass. As soon as he gets another glance at his foe, turning to come in from behind again, Johnson notices the enemy fighter is diving. Already close to the ground after the first long dive, Johnson pushes stick forward and *All Hell* streaks after the fleeing German. This time the chase is short. The crippled enemy fighter can't make top speed. The Thunderbolt walks right up on him in the dive, easing up through the smoke stream into point-blank range. The enemy fighter's wingspan fills the orange sight circle and Johnson fires again. Shells reach out to the German fighter. The 190 noses down, hit again. Now the earth is racing up, straight below. The enemy fighter doesn't pull out.

Suddenly Johnson sees an FW-190

163

on his wingman's tail. He hauls stick back and breaks off the chase, turns into the enemy fighter, drives him off.

Johnson is too low for comfort, and begins the long climb back to high altitude. His wingman is in position. He wonders if the 190 went straight in. In protecting his comrade, again, he lost sight of his foe at the critical moment. He can claim only a probable!

The two Thunderbolts slice upward through the clear sky and Johnson looks up in search of the bombers, and whatever action might be in progress. He sees nothing. Altimeter registers steady gains and the fighters soon find themselves back at altitude . . . 15,000, 16,000, 17,000 feet. Still climbing, he makes out bandits at two o'clock high. About six of them, FW-190's and ME-109's, are firing on a lone B-17. Johnson gives *All Hell* right stick and rudder and continues his climb . . . straight into the German fighters. His wingman sticks in position. Full throttle.

The distance closes rapidly and Johnson gets ready to open fire, coming up on their rear. The approaching fighters are now almost at the same altitude and Johnson puts his finger on the trigger. He lines up one of the bandits in his sight. Fire! His guns spit and *All Hell* shudders from the vibration. The Germans now break sharply left and go into a dive. Johnson rolls over to his right and starts down again, in another vertical chase following two 109's.

The enemy fighters have speed on the two P-47's and pull away. Johnson's two Thunderbolts keep them in sight and at full throttle rapidly increase speed. But Johnson knows he can't stay over Germany much longer at full throttle, with gasoline burning at a terrific rate. He has been taking on German fighters for a long time now, and his fuel supply is running low.

Still, he begins to gain gradually on the 109 directly ahead and decides to hang on a while longer. Slowly the enemy plane grows larger in his sight . . . speed building up in the roaring dive. Down and down they go, close to the deck again . . . and Johnson begins to approach firing range. Now almost ready to close the enemy, he spots two other bandits approaching, just as he begins to slacken the angle of dive, following the nearest bandit ahead.

The distance to the target is great, but Johnson is in a hurry. He opens with *All Hell's* eight wing guns. Shells streak out, marked by the flight of tracers. The Thunderbolt shudders. But he must break off the encounter. The enemy fighters coming to the rescue are almost on him, and Johnson turns in their direction. They flash by, as the great speed of each pair of fighters brings them together in seconds. Johnson doesn't turn to take after them. Never can he remember having started so many attacks in one day, only to have to break off before attaining victory. Today the sky is full

164

of Germans. He must start home without delay.

A glance at the enemy fighters shows they are pulling away to the east . . . they choose to fight again another day. Johnson is relieved. His ammunition is low, but fuel supply is his main problem. The North Sea ahead is quite wide when crossing it with limited fuel. Climbing once again, Johnson spots a flight of four P-47's not far away, heading west. He calls on the radio and identifies their marking; they're Keyworth Red Leader's second flight. They, too, have seen plenty of action. All six of the P-47's join up and head for England. Johnson orders each pilot to throttle back and use as little gas as possible.

One of the P-47's of the squadron is badly damaged. As they head west the pilot of the damaged Thunderbolt radios he can't make it. His engine has been hit and is through. Johnson tells him to bail out at 18,000 feet. But the pilot, Lt. Andrew B. Strauss, replies it's too cold at that altitude. He will go down to 5,000. The other pilots watch in sympathy, escort him down. He points his P-47's nose toward the deck for the last time, loses altitude rapidly. Then they hear him call — at 6,000 feet: "So long, you guys. I'm cutting off my radio, rolling over and dropping out." And he does.

Strauss's chute billows open and the stricken fighter spirals crazily down. His body swings back and forth, like a pendulum. Strauss can't arrest the motion. He drops closer and closer to the ground, still swinging back and forth, strikes the earth on the back of his neck and head. His comrades above circle and watch, hoping he will get up. He stands up, rubs his head and looks up. He sees his friends up where he was minutes before, who will soon be back at Halesworth. Then he puts his hands in his pockets and slowly walks away from the spot where he landed.

The rest of the 61st has to resume the flight home at once. Johnson points his growling fighter toward England. The others follow. The sky is now largely clear of German fighters. Johnson's Thunderbolts climb back to safe altitude and cross into Holland. Ahead they see a lone crippled Fortress, and provide an appreciated escort. Johnson wonders how many others won't come back this far. Soon they are out over the North Sea.

Watching gasoline gauges constantly during the last part of the flight, the 61st makes it across the North Sea, flashes in over England. In another 15 minutes the big fighters are landing at Halesworth. As they lose altitude and come down for a landing, Johnson notices the clock on his instrument panel. It is 1:51 P.M., still early in the day — and the wolf pack has been deep inside Germany, run into four big gaggles of enemy aircraft, and returned home. Big B has been an exciting mission.

In every country of occupied Europe there were resistance groups working against the Germans. They blew up bridges, derailed trains, sniped at German soldiers, sent valuable information to Great Britain and helped Allied airmen escape. Hitler's Gestapo worked hard in an attempt to curb this activity. In each of the occupied countries a register of the entire population was kept at Gestapo headquarters. The information in the registers was used to keep track of the residents, especially those who might be engaged in underground activities. Thousands were imprisoned and tortured or executed because of these Gestapo records.

Here are some details of the battle of the Royal Air Force against the Gestapo and its notorious records.

Pinpoint Bateson

Pat Pointon

THEY RECKONED that Bob Bateson could drop a bomb fair and square on a postage stamp. Flying so low that his Mosquito stirred the dust off the rooftops, this stocky, quiet-spoken group captain brought a touch of inspired genius to the attack of some of the most difficult targets of the whole war. He led his wing against the Gestapo headquarters in The Hague, Copenhagen, and Odense, where the objective, in all cases, was a single house in a single street in the center of a city.

With the shrewd skill that earned him the nickname of "Pinpoint," Bob Bateson invariably put his load smack in the center of the bull's-eye. Spurning the use of any aiming sight or scale, he relied on lightning coordination between eye and brain plus an uncanny sense of judgment in gauging precisely the right second to press the bomb button.

The war kept Bob Bateson abroad until 1943. They were years of peril, of hardship, and hairbreadth escapes against a wily adversary who held all the advantages in the air and on the ground. As Bob Bateson's experience grew, so, too, did his prowess. He returned to Britain as a pilot with an outstanding record for courage and bravery who had tackled sorties against all manner of targets.

In England, he found the Mosquito was just coming into its own as one of the fastest, most formidable air weapons of the war. He wriggled out of the "chairborne" job that was earmarked for him and even dropped back in rank to wangle himself on to "mossies." Toward the end of 1943 he found himself promoted to wing commander and given command of 613 Squadron which was then based as Lasham between Alton and Basingstoke in Hampshire.

For most of the time at that period, the squadron was engaged on low-level precision attacks in the "noball" offensive against the V-I sites. Compact, cunningly camouflaged, and strongly defended, these targets gave the squadron an ideal apprenticeship for the sterner tasks that they were destined to perform later.

Bateson kept his crews continuously on their toes. Morale was high, and he encouraged them to perfect their aiming accuracy by repeated practice. The average bombing error was whittled down to a mere 20 yards or less.

Soon the squadron was to face its greatest challenge. From the Gestapo headquarters in the heart of The Hague, an evil web of fear and tyranny spread throughout the Low Countries. The files and indexes that the Gestapo had built up had trapped many gallant resistance fighters. The Dutch underground appealed to the RAF to smoke out the hornets' nest. At first it seemed a hopeless plea. The headquarters was well defended, and consisted of a single 90-foot-high house of five stories wedged tightly among other buildings in the Schevengsche Weg, near its junction with Carnegie Plein, close to the Peace Palace. The dilemma was how to locate and strike such a difficult target. In the end it was decided to entrust Bob Bateson and the boys of 613 Squadron with the task.

Before Bateson or any of his crews were told of the daring project, however, weeks of research were carried out to evolve exactly the right type of bomb for the job. Contrary to popular belief, it was virtually impossible to destroy paper in bulk by fire. And the use of high-explosive bombs might destroy the building, but the contents of the filing cabinets would merely be scattered and could be collected again. High explosive dropped in sufficient amounts just to cause the collapse of the walls would serve only to bury the vital filing cabinets instead of destroying their contents. Eventually, the "boffins" produced a bomb which was a judicious mixture of high explosive and incendiary. An exact, scale model of the building was built from plaster of Paris and, from scraps of information filtered through from the Dutch underground, staff officers obtained details about the thickness and composition of the walls of the house, and the number and size of its windows.

Everything hinged on secrecy — plus accuracy. There was little margin for error if the killing or injuring of Dutch citizens was to be avoided. Right under the noses of the Gestapo, in the very house next door to the headquarters, was a group of resistance chiefs who supplied much valuable data for the raid. But it was out of the question to convey any warning to them in case the tip went astray and wrecked the whole scheme.

Not until the early days of April, 1944, was Bateson let into the secret preparations. To him was entrusted the actual planning of the attack.

He picked his crews and warned them to cram in some extra target practice, but he gave them no inkling of the real nature of the sortie that lay ahead. Privately he mapped out routes, turning points and landmarks. With the secret model at eye level, he patiently studied the exact appearance of the Gestapo HQ for hours on end until its image was riveted firmly in his mind. He wanted to make absolutely sure that he could identify the building correctly in a single glance when the right moment came.

At last everything was ready. At the head of six Mosquitoes, Bateson took off from Lasham in the early morning of April 11, 1944, on the secret mission. Each second was vital. Bateson had planned the attack so that if, at any stage, it had to be called off, the Germans would have no clue of what the original target had been.

Crossing the English coast at 260 mph., the Mosquitoes swooped right down to sea level. Before long they got their first — and only — real shock. Unknown to the formation, the Germans had recently opened the sluice gates on the Scheldt, flooding a vast area, and creating a false coast. Consequently, the pilots were surprised to find themselves making a landfall well ahead of their carefully timed sched-ule at a point which bore little resemblance to their maps. Had they blundered? Were they off track? It was hard to know what had gone wrong in the low-flying, fast-moving Mosquitoes. Bateson was baffled. So was his navigator. But a few minutes later their worries were routed when they spotted the real coast coming up ahead and they found to their relief that they were both on course and on time.

Over Holland the Mosquitoes streaked inland on a series of dogleg courses so that the final objective would not be revealed. Visibility was good; the cloud base was suitable. Everything was going like clockwork. The last turning point came up. Waggling his wings to indicate that the show was "On," Bateson kicked his rudder hard over and sent his plane wheeling around the sky in a tight, 130-degree turn as he headed its nose toward the house in The Hague. Behind him the rest of the formation took up stations in pairs of two . . .

Now those long hours patiently studying intelligence photographs were about to be repaid . . . Roof patterns and prejudged pinpoints flashed past in a neat, orderly succession, almost like a cinema film unwinding . . .

Hauling back on his control column, Bateson pulled his Mosquito sharply up to 400 feet for a lightning glance around a broader horizon to make absolutely certain that the formation was correctly aligned on its target, and then he plummeted back equally abruptly to rooftop height again.

Now they are on the final few hundred yards . . . the bomb doors swing open . . . they clip the spire on the Peace Palace so uncomfortably close that it almost slices off the port wing tip . . . the familiar outline of the Gestapo HQ is briefly silhouetted directly in front of the aircraft's nose.

Coolly, Bateson chooses his exact moment. His bombs drop away, cascading straight for the crucial point where the walls of the building meet the ground.

Flt. Lt. Peter Cobley, who was accompanying the leader, said afterward that he saw Bateson's bombs "go right in at the front door." A sentry on duty at the building who spotted the bombers streaking toward him, flung away his rifle and fled for his life. Immediately behind the house was a German barracks. When the Mosquitoes appeared on the scene, some of the German soldiers were on parade, while others were playing football. The game and the parade broke up abruptly in startled panic and confusion.

After a two-minute interval to give the delayed-action bombs of the leading pair time to explode, the second brace of Mosquitoes zoomed into the breach. They dropped incendiaries across the headquarters which was already partly obscured by smoke. Then the last pair went in and finished the attack.

All six Mosquitoes got back to base entirely unscathed. The Germans were completely caught napping. Not a single shot was loosed off at Bateson's force, nor was there any opposition from enemy fighters. The raid was overwhelmingly successful. In turn, high explosive, delayed-action and incendiary bombs had rent the house from its neighbors like a decayed tooth. Reconnaissance photographs later showed that while the building had been reduced to rubble, surrounding property suffered no more damage than broken windows and loosened tiles.

Almost exactly a year later, Bateson was picked to lead an even more hazardous enterprise against the Gestapo HQ at Copenhagen. Here again, the target was a single building in the center of a city, well defended and awkward to locate.

Bateson, now a group captain commanding 140 Wing in Belgium, returned to England with the crews he had chosen for the raid, and prepared his plans along similar lines to the Hague attack. Because of the greater distance involved, the Mosquitoes had to be fitted with extra fuel tanks. And they were given a fighter escort to protect them on their long sortie.

Much of the information on which the operation was based was supplied by a Danish army officer working secretly with the underground guerilla movement, whose identity must still remain anonymous. Contemptuously scorning personal danger, he risked his life a dozen times to make clandestine trips to England carrying plans of

169

the building, details of the Gestapo's daily movements, and the position of the local defenses.

In many ways it was an infinitely more delicate mission than the previous raid on the house in The Hague. For inside the Copenhagen headquarters, a group of key Danish underground leaders was imprisoned. They languished, starved and tortured, in cells on the top story. The bombs from the liberating Mosquitoes had to be placed with meticulous precision, otherwise the pilots would find themselves acting the role of executioner for the Germans. The raid was timed to coincide with a desperate attempt to free the prisoners by the local underground forces, which had previously managed to smuggle explosives inside to their doomed compatriots.

At last everything was ready, but adverse weather caused a last-minute hitch. A force of 18 Mosquitoes and 20 escorting fighters finally took off from a Norfolk base in March, 1945. The weather was bitterly cold, and during the long 350-mile sea crossing, spray blown off the waves by the heavy head winds caked in a solid layer of salt on the windscreen of the planes, seriously limiting the view from the cockpits.

The poor arc of visibility that was created was directly responsible for marring the complete success of the raid. At the approaches to Copenhagen, the Mosquitoes peeled off in pairs. Bateson and his companion at the head of the force dropped their bombs well and truly on the target, but another pilot miscalculated his run-in and crashed on a nearby school. Some of the others got off course and received a severe mauling when they strayed over the harbor where a German cruiser and several flak ships opened up at point-blank range.

While the escorting fighters effectively dealt with gun emplacements on surrounding rooftops, Bateson's boys regrouped behind their leader, and the Mosquitoes swept down the main street of the city well below the level of the buildings in a gesture of defiance before turning out to sea again.

The object of the raid was ideally achieved. The Gestapo HQ was wiped out and the incriminating documents that it contained were consumed in the fire that swept the place. But before it collapsed in a heap of charred ashes, the incarcerated underground chiefs won their way to freedom.

After the war when Bateson was feted by the Dutch underground and received a Danish award during a state visit to the country, he met several of the men who evaded the stupefied guards amidst the panic of exploding bombs and got safely away.

Among them was one resistance fighter who was actually strung up by his wrists undergoing torture, as the Mosquitoes screamed over the skyline of Copenhagen.

A month later Bateson hammered the Gestapo for the third time. The Nazi war machine was already reeling back eclipsed and vanquished, when the familiar pattern of attack was unleashed once more against a mansion at Odense on the island of Fyn, in Denmark. From his base at Melsbruck, in Belgium, Bateson led a force of about a dozen Mosquitoes over the North Sea and across the Dutch islands, below the cover of the German radar, to his final objective.

"The attack followed similar lines to the raids on The Hague and Copenhagen," Group Captain Bateson ex-plains. "In the case of Odense, though, the Germans had taken extraordinary measures to stop us spotting the Gestapo HQ. Clearly, they must have realized that it might be next on our list, and the target was extremely well camouflaged. The shadow of our planes must have passed over the place several times as we circled around trying to pick it out. But we made no mistake in our final identification, and we left the place a smoking ruin."

It isn't often that a large-scale air attack can be carried out with no losses to the attacking force. The Luftwaffe accomplished such a feat in June, 1944, when its bombers hit Poltava in what has been described as the best attack the Luftwaffe ever made against the United States Army Air Forces. Here is what happened.

Black Night at Poltava

Kenn C. Rust

BY THE MIDDLE OF 1944 the 8th United States Army Air Force was undisputed master of the day skies over Europe. The Luftwaffe had been spread out on three fronts and slowly decimated by day and by night under the weight of the surging tide of Allied air power. Yet, weakened though it was, the Luftwaffe was still capable of striking back when the opportunity arose. And so it was that, in June, 1944, 8th AAF Bomber Command suffered a blow which cost it its greatest single day's loss of the war. This is the story of that day's operations and the beginnings of project FRANTIC.

FRANTIC was the outgrowth of protracted talks with the Russians re-

This is the only picture taken during the highly successful Luftwaffe attack on the airfield at Poltava. It shows flares dropped by the German raiders, the antiaircraft fire of the Russians and some of the parked B-17s.

lating to the use of Russian airfields by U.S. aircraft to open up to AAF shuttle-bombing of enemy-held territory previously out of range. Secondarily it was hoped such shuttle operations would force further dispersal on the Luftwaffe and otherwise strain German resources in trying to meet the new attacks over a larger strategic area made up of German-held and controlled Polish territory.

Negotiations for such operations had begun in late 1943 but it was not until April of 1944 that the Russians finally allocated three airfields, instead of the

expected six, for use by the USAAF. The three airfields were located in the scorched earth area around Kiev, and it took all of April and May for American engineers to extend runways, build new base facilities, bring in supplies and in general rejuvenate the airfields so they could accept AAF aircraft. Of the three airfields, Poltava was best suited to handling heavy bombers, Mirgorod could handle some heavies, but Piryatin was capable of handling only fighters.

Project FRANTIC finally began on June 2, 1944, when 130 B-17's and 70

P-51 Mustangs of the Fifteenth AAF flew from Italy to bomb marshaling yards at Debrecen and then proceeded to .he FRANTIC airfields. On June 6 these forces sortied from Russia to bomb and strafe the airfield at Galatz, Romania, and on June 11, on their way back to Italy, they shuttle-bombed Foscani airfield in Romania. In the three operations only two B-17's and two Mustangs were lost. The stage was set to bring the 8th AAF into the shuttle-bombing operations.

Like all other air forces based in Britain in June, 1944, the 8th had been completely given over to tactical attacks in support of the troops on the Normandy bridgehead. However, by midmonth the ground situation was so well in hand that the 8th was able to swing back to its more normal course of strategic operations against the German heartland. As a part of these operations the 8th would begin its participation in FRANTIC on June 21.

The main target was Berlin, and a total force of some 2,500 bombers and fighters was dispatched. Targets assigned in Berlin were aircraft engine factories and marshaling yards in the outskirts of the city. On the way into the target a smaller force of 114 B-17's and 70 P-51 Mustangs broke off from the main group just as some 100 German day fighters made a concentrated attack. The main force fought its way through this attack and then through the heavy and accurate flak over Berlin to bomb its targets. The main force then returned to England with a loss of 44 heavy bombers. It was a heavy loss, yet not up to the high of 60 bombers lost the year before at Schweinfurt. But the day was not yet over.

The smaller force of B-17's and Mustangs, once separated from the main force, had proceeded to Ruhland, 75 miles south of Berlin, and bombed a synthetic oil plant against mild opposition. These aircraft then continued eastward, heading for the FRANTIC airfields around Kiev. They flew high through sunny skies, the sun behind them still well up over the western horizon.

But there was more than a sun in that sky. When German ground stations had recognized that this force had not headed back toward England, a single Heinkel HE-177 was ordered up. Now, hidden by distance and the sun, that Heinkel heavy bomber stalked its American counterparts, across eastern Germany and Poland to the Russian lines.

By late afternoon, the 8th AAF bombers and fighters were flying over the neat, bunched squares of collective farms; lush, spring green fields and the yellowed, burned-out remnants of razed hamlets and ravaged earth. Then the B-17's and Mustangs began letting down to the Kiev area. Most of the Mustangs landed at Piryatin while 73 B-17's landed at Poltava and the remaining aircraft landed at Mirgorod.

At Poltava the Flying Fortresses

These Soviet Yak 9 fighter planes were part of the force that guarded the American shuttle bases. They were unable to shoot down a single German plane during the attack on Poltava.

found a new 5,950-foot runway running north and south, diagonal to the original L-shaped runways of the Russian airfield. As the aircraft landed, aircrews noticed a few other AAF aircraft at the north end of the airfield, six C-47's, three photo reconnaissance planes, and a single P-38. To the east were hangars and a number of fighters and utility aircraft of the Russian air force.

As soon as they were down, the B-17's taxied to dispersal points around the main runway. Fourteen of them parked on the turf at the north end of the airfield; the other 59 spread out in a gentle arc parallel to the western side of the runway. Three of these were in the only blast-proof revetments, the others were spread out in the open and somewhat bunched because of the size of the field.

As the propellers stopped turning, a host of Russians, men and women, military and civilian, came out to greet the victorious American crews from England. It was a party atmosphere and soon the groups moved to the new building where they exchanged toasts and more compliments. Outside the sun was down and night folded its curtain over Poltava airfield.

Some crews turned in early, others continued the fraternal toasts with their hosts, while on the airfield guards stood by the aircraft and two oxygen service crews went about their work. Nearby, slit trenches had been dug, bombs were stored in perimeter revetments, and fuel drums were in dispersed piles just outside the airfield. By 22:00 hours all work was ended and the aircraft stood mute in the dark night.

Suddenly, at 23:35, Russian authorities notified American headquarters at Poltava that enemy aircraft had crossed the Russian front lines and were headed toward the Poltava area. Immediately air-raid alarms were sounded and the men took to the slit trenches and whatever other cover they could find. For almost 30 minutes they crouched in the dark against the damp earth; but nothing happened and slowly the tension began to break.

Then, just after midnight, the sound of aircraft engines became audible as 80 JU-88's and HE-111's, tipped off by the lone HE-177, arrived over the field. Immediately flares popped into brilliance in the night sky to drop lazily on their invisible parachutes. The B-17's, no more than one of which was camouflaged, suddenly glistened brightly in the flare light. Ten minutes passed, during which the garish lights grew brighter and more numerous, and then the first HE-111 began dropping demolition bombs.

Russian antiaircraft units, mostly of small caliber, fired continuously, and from a nearby airfield Russian night fighters were sent up. But no enemy aircraft had so far been shot down.

The high-altitude bombing from 10,000 feet and lower by single aircraft, continued for over an hour. A small quantity of high explosives and short-delay high-explosive bombs were followed by a large quantity of small incendiaries and antipersonnel bombs. All around the field B-17's were bursting into flames, becoming fresh markers to guide the Luftwaffe bombers, and one of the caches of fuel was hit to burst even brighter light and flame into the nightmarish night sky.

At 01:45 the bombing ceased almost as quickly as it had begun, but the Heinkels and Junkers continued to cruise over the field. Still not one had fallen to the defenses. Then, at 02:00, the JU-88's came screaming in at low level dropping antipersonnel bombs and strafing. More B-17's were hit and caught fire as the Junkers raced back and forth across the field sending out streaks of machine-gun and cannon fire and leaving behind them the telltale burst of small fragmentation bombs.

At 02:15 the last JU-88 roared across the field, spitting out death, and then climbed to disappear back into the night beyond the flames and smoke raging upward from the shattered airfield. Five minutes later a pair of HE-111's dropped flash bombs, took their photos, and departed. The attack was over.

For hours afterward, the Russians — refusing to allow the Americans to take part — fought the fires. But it was not until morning that the last fire was out and a complete assessment of the damage and losses could be made. Of the 14 B-17's at the north end of the airfield, seven had been destroyed, but the real disaster was along the western edges of the main runway. There, 40 of the 59 B-17's had been destroyed — including the three which had been in blast-proof revetments. In all, 47 B-17's were destroyed, and when that number was added to the losses suffered over Berlin, the number of heavy bombers lost by 8th AAF's Bomber Command for one operation reached 91, the highest total that force would know throughout the entire war.

And that was not all the damage at Poltava. The remaining 26 B-17's had all suffered damage, two C-47's had been destroyed along with a photo plane, and on the Russian side of the field one fighter plane had been destroyed and a further 25 aircraft damaged. More than 400,000 gallons of petrol had gone up in flames. Two Americans were killed and six wounded, while 30 Russians died and another 95 were wounded.

To accomplish this, the Luftwaffe had dropped 110 tons of bombs of which 15 tons were high explosive, 78 tons antipersonnel and 17 tons incendiary. And not a single German aircraft was lost, either to the wild Russian AA fire or their night fighters which had failed to make contact.

The Germans were to strike again, the next night at Mirgorod, but then

Some of the B-17s that were destroyed or damaged at Poltava.

the American planes were gone. The Luftwaffe had had its last moment of glory, and never again would it achieve so much on any single operation. As for the USAAF, FRANTIC was to continue spasmodically over two more months and then was forgotten. But no one who was there will ever forget that black night on the airfield at Poltava.

Two American airmen examine a B-17 after the disastrous raid.

*The mighty 42,000-ton Tirpitz was Germany's last surviving battleship.
Since her completion in 1942, she had been based in the Norwegian fiords
where she was a serious threat to the north Russian convoys of the Allies.*

The Sinking of the Tirpitz

A Picture Story

ALTEN FJORD

TIRPITZ

KAA FJORD

Reconnaissance pilots of the Royal Air Force kept a constant watch on the *Tirpitz*. This photo was taken in 1943 when she was moored in Kaa Fiord.

An enlarged reconnaissance photo of the *Tirpitz* shows that she has suffered damage in an RAF bombing attack. The line at the top is part of the antitorpedo boom that surrounded the battleship.

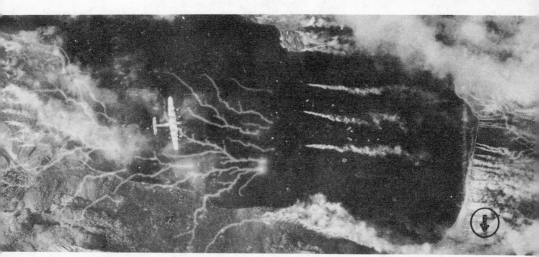

The *Tirpitz* was badly damaged by British midget submarines in September, 1943. After six months in Germany for repairs she was returned to Norwegian waters. In September, 1944, RAF Lancasters flying from bases in Russia attacked the *Tirpitz* (arrow) with 12,000-pound Tallboy bombs. A smokescreen was sent up to hide the battleship and the resulting poor visibility limited the success of the mission.

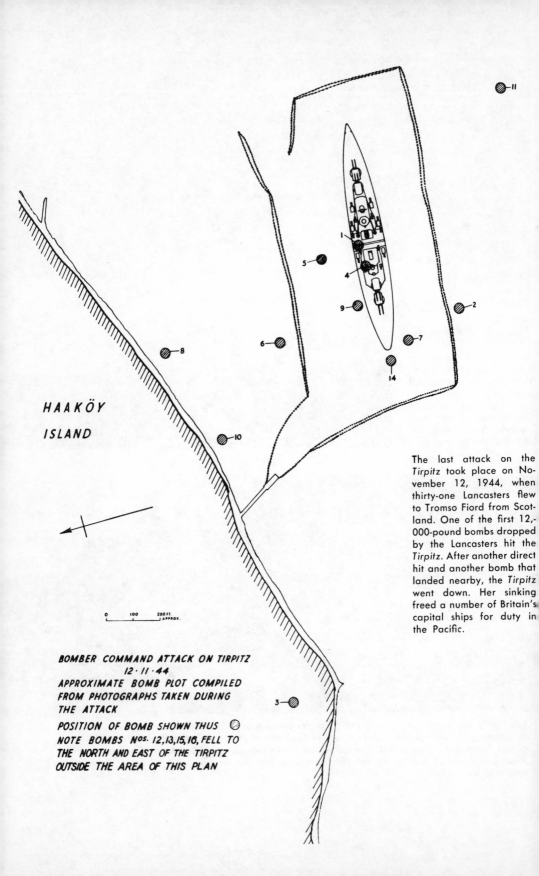

HAAKÖY
ISLAND

0   100   200 FT.
              APPROX.

BOMBER COMMAND ATTACK ON TIRPITZ
12·11·44
APPROXIMATE BOMB PLOT COMPILED
FROM PHOTOGRAPHS TAKEN DURING
THE ATTACK
POSITION OF BOMB SHOWN THUS ◉
NOTE BOMBS Nᵒˢ. 12,13,15,16, FELL TO
THE NORTH AND EAST OF THE TIRPITZ
OUTSIDE THE AREA OF THIS PLAN

The last attack on the *Tirpitz* took place on November 12, 1944, when thirty-one Lancasters flew to Tromso Fiord from Scotland. One of the first 12,000-pound bombs dropped by the Lancasters hit the *Tirpitz*. After another direct hit and another bomb that landed nearby, the *Tirpitz* went down. Her sinking freed a number of Britain's capital ships for duty in the Pacific.

PART FOUR

GREAT AIR BATTLES OF WORLD WAR II: THE PACIFIC

Introduction

WORLD WAR II began in the Pacific as it had in Europe — with a surprise air attack, the forerunner of fierce aerial battles that were to be waged across the vast expanses of the Pacific Ocean. These battles were fought by two types of planes — those based on widely scattered land areas and those based on the aircraft carriers which in World War II took over the important position once occupied by the battleship. In the most important sea battles of the war all of the offensive fighting was done in the air.

The attack on Pearl Harbor on December 7, 1941, was followed by a rapid extension of Japanese control throughout the whole Pacific area. Early in 1942 the United States was able to begin the long, slow process of first halting the enemy's advance and then, island by island, forcing her back across the Pacific. This gradual movement toward Japan was made possible by the fact that the Allies were able to wrest control of the air from the Japanese. Without that control troops could not be moved and landed and beachheads could not be held.

The Japanese fought hard to hold their installations in the Pacific area. Zeros, Vals, Judys, Zekes and many other combat planes rose from island bases and aircraft carriers in an attempt to halt the Allied advance. In a last desperate effort the Kamikazes, or suicide pilots, were thrown into the struggle.

Opposing the formidable air might of Japan were the A-20, B-17, B-25, and B-24 bombers of the United States and an array of fighters including the F6F Hellcat, the F4U Corsair, the P-38 and the P-47. And in 1944 the B-29 went into action. It was the plane that carried the war to Japan itself.

A war as long and difficult as that fought in the Pacific produced a great many important air battles, each one contributing its share to the final outcome. And that outcome could not have been foreseen when the fighting began. The detailed plans that had been drawn up for an invasion of Japan were never needed. The successful air attack, which finally brought destruction to the cities of Japan, made invasion unnecessary.

The *Prince of Wales* and the *Repulse* under attack from twenty-seven Japanese bombers and sixty-one torpedo bombers. The second torpedo to strike the *Prince of Wales* sealed its doom; five attacks on the *Repulse* sent it down.

Just three days after dealing a disastrous blow to the United States fleet at Pearl Harbor, Japanese bombers attacked and sank the only two British battleships in Far Eastern waters, the new, 35,000-ton Prince of Wales *and the 32,000-ton* Repulse. *Because the few British fighters in the area were needed elsewhere, the* Prince of Wales *and the* Repulse *had put out to sea without their usual protective air cover. They were headed for Malaya in an attempt to prevent the Japanese from landing troops.*

When the ships were only 50 miles from their destination, they were spotted by a Japanese reconnaissance plane. Information was immediately flashed to Japanese torpedo bombers already in the air. The resulting air-sea battle is described by a leader of one of the torpedo squadrons, who kept detailed notes of his experiences. In this one engagement the Japanese bombers destroyed the power of the British Asiatic Fleet.

The Sinking of the Prince of Wales and the Repulse

Masatake Okumiya and Jiro Horikoshi with Martin Caidin

AT 12:20 P.M. my wireless operator informed me that he had just received a message. I instantly left the pilot's seat and used the code book to decipher the message, which revealed that the enemy fleet had been found! On the face of everyone aboard the plane there appeared excitement and a joy at having finally discovered the enemy. Soon there would be battle! The message read: "Sighted two enemy battleships. Seventy nautical miles southeast of Kuantan. Course south-southeast. 1145."

Our new heading was north-north-west. Anticipating the coming battle, all planes moved in and took up a close formation. We were flying just above 8,300 feet. Clouds had begun to fill the sky, but they did not restrict our view of the ocean below. In spite of repeated warnings to the crew members not to relax for a moment their vigilance to the rear and above our airplanes, everybody was straining to look ahead of our bomber to sight the enemy fleet. Everybody wanted the honor of being first to see the British warships.

It was just past one o'clock. Low clouds were filling the sky ahead of us. Fully five hours had passed since we left Saigon that morning. The enemy fleet should become visible any moment. I became nervous and shaky and could not dismiss the sensation. I had the strangest urge to urinate. It was exactly like the sensation one feels before entering a contest in an athletic meet.

At exactly 1:02 P.M. a black spot directly beneath the cloud ahead of us was sighted. It appeared to be the enemy vessels, about 25 miles away. Yes — it was the enemy! Soon we could distinguish the ships. The fleet was composed of two battleships, escorted by three destroyers, and one small merchant vessel. The battleships were the long-awaited *Prince of Wales* and the *Repulse*.

The 1st Squadron picked up speed and moved ahead of my squadron. Lt. Comdr. Nakanishi ordered, "Form assault formation!" A little later, "Go in!"

The enemy fleet was now about eight miles away. We were still flying at 8,300 feet and were in the ideal position to attack. As we had planned, Nakanishi's bomber increased its speed and began to drop toward the enemy fleet. He was headed to the right and a little ahead of the warships. Trying to maintain the same distance and not be left behind, the bombers of my squadron also increased their speed as I started a gradual dive. I headed toward the left flank of the enemy formation. It was a standard practice among us for the 1st Squadron to attack the largest vessel, and the 2nd Squadron the next largest.

All crew members searched the sky vigilantly for the enemy fighters which we expected would be diving in to attack us at any moment. Much to our surprise not a single enemy plane was in sight. This was all the more amazing since the scene of battle was well within the fighting range of the British fighters; less than 100 nautical miles from both Singapore and Kuantan.

Except for the planes which at this moment were screaming in to attack, no other aircraft could be seen. We learned later that the third reconnaissance plane, piloted by Ensign Hoashi, had first sighted the enemy battleships and alerted all the bombers. As soon as he had reported the presence of the enemy fleet and was informed that our bombers were rushing to the scene, Hoashi left the area to bomb the Kuantan air base, to prevent the enemy fighters from taking off.

Without interference from enemy fighters we could make our attacks freely. Coordinating my movements with those of the 1st Squadron, I led my squadron to the attack so that the enemy ships would be torpedoed from both flanks. The 1st Squadron was circling about four miles to the left and forward of the enemy ships and was about ready to begin its torpedo run. Antiaircraft shells were exploding all around the circling bombers. The planes could be seen between the flashing patches of white smoke as the shells exploded.

I was nervous and upset, and starting to shake from the excitement of the moment. We turned and flew into the clouds again. We changed course while in the clouds to confuse the enemy and finally came out from beneath the clouds in attack position. This was possible because of a stratum of scattered clouds between 1,000 and 1,700 feet.

We began the attack at an altitude of 1,000 feet and about a mile and a half from the enemy. No sooner had we emerged from the protection of the clouds than the enemy gunners sighted our planes. The fleet opened up with a tremendous barrage of shells, trying to disrupt our attack before we could release our torpedoes. The sky was filled with bursting shells which made my plane reel and shake.

The second battleship had already started evasive action and was making a hard turn to the right. The target angle was becoming smaller and smaller as the bow of the vessel swung gradually in my direction, making it difficult for me to release a torpedo against the ship. It was expected that the lead torpedo bomber would be compelled to attack from the most unfavorable position. This was anticipated, and it enabled the other planes following me to torpedo the target under the best conditions.

The air was filled with white smoke, bursting shells, and the tracers of anti-aircraft guns and machine guns. As if pushed down by the fierce barrage thrown up by the enemy, I descended to just above the water's surface. The airspeed indicator registered more than 200 knots. I do not remember at all how I was flying the airplane, how I was aiming, and what distance we

were from the ship when I dropped the torpedo. In the excitement of the attack I pulled back on the torpedo release. I acted almost subconsciously, long months of daily training taking over my actions.

A giant battleship suddenly loomed before the plane. Passing very close to the towering stern I swung into a hard turn and sped away from the warship. I began a wide circling turn in a clockwise direction, hastily easing the complaining bomber out of its steep climbing turn.

Not many shells appeared to be bursting about us. The engines were still roaring loudly and only moderate damage had been inflicted upon my airplane. I pulled up again in a steep climb and leveled off, once we were within the clouds. I took a deep breath, and forced my taut muscles to relax.

Suddenly my observer came stumbling forward through the narrow passageway, crying "Sir! Sir! A terrible thing has happened!" When I looked at him in surprise, he shouted, "The torpedo failed to release!"

I felt as though cold water had been dashed over my head and entire body. We were still carrying the torpedo! I forced myself to be calm and reversed our course at once. I passed on my new orders to the men. "We will go in again at once."

I began to lower our altitude as we flew through the clouds. The second torpedo run on the battleship would be very dangerous; the enemy gunners were fully alert and would be waiting for us. I did not like the idea of flying once again through a storm of anti-aircraft fire which would be even worse than before.

We dropped below cloud level. We were on the side of the enemy battleship, which was just swinging into a wide turn. Our luck was good — no better chance would come!

I pushed the throttles forward to reach maximum speed and flew just above the water. This time I yanked hard on the torpedo release. Over the thudding impact of bullets and shrapnel smashing into the airplane, I felt the strong shock through the bomber as the torpedo dropped free and plummeted into the water. It was inexcusable that we did not notice the absence of this shock during the first torpedo run.

The 1st Squadron commander was sending out the attack reports by radio. "Many torpedoes made direct hits," and "The lead battleship is listing heavily but is returning to normal position," etc.

As the outcome of my squadron's attack was impossible for me to determine, I merely radioed, "The 2nd Squadron has finished its torpedo runs."

I banked my airplane and studied the battle scene below us. White smoke poured from the second large battleship. This was due to a direct torpedo strike scored about 20 minutes before we attacked; the hit had been made by Lt. Yoshimi Shirai's bomber squad-ron of the Mihoro Air Corps. The level bombers had made their attack from a height of 11,700 feet, and in the first bombing run a 550-pound bomb scored a direct hit. In the second attack two 550-pound bombs scored near-misses.

By now the *Repulse* was a shattered hulk. It was still moving, but slowly, and was gradually losing speed. It had completely lost all fighting power and was no longer considered a worthwhile target. It was only a matter of minutes before the battle cruiser went down.

To all appearances, the *Prince of Wales* was intact, and defending herself furiously with an intense antiaircraft barrage. She was selected as the next bombing target. Fourteen 1,110-pound bombs were dropped; several scored direct hits on the enemy warship. The bombs struck directly in the center of the battleship.

All the bombs of one squadron were wasted. While attempting to obtain an accurate bombing fix on the *Prince of Wales*, the squadron leader accidentally tripped his bomb release. He was still far from the enemy battleship when his bombs dropped; the other planes in the squadron, when they saw the bombs falling from the lead aircraft, immediately released their own bombs, which fell harmlessly into the sea.

Ensign Hoashi's plane caught the dramatic last moments of the two battleships. Minute by minute, as he circled above the stricken warships, he radioed back a vivid report of what was happening far below him. Twenty minutes after being hit by torpedoes, the *Repulse* began to sink beneath the waves. By 2:20 P.M. the great ship was gone.

A few minutes later a tremendous explosion ripped through the *Prince of Wales*. Twenty minutes after the *Repulse* had sunk, the *Prince of Wales* started her last plunge and disappeared quickly.

All pilots and crew members in the bombers returning to their bases were jubilant and flushed with victory. We happily listened to each of Ensign Hoashi's radio reports as he told how the burning and exploding enemy ships were sinking.

Back at the airfields in French Indochina, a second wave of bombers were being readied for another assault on the enemy battleships. The base had not been able to obtain accurate information on the progress of the battle, and was prepared to launch another mass attack. However, as soon as it received the reports from Ensign Hoashi's plane as he circled the area, the attack was called off.

While he observed the sinking *Prince of Wales*, Hoashi sighted eight enemy fighters racing to the scene. Their belated appearance was of no avail, for the *Repulse* and the *Prince of Wales* had already disappeared beneath the waves.

Hoashi immediately fled to the protection of nearby clouds. As the enemy fighters searched vainly for his reconnaissance plane, he skillfully eluded his pursuers and returned safely to base.

This was indeed fortunate for us. Had Hoashi's plane failed to confirm the results of the battle, our future operations would necessarily have been based on the assumption that the two mighty warships had not been destroyed. Our freedom of action would have been severely curtailed, for we dared not send surface units in an area in which the big guns of the British warships might destroy them.

The great ability of our pilots to wrest every possible mile of range out of their bombers was soon made apparent in dramatic fashion. We feared that many of our planes would be compelled to make forced landings at Kota Bharu, since we had flown beyond our calculated "point of no return" and then engaged in fuel-consuming battle maneuvers. Actually, not a single plane was forced to make an emergency landing at Kota Bharu, and all bombers were able to return to their respective bases in Indochina.

Furthermore, only the three planes which fell in flames during the sinking of the enemy warships failed to return. And all three planes had managed to crash into the battleships. It was a great and glorious victory.

A Navy gun crew watches one of the B-25's leave for Japan.

The days following Pearl Harbor were dark ones for the United States; the Japanese were moving steadily across the Pacific, taking island after island with surprising ease, while the Japanese homeland seemed invulnerable to attack. Something had to be done to bring the war home to the Japanese and at the same time raise the sagging morale of the American people. The solution was an air attack on Japan launched from an aircraft carrier.

Once the decision to attack Japan had been made things moved rapidly. Lt. Col. James K. Doolittle was chosen to lead the daring raid. Twenty-four crews were selected from the many men who volunteered for a "secret" mission. During an intensive training period at Eglin Field in Florida they learned to take heavily loaded B-25's off the ground after a run of only 700 to 750 feet. Bombardiers practiced bombing from the low altitude of 1,500 feet. On April 2, 1942, 71 AAF officers, 130 enlisted men, and 16 B-25's sailed from Alameda, California, aboard the aircraft carrier Hornet.

The Hornet was able to carry the Tokyo raiders to within 800 miles of the coast of Japan. Doolittle had hoped that it would be 450 miles. He felt that 650 miles was the maximum distance for a successful attack, but it had been agreed that the B-25's would leave the Hornet if she was spotted by the enemy.

The early take off meant that the bombers would have only a slight chance of reaching the airfields in unoccupied China where they were to land when the raid was over. Not one of them made it. Fourteen of the crews survived but all of the planes were lost.

This is the firsthand account of the famous Tokyo raid by one of the survivors. After successfully dropping his bombs on the target he was forced to crash-land his B-25 on the Chinese coast.

Thirty Seconds Over Tokyo

Ted W. Lawson

I SLEPT FROM about ten o'clock until battle stations the next dawn — which regrettably and unexpectedly turned out to be the day of the raid. That was April 18.

After battle stations early that morning I went back to the room to wait for breakfast. I thought it would be a good idea to see just how much equipment I could get in my B-4 bag. All of us had B-4's. It's a valise, canvaslike, which is packed in a flat, spread-out fashion, then folded into handier carrying shape. It can be hung up, unfolded, to keep your stuff pressed.

I tried putting in my raincoat, shaving kit, shoes, shirts, shorts, handkerchiefs, blouse, trousers, and a few other things. It was about 7:30 A.M., bitterly cold and rough.

That's when it happened. First there was a muffled, vibrating roar, followed immediately by the husky cry of battle stations. "Nig" jumped for the door and I went right after him. We were three decks down. Scrambling after "Nig" as fast as I could, I found other Army boys racing for the top. We flung questions at one another, but got no answers. And twice before I could get up on top, the *Hornet* vibrated and echoed with the sound of heavy gunfire nearby.

I got out on the flight deck and ran around a B-25 just in time to see the cruiser off to our left let go another broadside of flame in the direction away from us. And presently, down near the horizon, a low-slung ship began to give off an ugly plume of black smoke. Dive bombers were wheeling over it.

I must have asked two dozen questions in one minute. One of the Navy boys, hurrying past, said it was a Japanese patrol boat and that our gunnery had accounted for it within three minutes after engaging.

"Let's go!" somebody yelled at me above the bellow of the cruiser's guns, the crashing sea, the sound of the wind and the cries of excited, jubilant men. I turned and saw it was "Nig." He was racing back over the route we had covered just a few minutes before.

I was on his heels, saying nothing. This was it, and before we wanted it. We'd have to take off now. Not Sunday evening. Now, Saturday morning. We were forced to assume that the Japanese ship had had time to flash the warning about us. All hope of surprising the Japanese had now fled, I thought. Surprise was our main safety factor, Doolittle had often drummed into our heads. We had no way of knowing that no warning was sent. Apparently the ship either did not see the B-25's spread all over the deck of the *Hornet*, or just couldn't believe that it was possible, or maybe the Navy sank it too soon.

The *Hornet* leaped forward, boring a hole in the head wind. I could feel its turbines take up a faster beat and felt that it was straining forward as fast as it could, to get us a minute closer — a gallon nearer.

I felt this, too: that our Navy had done all that it could — and it had done it in a way that made a fellow proud of belonging to the same country. I thought of Halsey with that tough jaw jutting out, standing high up in the island of the *Hornet*, and I wondered, as I began stuffing something in my bag, how long it would take the long-range Japanese bombers to come out after our carrier.

I don't really remember what I

stuffed in my bag. Whatever it was it was handy to reach. Now I was thinking about our gas, and the junking of so many of our long-discussed plans. We had based so much of our hope of getting to China on the presumption that the Navy could run us up to within about 400 miles of the Japanese coast. Even then it was going to be a tight fit.

Now we were going to take off about 800 miles off the coast. It took some figuring — quick figuring. And the sums I arrived at, in my buzzing head, gave me a sudden emptiness in the stomach. I thought of the preparations the Japanese must be making for us, and I thought of that turret that just wouldn't work. But most of all I thought of our gas.

"Army pilots, man your planes! Army pilots man your planes!" the loudspeakers brayed. But I already knew the time had come. "Nig" was a great help. He helped me round up my gun, compass, medical stuff, and the whisky. Lt. Thomas R. White, the mission's flight surgeon — and, inevitably "Doc" to everybody — had brought along 80 quarts of GI bourbon — a quart for each man who was going on the raid. On the ship, Doc traded it in for pints of Navy medicinal rye. Easier to carry, if we had to bale out.

"Nig" and I started up top with our arms filled. "Nig" was pretty talkative. I guess he could see I was nervous. He asked me if I thought it would be a good idea to relax a moment and take a drink out of one of the pints. I don't even remember answering him.

I went right to my plane. The crew was there. I shoved the whiskey and some of the other stuff in McClure's navigating compartment, just behind and a step lower than the pilot's compartment.

The flight deck of the *Hornet* was alive with activity, while the big voice of the looming island barked commands. The man I thought was responsible for our bad turret hurried by and I stopped him long enough to tell him what I thought of him. And was sorry, as soon as I did. Nothing was important now except getting off that wet, rolling deck.

Lt. Jack "Shorty" Manch, a Virginian who must be the tallest fellow in the Air Force, ran up to our plane, carrying a fruitcake tin.

"Hey, Clever," he said to our bombardier, "will you-all do a fellow a big favor and carry my phonograph records under your seat? I'll take my record player along in my plane and we'll meet in Chungking and have us some razz-ma-tazz," and Shorty practically trucked on away from us through the turmoil. Clever shrugged and put the can of hot records under his seat.

The Navy was now taking charge, and doing it with an efficiency which made our popped eyes pop some more. Blocks were shipped out from under wheels. The whirring little "donkey" — the same one that was supposed to have broken loose and smashed my plane — was pushing and pulling the B-25's into position.

In about half an hour the Navy had us crisscrossed along the back end of the flight deck, two abreast, the big double-rudder tail assemblies of the 16 planes sticking out of the edges of the rear of the ship at an angle. From the air, the *Hornet*, with its slim, clean foredeck, and its neatly cluttered rear deck, must have looked like an arrow with pinfeathers bounding along the surface of the water.

It was good enough flying weather, but the sea was tremendous. The *Hornet* bit into the roughhouse waves, dipping and rising until the flat deck was a crazy seesaw. Some of the waves actually were breaking over the deck. The deck seemed to grow smaller by the minute, and I had a brief fear of being hit by a wave on the takeoff and of crashing at the end of the deck and falling off into the path of the careening carrier.

The *Hornet*'s speed rose until it was making its top speed, that hectic, hurried perfect morning of April 18. The bombs now came up from below and rolled along the deck on their low-slung lorries to our planes. It was our first look at the 500-pound incendiary, but we didn't waste much time on it except to see that it was placed in the bomb bay so that it could be released fourth and last.

The Navy had fueled our planes previously, but now they topped the tanks. That was to take care of any evaporation that might have set in.

When the gauges read full, groups of the Navy boys rocked our planes in the hope of breaking whatever bubbles had formed in the big wing tanks, for that might mean that we could take a few more quarts. The *Hornet*'s control tower was now beginning to display large square cards, giving us compass readings, and the wind, which was of gale proportions.

I saw our takeoff instructor, Lt. Miller, trot up to Doolittle's plane and climb in the bottom opening. For a time I thought that he was going along, but after a bit he came out and began visiting each of the other B-25's. We were in the *Ruptured Duck* now, all of us, and when Miller came up to the pilot's compartment he must have stood there a half minute with his hand stuck out at me before I came back to life and shook hands with him. I had so much on my mind. Miller wished all of us good luck, and he said, "I wish to hell I could go with you."

It was something of a relief when five additional five-gallon tins of gas were handed in to us. We lined them up in the fuselage beside the ten cans Doolittle had already allotted us. It was a sobering thought to realize that we were going to have to fly at least 400 miles farther than we had planned. But my concern over that, as I sat there in the plane waiting to taxi and edge up to the starting line, was erased by a sudden relief that now we wouldn't have to worry about running into barrage balloons at night. This,

Captain Marc A. Mitscher (foreground, holding paper) the skipper of the *Hornet* and the men who will bomb Tokyo. Lt. Col. Doolittle is on Mitscher's right.

of course, was going to be a daylight raid. It was only a few minutes after eight in the morning.

Comdr. Jurika and "Nig" also came up to say good-bye and to shake hands. When they had gone I suddenly remembered that none of my crew had had breakfast and that all of us had lost sight of the fact that we could have taken coffee and water and sandwiches along. I was tempted to send Clever below to get some food, but I was afraid that there would not be time. Besides, Doolittle's ship was being pulled up to the starting line and his and other props were beginning to turn. The *Hornet*'s deck wasn't a safe place. I found out later that one of the Navy boys had an arm clipped off by a propeller blade that morning.

Doolittle warmed and idled his engines, and now we got a vivid demonstration of one of our classroom lectures on how to get a 25,000-pound

195

bomber off half the deck of a carrier.

A Navy man stood at the bow of the ship, and off to the left, with a checkered flag in his hand. He gave Doolittle, who was at the controls, the signal to begin racing his engines again. He did it by swinging the flag in a circle and making it go faster and faster. Doolittle gave his engines more and more throttle until I was afraid that he'd burn them up. A wave crashed heavily at the bow and sprayed the deck.

Then I saw that the man with the flag was waiting, timing the dipping of the ship so that Doolittle's plane would get the benefit of a rising deck for its takeoff. Then the man gave a new signal. Navy boys pulled the blocks from under Doolittle's wheels. Another signal and Doolittle released his brakes and the bomber moved forward.

With full flaps, motors at full throttle, and his left wing far out over the port side of the *Hornet*, Doolittle's plane waddled and then lunged slowly into the teeth of the gale that swept down the deck. His left wheel stuck on the white line as if it were a track. His right wing, which had barely cleared the wall of the island as he taxied and was guided up to the starting line, extended nearly to the edge

The take-off from the *Hornet* on the morning of April 18. The first B-25, carrying Col. Doolittle, left at 8:18; the last plane cleared the deck at 9:21.

of the starboard side.

We watched him like hawks, wondering what the wind would do to him, and whether we could get off in that little run toward the bow. If he couldn't, we couldn't.

Doolittle picked up more speed and held to his line, and, just as the *Hornet* lifted itself up on the top of a wave and cut through it at full speed, Doolittle's plane took off. He had yards to spare. He hung his ship almost straight up on its props, until we could see the whole top of his B-25. Then he leveled off and I watched him come around in a tight circle and shoot low over our heads — straight down the line painted on the deck.

The *Hornet* was giving him his bearings. Adm. Halsey had headed it for the heart of Tokyo.

The engines of three other ships were warming up, and the thump and hiss of the turbulent sea made additional noise. But loud and clear above those sounds I could hear the hoarse cheers of every Navy man on the ship. They made the *Hornet* fairly shudder with their yells — and I've never heard anything like it, before or since.

Travis Hoover went off second and nearly crashed. Brick Holstrom was third; Bob Gray, fourth; Davey Jones, fifth; Dean Hallmark, sixth, and I was seventh.

I was on the line now, my eyes glued on the man with the flag. He gave me the signal to put my flaps down. I reached down and drew the flap lever back and down. I checked the electrical instrument that indicates whether the flaps are working. They were. I could feel the plane quaking with the strain of having the flat surface of the flaps thrust against the gale and the blast from the props. I got a sudden fear that they might blow off and cripple us, so I pulled up the flaps again, and I guess the Navy man understood. He let it go and began giving me the signal to rev my engines.

I liked the way they sounded long before he did. There had been a moment, earlier, when I had an agonizing fear that something was wrong with the left engine. It wouldn't start, at first. But I had gotten it going, good. Now, after 15 seconds of watching the man with the flag spinning his arm faster and faster, I began to worry again. He must know his stuff, I tried to tell myself, but when, for God's sake, would he let me go?

I thought of all the things that could go wrong at this last minute. Our instructions along these lines were simple and to the point. If a motor quit or caught fire, if a tire went flat, if the right wing badly scraped the island, if the left wheel went over the edge, we were to get out as quickly as we could and help the Navy shove our $150,000-plane overboard. It must not, under any circumstances, be permitted to block traffic. There would be no other way to clear the forward deck for the other planes to take off.

After 30 blood-sweating seconds the Navy man was satisfied with the sound of my engines. Our wheel blocks were jerked out, and when I released the brakes we quivered forward, the wind grabbing at the wings. We rambled dangerously close to the edge, but I braked in time, got the left wheel back on the white line and picked up speed. The *Hornet*'s deck bucked wildly. A sheet of spray rushed back at us.

I never felt the takeoff. One moment the end of the *Hornet*'s flight deck was rushing at us alarmingly fast; the next split second I glanced down hurriedly at what had been a white line, and it was water. There was no drop nor any surge into the air. I just went off at deck level and pulled out in front of the great ship that had done its best to plant us in Japan's front yard.

I banked now, gaining a little altitude, and instinctively reached down to pull up the flaps. With a start I realized that they were not down. I had taken off without using them.

I swung around as Doolittle and the others before me had done, came over the nine remaining planes on the deck, got the bearing and went on — hoping the others would get off and that the *Hornet* — God rest her — would get away in time.

There was no rendezvous planned, except at the end of the mission. Those who took off early could not hover over the ship until a formation was formed because that would have burned too much gas in the first planes. This was to be a single file, hit-and-run raid — each plane for itself.

And at levels which still are hard to believe.

Once on our way, we immediately started topping the wing tanks with the auxiliary gas. We began with the big emergency tank. I knew all there was to know about the appetite of our Wrights, but it was still depressing to figure that they had burned the equivalent of eight of our five-gallon tins during the warming up and takeoff. Forty precious gallons gone before we were on our way!

About 2,200 miles of nonstop flying, I hoped, lay ahead of us. I tried now to visualize the end of the trip, the airport at Choo Chow Lishui. I thought again of the tremendous planning behind the whole raid when I recalled that I must not miss the signals at Choo Chow Lishui or the other Chinese fields I might be tempted to choose. All of them were close to Japanese-occupied territory. There was always the chance that even while we were en route the Japanese might seize these fields. If that happened, the Chinese were to signal "Don't land" by a simple but effective system.

But there were more pressing things to think about now as I kept the clean nose of the *Ruptured Duck* about 20 feet above the water and settled into the gas-saving groove. If all went well on the way in, I would hit Tokyo about a half hour after Doolittle. I figured that if by some improbable miracle the first few planes got in unmolested, every Japanese fighting plane and antiaircraft gun would be ready for me, and for the others behind me.

That made me think about the turret. I pushed the button on the interphone and told Thatcher to give it one more test. He did and said it was still on the blink. Then I switched on the emergency juice, but that wouldn't work either. I hadn't built up enough power as yet. Our two .50-caliber rear guns were pointing straight back between the twin rudders and would be unable to budge one way or the other in case of attack. I spoke to Thatcher again and said that, at least, we'd test the guns. So I raised the nose of the plane and, when the tails slanted down at the right angle, Thatcher fired a short burst into the water behind us.

We plowed along at a piddling speed for a B-25. The controls were very sloppy at that speed. Nobody wanted to say anything. We were busy, or thinking. The flying weather was good — disgustingly good.

Suddenly a dazzling, twisting object rushed past our left wing. It was startling until I realized it was a five-gallon can discarded by one of the planes in front of me. I could see two planes, and Thatcher said he could see two behind us. The can would have downed us if it had hit a prop. What a climax that would have been!

An hour and a half after we took off we came into view of a large Japanese merchantman. It was about three miles off to our left as we spun along just over the waves.

"Let's drop one on it," Davenport said into the phone.

"Let's do," somebody else said. I let them talk. I had better use for the bombs.

"O.K.," McClure said, "but I bet that guy is radioing plenty to Tokyo about us." It was the only ship we saw on the way in, but no one doubted by now that the whole coast of Japan knew we were en route.

Our emergency tank was used up by now and we were well into our other stores. We drummed along, expecting to see planes every minute, but saw none. I tried the turret again, and it worked. I had enough power. It had to be used clumsily in that the emergency power had to be turned on in the pilot's compartment. I couldn't see Thatcher in the back of the plane, so it had to be done over the phone. The emergency power would last such a short time that the turret would have to be used sparingly. Only during actual attack could I afford to turn it on.

We kept going in and, after two or three hours, it got tiring. I was keyed up enough, but at our low-level and sluggish speed it was a job to fly the ship. I called Clever on the phone, out in the snout of the bombardier's section, and asked him to turn on our automatic pilot. He did, but when I took my hands off the controls the *Ruptured Duck* slipped off dangerously to the left. The automatic pilot wasn't working.

So Davenport and I took turns at the controls, and I happened to have them in my hands, at 2 P.M., our time, when we sighted the coast of Japan.

It lay very low in the water in a slight haze that made it blend lacily into the horizon. I had an ingrained, picture-postcard concept of Japan. I expected to spot some snow-topped mountain or volcano first. But here was land that barely rose above the surface of the water and, at our 20 feet of height, was hardly distinguishable. I headed straight for the beach.

Many small boats were anchored off the beach and, as we came in closer, I was surprised to see that they were motorboats and nice-looking fishing launches instead of the junks I expected. I had to keep low to avoid spotters as much as possible and to keep out of range of any detecting device which the Japanese might have. So I braced myself as we came close to the masts of the little boats offshore, waiting for a burst of machine-gun fire.

We thundered up to and just over them. Instead of bullets, I got a fleeting, frozen-action look at a dozen or so men and women on the little boats. They were waving at us. You see, the emblems on our plane were the old style: blue circle with white star and a red ball in the middle of the white star. Maybe that's what confused them. I'm sure we weren't being hailed as liberators.

White beaches blended quickly into soft, rolling green fields. It was the first land I had seen in nearly three weeks. It looked pretty. Everything seemed as well kept as a big rock garden. The little farms were fitted in with almost mathematical precision. The fresh spring grass was brilliantly green. There were fruit trees in bloom, and farmers working in their fields waved to us as we pounded just over their heads. A red lacquered temple loomed before us, its coloring exceedingly sharp. I put the nose of the ship up a little, cleared the temple, and got down lower again.

It was all so interesting that I believe none of us thought much about our danger. What brought that to us, a few minutes after we came over the land, was the sudden sight and disappearance of a large flat building which literally erupted children as we came up to it. A lot of them waved to us. I caught a fleeting glimpse of a playground — and then a sharp, quick look at a tall flagpole from which fluttered the Japanese flag.

It was like getting hit in the chest very hard. This was for keeps. I listened with new interest to the voice of the engines. A lot of the unreal beauty left the land below us. We just could not have a forced landing now.

I clicked on the interphone and said, "Keep your eyes open, Thatcher."

"I'm looking," Thatcher said.

I found a valley leading more or less toward Tokyo and went down it lower than the hills on either side. But McClure checked our course and found that it was leading us off, so I lifted the nose over a hill and found another valley that compensated and straightened us out again. McClure held a stopwatch on the valleys that went off on tangents. He'd let me go 15 seconds down one, then I'd hop the ridge and find one that brought us back on our imaginary beam. We kept very low.

Davenport, Clever, and I saw the Zeros simultaneously. There were six of them, flying in two tight V's. They were at about 1,500 feet, coming straight at us. Our eyes followed them as they came closer and closer. They looked like one of our American racing planes, with their big air-cooled engine and stubby wings. I kept just over the tops of a forest of evergreens.

The first echelon of Zeros swept up our transparent nose and disappeared in the metal top that shut off our view. The second V of Japanese planes was now doing likewise, but just before I lost sight of them overhead the Zero on the left end peeled off and started to dive for us.

I clicked the interphone just as Thatcher did. "I saw him," he said.

I was relieved, until I thought again about the turret. I told Thatcher to tell me when he wanted the power on.

Five or six interminable seconds dragged by. Then I asked Thatcher if he wanted the turret on now.

"No, wait awhile," he said.

My mind was making pictures of that Zero diving on our tail with cannon and machine-gun fire. I called Thatcher again. There was no answer. I thought that something might have gone wrong with the interphone and

that Thatcher even now might be yelling into a dead phone that he needed the turret. I was just about to take a chance and switch it on when Thatcher came back on the phone again.

"I don't know what happened to him," he said. "I can't see him now. I think he must have gone back in the formation."

We skimmed along. We went over the rooftops of a few small villages, and I began to worry. Twenty minutes was what it was supposed to take to reach Tokyo from the point where we came in. Now we had been over land for nearly 30 minutes, and no sign of the city. I saw one fairly large town off to the left, however, and I said to myself that if worst came to worst and we couldn't find Tokyo, I'd come back there and do at least some damage.

But just then we came up over a hill, dusting the top of another temple, and there before us, as smooth as glass, lay Tokyo Bay.

It was brilliant in the midday sun and looked as limitless as an ocean. I came down to within about 15 feet, while McClure checked our course. I kept the same slow speed, gas-saving but nerve-racking when I thought occasionally of the 400 mph plus diving speed of the Zeros.

We were about two minutes out over the bay when all of us seemed to look to the right at the same time and there sat the biggest, fattest-looking aircraft carrier we had ever seen. It was a couple of miles away, anchored,

201

and there did not seem to be a man in sight. It was an awful temptation not to change course and drop one on it. But we had been so drilled in what to do with our four bombs, and Tokyo was now so close, that I decided to go on.

There were no enemy planes in sight. Ahead, I could see what must have been Davey Jones climbing fast and hard and running into innocent-looking black clouds that appeared around his plane.

It took about five minutes to get across our arm of the bay, and, while still over the water, I could see the barrage balloons strung between Tokyo and Yokohama, across the river from Tokyo.

There were no beaches where we came in. Every inch of shoreline was taken up with wharves. I could see some dredging operations filling in more shoreline, just as we were told we would see. We came in over some of the most beautiful yachts I've ever seen, then over the heavier ships at the wharves and low over the first of the rooftops. I gave the ship a little more throttle for we seemed to be creeping along.

In days and nights of dreaming about Tokyo and thinking of the eight millions who live there, I got the impression that it would be crammed together, concentrated, like San Francisco. Instead it spreads all over creation, like Los Angeles. There is an aggressively modern sameness to much of it and now, as we came in very low

over it, I had a bad feeling that we wouldn't find our targets. I had to stay low and thus could see only a short distance ahead and to the sides. I couldn't go up to take a good look without drawing antiaircraft fire, which I figured would be very accurate by now because the planes that had come in ahead of me all had bombed from 1,500 feet. The buildings grew taller. I couldn't see people.

I was almost on the first of our objectives before I saw it. I gave the engines full throttle as Davenport adjusted the prop pitch to get a better grip on the air. We climbed as quickly as possible to 1,500 feet, in the manner which we had practiced for a month and had discussed for three additional weeks.

There was just time to get up there, level off, attend to the routine of opening the bomb bay, make a short run and let fly with the first bomb. The red light blinked on my instrument board, and I knew the first 500-pounder had gone.

Our speed was picking up. The red light blinked again, and I knew Clever had let the second bomb go. Just as the light blinked, a black cloud appeared about 100 yards or so in front of us and rushed past at great speed. Two more appeared ahead of us, on about the line of our wing tips, and they too swept past. They had our altitude perfectly, but they were leading us too much.

The third red light flickered, and, since we were now over a flimsy area in the southern part of the city, the fourth light blinked. That was the incendiary, which I knew would separate as soon as it hit the wind and that dozens of small fire bombs would molt from it.

The moment the fourth red light showed I put the nose of the *Ruptured Duck* into a deep dive. I had changed the course somewhat for the short run leading up to the dropping of the incendiary. Now, as I dived, and looked back and out I got a quick, indelible vision of one of our 500-pounders as it hit our steel-smelter target. The plant seemed to puff out its walls and then subside and dissolve in a black and red cloud.

Our diving speed picked up to 350 mph in less time than it takes to tell, and up there in the front of the vibrating bomber I dimly wondered why the Japanese didn't throw up a wall of machine-gun fire. We would have had to fly right through it.

I flattened out over a long row of low buildings and homes and got the hell out of there. I felt satisfied about the steel smelter and hoped the other bombs had done as well. There was no way of telling, but I was positive that Tokyo could have been damaged that day with a rock.

Our actual bombing operation, from the time the first one went until the dive, consumed not more than 30 seconds.

We were very low now, snaking back and forth, expecting a cloud of Zeros from moment to moment.

I pushed the interphone button and asked Clever if he was sure the bombs were all away.

"Sure," he said. McClure set our course due south. Thatcher, looking behind us, said that smoke was beginning to rise. I told him to watch out for planes and let me know when he wanted the turret.

I nosed down a railroad track on the outskirts of the city and passed a locomotive close enough to see the surprised face of the engineer. As I went by I could have kicked myself for not giving the locomotive's boiler a burst of our forward .30-caliber guns; then I remembered that we might have better use for the ammunition. A string of telephone wires shone like silver strands in the sunlight. It wasn't difficult to imagine the excited voices coursing over them, giving our direction to those waiting for us ahead.

It was McClure who spotted the six Japanese biplane pursuits, ugly black crates that look as slow as observation planes. They were flying well above us in close formation. We watched them, waiting for them to dive and hoped that if they did so our extremely low altitude would cause enough of them to crash before they could pull out.

But the planes stayed where they were, and we were in no mood to go up there and fight them.

There was the gas to consider. All our auxiliary gas was gone now. We were starting in on the wing tanks. With the city behind us, I dropped the speed.

Presently we were out over water again, for the coastline of Honshu, the main island on which Tokyo is located, slants to the southwest. We were going due south because it was part of the plan to confuse possible pursuers and to keep from tipping off our eventual intention of swinging westward to China.

Thatcher now got a chance to use his guns, but not on a plane. A big yacht loomed up ahead of us and, figuring it must be armed, I told Thatcher to give it a burst. We went over it, lifted our nose to put the tail down and Thatcher sprayed its decks with our .50-caliber stingers.

Not much later, as we edged along about 20 feet over the water, I looked ahead and four or five miles immediately in front of us three Japanese cruisers appeared. They were coming our way, fast. They spotted us about the exact instant we spotted them. I looked down at the water a moment, gauging my clearance, and, when I looked up again, the three cruisers were turning with amazing precision, leaving big white wakes for tails, to face us broadside.

I wanted no part of them. I skirted deeply around them, and they didn't fire a shot.

McClure got us back on our course. Now, in line with the long-rehearsed plan, we altered our course to southwest. The island of Honshu has a lumpy, half-submerged tail of islands curling southwestwardly from it. Our marker was the volcanic mass named Yaku Shima which rises out of and forms a kind of eastern barrier of the China Sea.

We bored along our course through the long bright afternoon, all of us under considerable strain. Then, with a yell, we spotted what was unmistakably Yaku Shima and the smaller nearby Sumi Gunto. I flew between their wide-set gorge, held the course a bit longer, and then turned due west. We were now on the 29th parallel and winging out over the China Sea for our still-distant Choo Chow Lishui.

The Battle of Midway in 1942 was one of the decisive air engagements of World War II. It was a battle fought at sea but air action alone determined the outcome. In three days of fighting United States air power based on carriers and on Midway Island destroyed four Japanese carriers. This was enough to shift the balance of carrier strength to the United States and to end any hopes the Japanese had for further expansion in the Pacific.

The Battle of Midway

Adrian O. Van Wyen

THE UNITED STATES had been at war for six months. Such damage as its forces had inflicted on the enemy was more temporary than permanent, and successes in battle were more psychological than real. There was little promise of the overwhelming victory that eventually would be ours.

The attack on Pearl Harbor had crippled both the Pacific Fleet and its principal base outside the continental limits. Wake and Guam had been lost, the Philippines had been overrun, and the red glow of the Rising Sun had spread swiftly and easily down the Malayan Peninsula, through the East Indies, across New Guinea and was moving into the Solomons. To oppose it, the United States, employing five different carriers, never more than two at a time, had made hit-and-run raids on enemy outposts, had carried Army Air Force bombers to within range of Tokyo and, in the Battle of the Coral Sea, had slowed the Japanese advance in the South Pacific.

To achieve even that small measure of success, the cost had been high. The *Lexington* had been lost and the *Yorktown* badly mauled by enemy air attack; *Saratoga* had been put in the yard by a torpedo. Only *Enterprise* and *Hornet* were in good shape and *Hornet* had yet to taste battle.

In that situation, Adm. C. W. Nimitz, Commander in Chief of the Pacific, was informed by naval intelligence that the Japanese were assembling a strong naval force for yet another advance. Dismaying as the news must have been, advance knowledge of enemy plans and timetables gave Adm. Nimitz an advantage which he was not slow to use. The advance would be two-pronged, one against the Aleutians and the other on the island of Midway. Of these, Midway was by far the most important to the future prosecution of the war. Its suc-

The *Yorktown*, already damaged and under tow, goes down on the morning of June 7, 1942, after receiving two direct torpedo hits.

cessful occupation by the enemy would not only extend the perimeter of his control in the central Pacific and strengthen his outer defenses, but would seriously threaten, if not neutralize, our base at Pearl Harbor.

Strengthening of Midway defenses began immediately. The island was fortified and its garrison reinforced. Its commander was given all the aircraft the island could operate effectively. Fleet forces were also assembled. The *Yorktown*, damaged survivor of the Battle of the Coral Sea, was rushed to the yard for repairs.

Enterprise and *Hornet* with their cruisers and destroyers, only days out of Pearl Harbor on their way to the South Pacific, were recalled. Availability of the *Saratoga*, out of the yard after repairs but not fully ready for sea, was doubtful unless the enemy delayed his movement.

Ships available to Adm. Nimitz were organized into three forces. One, composed of five cruisers and four destroyers, was sent to the North Pacific to defend against the advance toward Alaska. Two were organized for the immediate defense of Midway. Of these, Task Force 17, under command of Rear Adm. Frank Fletcher, was composed of the *Yorktown* with two cruisers and six destroyers, and the other, Task Force 16, under Rear Adm. Raymond A. Spruance, was composed of *Enterprise* and *Hornet* with six cruisers and nine destroyers.

In the two task forces, Adm. Nimitz had 233 F4F, SBD, and TBD aircraft. He had another 115 aircraft on Midway Island, including Navy PBY's and TBF's, Marine Corps F2A's, F4F's, SB2U's, and SBD's, and Army Air Force B-26's and B-17's. To intercept the enemy fleet and to give early warning of its approach, he had 19 submarines fanned out over the westward and northward approaches to Midway.

This was by far the most formidable U.S. naval force assembled for battle up to this point of the war. Compared to its prospective opponent, however, it was puny and in some respects had the look of a "pickup team." Although *Yorktown* had full operating capability, she had been hastily repaired and much of the work was temporary. A 90-day repair job had been done under crash conditions in two days and two nights. Her air group, which had been at sea for four months, had suffered losses in action and was in need of a rest.

The *Hornet* was in excellent shape but without battle experience. Her commanding officer, Marc A. Mitscher, was held over for command during the battle in spite of his promotion to rear admiral. The two task forces were commanded by nonaviators, one of whom had had comparatively extensive experience in carrier combat command and the other, sent in as an alternate for the ailing Adm. Halsey, had none. But under the severest of tests, this "pickup team," commanders and individuals alike, fought with the skill of old pro's and forged a victory that would be acclaimed as the turning point of the Pacific War.

The opponent was strong and experienced. Adm. Yamamoto, Commander in Chief of the Combined Fleet, had 11 battleships, 12 cruisers, 35 destroyers, 16 submarines, 6 aircraft carriers, 3 seaplane carriers, 12 transports, and numerous support ships under his immediate command. His aircraft strength numbered 312, of which 284 were carrier types and 28 scout-observation types, plus additional scouts on battleships and cruisers.

His plan of battle called for the use of his submarines as advance scouts and for the employment of his other ships in four separately operating elements, each to be committed to action in turn. One element, built around two aircraft carriers, was responsible for the attack on Dutch Harbor and the occupation of Kiska and Attu which, as the opening move of the battle, was intended to draw U.S. fleet forces northward, leaving the approach to Midway clear of opposition.

The attack on Midway itself would be initiated by a Carrier Striking Force built around four carriers under command of Vice Adm. C. Nagumo, veteran carrier commander of the attack on Pearl Harbor and of actions which had spearheaded the Japanese advance in the southwest Pacific. This force would destroy the island defenses and clear the way for the occupation and support group standing off to the west. The main body and fourth element, containing heavy surface units, and one small carrier, was to operate in reserve ready to pounce upon whatever U.S. ships ventured forth to oppose the occupation.

When early action by the U.S. fleet against the Striking Group upset enemy calculations and the Japanese either refused or were unable to alter their basic plan, only one element of their total force was pitted against the entire U.S. force, and the battle was fought on nearly equal terms.

Adm. Nimitz deployed his forces early. Spruance, with *Hornet* and *Enterprise,* put to sea on May 28, 1942; Fletcher with *Yorktown* sailed two days later. On June 2 the two forces joined at sea about 325 miles northeast of Midway, at which time Adm. Fletcher assumed tactical command. Carrier air search began on June 1 covering the area of suspected approach. Search from Midway by PBY's and B-17's began May 30 over the western approaches to Midway and to the northwest as far out as the weather front permitted. Information of the enemy's approach was essential.

The battle opened according to Japanese plan. Early on the morning of June 3, 1942, the carriers *Ryujo*

and *Junyo* launched their attack on Dutch Harbor. Contrary to Japanese expectations, this attack did not draw fleet forces out of the Midway area, but rather was met by those already in the north Pacific. Neither the attackers nor the defenders scored very heavily, and what took place in that area had little effect on the outcome of the main battle.

At about the time the first air strike on Dutch Harbor was returning to its carriers, a PBY from Midway reported an enemy force of 11 ships on an easterly course, about 700 miles west of Midway. This force was attacked by B-17's in the afternoon and by four PBY's armed with torpedoes after midnight. The PBY's scored one hit.

Dawn of June 4 broke clear in the Midway area. With it came a report of enemy carriers to the northward, followed shortly by another report that many enemy planes were approaching Midway. The flight — 108 planes that had taken off from the four carriers at 0430 — was met 30 miles out by Marine fighters, but the Marines were so outnumbered and outmaneuvered that of the 26 F2A's and F4F's intercepting, only nine returned to base and seven of those were badly damaged. The attack was not stopped and at 0630 came in big and strong. Many buildings were hit, the command post was destroyed, gasoline tanks were blown up, but either by design or poor marksmanship, the runways were unharmed. Damage was extensive, but when the attack leader reported that a follow-up strike was necessary, it was clear that the objectives had not been achieved.

That report which Adm. Nagumo received at 0700, set off a chain of circumstances important to the outcome of the battle. The admiral had held 93 planes in reserve, specially armed and ready to attack any ships discovered in his general vicinity. Shortly after receiving the report, he ordered that these aircraft be rearmed and made ready for the second strike.

Nagumo's decision may have been helped by the attack of Midway-based aircraft which began at 0710 as four B-26's and six TBF's attacked with torpedoes. He fought them off without difficulty; only two bombers and one torpedo plane survived to return to Midway. That attack was followed at 0755 by 16 Marine SBD's, then by 15 B-17's from high level and then by 11 Marine SB2U's. Each time he escaped damage. Although the battle was going very much in his favor, all was not serene.

Shortly after the torpedo attack, one of his search planes, which had been out since early morning, reported sighting ten enemy ships, and he faced the question of whether his order to rearm for a second Midway strike should be rescinded. Before the first dive bombers came in, he had decided that the ships were a more important target, and rather than take the time to rearm again, he would launch the attack with whatever ordnance the planes then had. As the last dive bomber attack came in, he was informed that a carrier was among the ten ships reported and his new decision became irrevocable. At this point his planes began returning from Midway and any plans for launching had to be postponed for the recovery. As it was completed, he pulled away from Midway by ordering at 0905 a 90-degree change of course to ENE. His planned strike was brought up on deck but before it could be launched, there would be other things requiring his attention.

In the meantime, Adm. Fletcher, having heard the early reports of aircraft sighting the enemy carriers, sent Spruance in to the attack. Spruance set course to reduce the range, and at 0702, *Hornet* and *Enterprise* began launching all aircraft except those needed for close air patrol. The strike was composed of 20 F4F's, 67 SBD's, and 29 TBD's. Within an hour after it departed for the attack, a *Yorktown* group of 6 F4F's, 17 SBD's, and 12 TBF's was also in the air. En route the torpedo squadrons flew at low altitude to conserve fuel, and the dive bombers and fighters flew above them. With scattered clouds between them, the squadrons became separated and arrived at the predicted enemy position at different times. Upon reaching it, they found nothing but empty sea. Unknown to the strike leaders, the reported enemy location was off by about 40 miles and, further, the enemy ships were no longer on the reported course. *Hornet* fighters and dive bombers continued onward and never found the enemy carriers. Some landed on Midway, some ditched; none took part in the day's battle.

At this point, Lt. Cmdr. John Waldron, leading the *Hornet* torpedo squadron, sighted smoke over the horizon and using it as his guide found the enemy carriers at 0925. But the enemy was also alert and began the counterattack while Torpedo Eight was still eight miles out. With no fighter protection and without benefit of coordinated action by other squadrons, the 15 planes of VT-8 went in alone. Through a hail of antiaircraft fire and beset on all sides by the Japanese fighters, they continued their gallant attack from which no plane returned and only one man survived. Minutes later, *Enterprise*'s VT-6 sighted the force and went in, meeting an almost similar fate — ten of 14 planes shot down. At 1000, VT-3 of the *Yorktown* attacked with fighter escort. These three determined attacks scored no hits. Of the 41 torpedo planes involved, only six returned.

It was a sacrifice but one which opened the way to victory. The attack forced the enemy carriers into such radical maneuvering that they could not launch their own planes and it pulled down the Zero fighters, leaving an opening overhead for our dive bombers which attacked next with devastating effect.

Yorktown and *Enterprise* dive bombers arrived on the scene almost simultaneously and from different directions. Without prearrangement, they selected separate targets for their bombs. *Enterprise* took on *Kaga* and *Akagi*. Coming down from above with no fighter interference and little antiaircraft fire, they plunked a near-miss ten yards abeam of the bridge, put one bomb through the flight deck near the amidship elevator, and another among the fueled and armed planes on the flight deck aft. These were enough to finish the *Akagi*. Four direct hits took care of the *Kaga*.

Yorktown SBD's hit the *Soryu* with three bombs, and the ship was abandoned in 20 minutes. Three carriers had fallen to the attack; sixteen dive bombers were lost. But *Hiryu* was overlooked, and it would prove an expensive oversight. Within half an hour after the attack, she launched 18 dive bombers and six fighters. It was not the strike over which Adm. Nagumo had deliberated earlier in the morning, but it was now the best he could do.

As our planes returned to their respective carriers, *Yorktown* radar reported 30 or 40 enemy planes approaching from 40 miles out. It was a few minutes before noon. The SBD's not yet landed were ordered to clear out, and the force made ready for the attack. Close air patrol took care of nine or ten of the attackers, and the destroyers shot down a couple of others, but six Val dive bombers broke through and scored three hits which put the *Yorktown* dead in the water in 20 minutes. The fires were brought

Another victim of the Battle of Midway, a Japanese cruiser, lies dead in the water after being bombed by the U.S. Navy's carrier-based aircraft.

under control, and in little more than an hour, she was under way at 20 knots and refueling fighter planes.

At this critical point, a second attack from *Hiryu* came in. Eight F4F's were launched with an average of only 25 gallons of fuel each, to join four others already in the air. They met six fighters and ten torpedo bombers. Neither the interceptors nor ships' AA could stop the attack, and at 1442, two torpedoes opened *Yorktown* on the port side, causing an immediate list of 17 degrees, that was increasing. The ship lost all power and was unable to counterflood. As she seemed about to capsize, the order was given to abandon ship.

A *Yorktown* search group of ten SBD's, which had been sent out to look for additional enemy carriers, had been out about three hours. Just as the *Yorktown* was heeling over from the torpedo hits, the pilot on the extreme left sector of the search found the *Hiryu* and reported her location.

Enterprise launched 24 SBD's, ten of which were from the *Yorktown,* and at 1700 this group went in for their second attack of the day. *Hiryu* was running at full speed, but she could not escape. She took four hits, one of which blew off the forward elevator platform and smashed it against the island. She was finished. Finished also was the decisive part of the battle, but there was more action to follow.

Adm. Yamamoto, still in the background with his heavy surface units, ordered the Aleutian force with two carriers to join up with his ships, pulled the transports of the Midway occupation force northwestward, and moved his heavy surface strength forward to support his badly wounded striking force. Battleships, cruisers, and destroyers of the Occupation Covering Force were already en route. Yamamoto was looking for battle with what he considered the remnants of the U.S. force. He ordered all ships to prepare for a night engagement. But as more reports came in, he could no longer ignore the fact that his air power was gone, and at 0255 on the morning of June 5, he accepted the situation and ordered a general retirement.

Adm. Spruance, also aware of the possibilities as well as the dangers of a night engagement, withdrew eastward during early hours of the night. At midnight he reversed course to be in position next morning to either follow up attacks on the retiring enemy or to oppose a landing on Midway if one was attempted.

The death throes of the stricken ships carried into the night. Fires raging on the *Akagi* were described by a survivor as "just like hell." She was abandoned at 1915 and sunk by a Japanese torpedo before sunrise. *Kaga* was also a mass of flames. About three hours after the attack, she exploded and at 1925 sank. *Soryu,* burning so fiercely that she was abandoned 20 minutes after the attack, sank at 1913. The submarine *Nautilus* was initially credited with an assist in her sinking, but later evidence indicates that *Soryu* went down from air attack alone. The *Hiryu,* last to be hit, was also the last of the enemy carriers to sink. As a result of uncontrollable fires and explosions, she was abandoned at 0315 and, after two Japanese destroyers hit her with torpedoes, she sank at 0900 on the morning of June 5.

That same morning *Yorktown* was still very much alive. The destroyer *Hughes,* which had stood by during the night, reported that the fires had burned out and that salvage seemed possible. A small party was put on board and about noon she was under tow by the minesweeper *Vireo* barely making headway. Before dawn on June 6, the destroyer *Hammann,* with a salvage party made up from the *Yorktown* crew, secured alongside to supply the power needed to trim up the ship. But shortly after noon, the submarine I-168 got inside the destroyer screen and at 1330 fired four torpedoes. One missed, two passed under *Hammann* to explode against the *Yorktown,* one hit the *Hammann* amidships. The combined effect literally blew the *Hammann* apart, and she sank in four minutes. *Yorktown* was also finished, and at 0600 on June 7, she went down.

Meanwhile, opposing forces sought contact. Early on June 5 a PBY from Midway reported the location of ships which were the cruisers *Mikuma* and *Mogami* limping homeward after being damaged in a collision during the night. A group of B-17's sent out to attack reported at 0615 that the reported ships could not be found. Twelve Marine SBD's and SB2U's went out next and, by following an oil slick which *Mikuma* was trailing, found the targets at 0805 and scored six near-misses. One SB2U, piloted by Capt. Richard E. Fleming, crashed on an after turret of the *Mikuma.*

Adm. Spruance also received reports of ship sightings, but none proved very productive. On the basis of a submarine report that cruisers and destroyers were approaching Midway, he set an interception course at 0420. Two hours later he learned that the force had turned about and was retiring and at the same time received another report that a large disposition of ships was retiring 200 miles to the northwest. He changed course to give it stern chase, but a search group of 32 SBD's launched at 1543 found nothing but a lone destroyer which they attacked without success.

With nothing to show for a full day's effort, Spruance turned once more to chase the crippled cruisers. Search planes launched before sunup found the targets and successive strike groups were launched. *Hornet* sent off 26 SBD's and 8 F4F's at 0800 and another 24 SBD's and 8 F4F's at 1330. *Enterprise* launched 31 SBD's, 3 TBD's and 12 F4F's at 1045. These attacks successfully finished the *Mikuma* and were thought to have sunk the *Mogami,* but she reached Truk.

By sundown Adm. Spruance, having reached a position about 400 miles west of Midway, turned about and retired to Pearl Harbor. Adm. Yamamoto was still hunting. All day on the 6th he was on course intended to intercept Spruance, but he was unsuccessful. Early on the 7th, he too retired. The battle was over.

The defeat was decisive. In terms of ships and aircraft, the final score stood at one carrier, one destroyer and 150 aircraft lost by the United States and four carriers, one heavy cruiser and 250 aircraft lost by Japan. In less tangible results, the outcome of the battle was disastrous to the Japanese. Loss of four carriers and some 100 first-line carrier pilots not only deprived them of the powerful striking force with which they had achieved their early successes, but also deprived them of the flight decks from which their remaining experienced air groups could operate. Lack of these decks made it necessary to assign carrier pilots to shore bases where their highly specialized skills could not be utilized effectively. Many were assigned to Truk and to Rabaul from whence they were committed piecemeal to the campaign in the Solomons. When Japanese carriers were again available in the numbers needed for aggressive action, hastily trained units were on board that lacked both the ability and skill of the earlier groups. The outcome of the battle therefore had more than immediate effect and it was truly the turning point of the war in the Pacific.

Captain Thomas G. Lanphier of the U.S. Thirteenth Air Force who shot down a bomber carrying the famous Japanese Admiral Isoroku Yamamoto. The plane behind Lanphier is a P-38.

214

In one of the most extraordinary air battles of World War II, Capt. Thomas G. Lanphier of the United States Thirteenth Air Force shot down a bomber carrying Adm. Isoroku Yamamoto on an inspection trip of Japanese bases. The admiral was the hero of all Japan because of his successful attack on Pearl Harbor. Since then he had directed the Japanese navy with great skill. His death was a severe blow to his country. The Japanese blamed it on bad luck; instead, it resulted from a combination of good intelligence work and a perfectly planned and executed mission.

How They Got Yamamoto

Gene Gurney

IN THE LATE AFTERNOON of April 17, 1943, a top secret message was flashed from Washington to the Army Air Forces on Guadalcanal. Naval Intelligence, via its varied channels, had learned that on the next morning Adm. Isoroku Yamamoto, commander in chief of the Imperial Japanese Navy, would be traveling from Rabaul to Bougainville. The admiral was on an inspection tour of Japan's far-flung outposts, and this leg of his itinerary brought him within range of the Army's P-38 Lightnings on Guadalcanal.

The blue tissue cablegram was ultimately delivered to Maj. John W. Mitchell, of Enid, Mississippi, and Capt. Thomas G. Lanphier, Jr., born in Panama, Canal Zone. The Navy used blue only for top priority messages; so it was no great surprise to find it signed simply "Knox." The Secretary of the Navy, in terse words, outlined the admiral's trip, giving exact time of takeoff and landing. It ended simply but emphatically: "Maximum effort should be made to destroy Yamamoto."

This was the man who had engineered and carried out the attack on Pearl Harbor, for which he received the personal congratulations of Emperor Hirohito. This was the man who boasted he would "dictate the terms of peace from the White House."

Adm. Yamamoto harbored an intense hatred for America and the West. It was inherited from his father, who told him bedtime stories of "the barbarians who came in their black ships, broke down the doors of Japan, threatened the Son of Heaven and trampled on the ancient customs." More than anything else, he wanted to return Adm. Perry's visit and bring about the complete destruction of America.

Yamamoto believed this could be achieved through a combination of air and sea power, and long before December 7, 1941, he began to amass an armada of aircraft carriers. Pearl Harbor proved his belief that "the fiercest serpent can be overcome by a swarm of ants." The British, if they entertained any doubts, felt his sting in the China Sea where the *Prince of Wales* and the *Repulse* were left sinking in his wake. By early 1943 his many successes convinced Americans and British alike that this was the canniest, ablest, and most ruthless leader they faced in the Pacific. When the opportunity came to get him, the Americans pounced on it.

It was ironic that Yamamoto himself played the most important part in his destruction. He was stiffly schooled in the Spartan tradition, and one of his pet fetishes was punctuality. If his schedule called for him to be at a certain place at a certain time, he would be there. If he wasn't, some hapless underling's hara-kiri knife was busy that night. No wonder that in spite of the uncertainties of wartime travel, Capt. Lanphier and Maj. Mitchell had reasonable hopes for successfully intercepting him, even though it called for almost split-second timing.

Mitchell and Lanphier were a logical choice to set up and carry out the mission. They had flown hundreds of combat hours together; their daring and ingenuity were well known. Even this early in the war they had jointly accounted for 14 enemy planes —

more than enough to qualify each as an ace, the Air Corps' designation for pilots with five enemy kills. Lanphier had six Japs to his credit, and Mitchell had already downed eight Japanese aircraft.

The message from the Secretary of the Navy reached Lanphier and Mitchell late in the afternoon. Little time was left before the meeting was to take place.

Two reasonable plans of attack grew out of the discussion Mitchell and Lanphier had with members of their own group and the naval officers then established on the Canal. The latter favored catching the admiral after he reached Kahili when he was scheduled to cross Shortland Harbor on a submarine chaser. Both Mitchell and Lanphier opposed this. Numerous Japanese craft could be expected in the water around Kahili, and neither they nor any members of their group were qualified to identify a submarine chaser. They didn't want to run the risk of getting the wrong ship and letting their prize escape.

The naval detachment finally came around and agreed with the plan proposed by Mitchell and Lanphier: to meet the admiral before he reached Kahili.

The islands of Guadalcanal, Bougainville, and New Britain — especially from Rabaul — lie pretty much in a straight line with Guadalcanal at the southeast end. This meant the Americans would have to meet the admiral head on, which added to the peril.

There was the danger of observation as they passed Jap-held Bo⟩gainville to intercept Yamamoto's group before he reached that island. A wide arc, by-passing the island considerably, was out of the question because it would exceed the cruising range of the P-38's. Henderson Field on Guadalcanal was more than 300 miles from Kahili. Another 100 miles had to be added to this because they would have to fly a circuitous route to avoid detection by radar. This was within the range of the Lightnings, but it didn't allow time for sightseeing. A spot 35 miles from Kahili airdrome was finally decided on.

The big factor, the admiral's punctuality, reared its head again. If they were seen and had to spend more than a few minutes waiting around for his lordship — well, they preferred not to think about what would happen. Their success depended on finding the admiral fast, hitting him fast, and then getting the hell home — fast!

A Mitsubishi cruising did about 210 mph, or 3½ miles a minute. According to the Navy Secretary's cablegram, the admiral was scheduled to arrive at Kahili at 9:45 A.M. If he maintained his schedule, this would put him at the rendezvous area around 9:34. If the Lightnings were in formation and under way at 7:30 — and not a moment later — they figured they could keep the rendezvous.

In spite of the importance of the mission, only 18 P-38's were available to carry it out. They accepted as a fact that they would be outnumbered. A VIP of Yamamoto's rank, out visiting the boys at their home away from home, warranted a big reception. By meeting him 35 miles out, they hoped to have only the admiral's entourage to cope with. They estimated his personal following would outnumber them considerably and had no desire to couple it with the strength of the local boys up to join the party.

As it turned out, the admiral's cover was greatly overestimated. It was a reasonable mistake, however, and one often committed, for at that time many attack groups arrived to find the cards had been reshuffled in their favor. The Rising Sun had reached its zenith, but it took a while for the Allies to realize it.

The pilots available outnumbered the planes by more than two to one. Mitchell had the unpleasant duty of choosing and eliminating, for each man was eager to participate.

The outfit was divided into two sections. The attackers, who figured on coping with no more than a dozen Zeros — if indeed that many — numbered four Lightnings. Lanphier led this section; so the selection of the other three was easy. He picked Lt. Rex Barber as his wingman; Lt. Joseph Moore, second element leader; and Lt. James McLanahan, his wingman. They had flown so many missions together they operated as smoothly as Notre Dame's backfield.

The choice of the covering section was not so easy. Although this unit expected to run into upwards of 100 Zeros, each of the 40-odd flyers was eager to man one of the 13 remaining planes. The pilots finally selected were: Capt. Besby Holmes, of San Francisco, California; Lt. Raymond Hines, Indianapolis, Indiana; Capt. Roger J. Ames, Laramie, Wyoming; Capt. Delton C. Goerke, Burr, Nebraska; Capt. Juliun Jacobson, San Diego, California; Maj. Louis R. Kittel, Casselton, North Dakota; Capt. Everett H. Anglin, Harlingen, Texas; Capt. Douglas S. Canning, Wayne, Nebraska; Capt. Lawrence A. Graebner, St. Paul, Minnesota; Capt. Eldon E. Stratton, Anderson, Missouri; Lt. Albert R. Long, Taft, Texas; Lt. Gordon Whitaker, Goldsboro, North Carolina; and Lt. William E. Smith.

Briefings were tense and thorough. Forecast for the coming day: sunny and quiet. Takeoff at 7:25; in formation and underway at 7:30. Hug the waves for two hours. Airspeed 210 mph. Maximum altitude a scant 30 feet above sea level — get above that and the enemy radar had you tuned in. At a little before 9:30 they should be in the rendezvous area. A quick climb to 10,000 feet to put the attackers in position to attack from the sun. The covering section had to gain twice this altitude. At this point Yamamoto should enter. Destroy the target at any cost. Break off and return home, evading further action.

As they filed out of the briefing room, each flyer was given a bag of English shillings — to be used in dealing with the friendly Solomon Islanders if they were lucky, or unlucky, enough to be shot down in their vicinity.

True to prediction, the morning of the 18th dawned clear and cloudless. It was 7:25 when the P-38's, encumbered as they were with their auxiliary tanks, rumbled down the runway. Lanphier and Barber had just cleared the strip when they looked back to see Moore taking off alone. McLanahan had blown a tire while taxiing to the runway. There was nothing to do but leave him behind. The loss of one plane did not materially reduce their chances as completely as the loss of time for repairs would. The remaining three attackers circled the field and joined Mitchell's section. The time, 7:30 A.M.

A few minutes later, 7:32 to be exact, Lt. Moore pulled up beside Capt. Lanphier and dipped his wings in a frantic gesture. His auxiliary tanks, which were to take him to Bougainville, weren't feeding his engines. A one-way ticket was no good. Lanphier signaled that he understood. Moore dropped out of the formation, and the attack section was pared to two.

Radio silence was strictly observed; so it took several anxious and desperate signals before Mitchell read Lanphier's message. Mitchell, in turn, designated Lts. Holmes and Hines to join Lanphier and Barber, men neither had flown with before.

For two interminable hours the squadron silently skimmed the waves.

The ocean stretched endlessly around them as they swung on an arc to by-pass all Jap-held islands. The emptiness of the Pacific sky and the incessant heat of the sun made the confines of the cockpits almost unbearable. It had an unnatural quality that only the sudden and recurring awareness of the stark reality of the mission could shake. Mechanically they followed each twist and turn Mitchell made.

It is difficult to overestimate the role played by Mitchell in the ultimate success of the mission. With only a compass and an airspeed indicator to guide him, he led the mission 435 miles to arrive at a special spot in the Pacific — and on the dot! As they approached Bougainville's southeastern shore and began their climb, Capt. Lanphier looked at his watch. It was 9:33 A.M.

Less than a minute later radio silence was dramatically broken.

"Bogey. Ten o'clock high."

The warning came from Capt. Canning in Mitchell's section. Lanphier looked up. Several thousand feet above him and about five miles off was the faint outline of planes against the blue. He counted two Mitsubishis and six Zeros. Adm. Yamamoto was on time!

If they had been a few minutes earlier, the tactical situation would have been perfect. Because they had to attack from below, climbing at full throttle, they were at a disadvantage. Lanphier released his belly tanks as he prepared for action, when Holmes's voice suddenly broke through:

"My belly tanks! I can't drop them."

He looked back to see Holmes leveling off and wriggling frantically, in an attempt to dislodge the cumbersome fuel tanks. Hines, Holmes's wingman, was compelled to break off and follow him. Nothing else could be done. The extra tanks reduced the Lightning's speed and maneuverability so much that Holmes would have been a sitting duck for the Zeros. It was Lanphier's and Barber's show.

It was a near miracle, but for some reason the Japs did not see the approaching Americans. In earlier encounters Lanphier had approached Japs, and they had acted as if nothing untoward had happened. Once he led a formation of Lightnings against three Zeros at 30,000 feet. He was positive he was seen, but the Zeros continued on their course until they were attacked. Lanphier promptly shot one down as the remaining two went into their stock maneuver of a sharp climb. The Americans had caught on to this tactic long before, and a group following above Lanphier picked off both of them without any trouble.

This time, however, Mitchell and his boys had not gained enough altitude to intercept them if they went into their climb, and the Japs weren't playing possum with his imperial lordship to guard. They simply didn't see what was coming until it was too late. Perhaps because they were so close to their destination, they didn't think

219

the Americans had the audacity to attack. It was a full two minutes before they sighted them, and by that time Lanphier and Barber were almost level with the planes clustering around Yamamoto's Mitsubishi and about two miles to the right.

The Japs must have been shocked and must have wondered what brought two lone Lightnings out of nowhere to attack his imperial lordship in his own backyard. As they dropped their belly tanks, Lanphier and Barber closed in. The three Zeros on Yamamoto's right peeled off to meet the Americans head on, and Yamamoto's cover from the left — the other three Zeros — circled around to space themselves between the admiral and the Americans.

Lanphier swung his plane sharply and brought the leading Zero into his gunsights. His excitement, after the long wait, caused him to fire prematurely. The Zero immediately returned fire, and his aim was just as bad. The exchange calmed Lanphier's nerves, and the next time he brought his guns to bear the stream of .50-caliber bullets tore one of the wings from the Zero. It burst into flames and the other two Zeros, unprepared for this turn of events, hurtled past Lanphier. There was a short innocuous spatter of gunfire as they passed.

Lanphier went into a spin, the Lightning's belly glistening in the sun. Below he caught the shadow of the lead Mitsubishi on the treetops. There is probably a Japanese saying comparable to "Discretion is the better part of valor." If not, a similar thought had crossed the mind of Yamamoto and his pilot. They had left the gunplay for the younger fellows and headed inland, hugging the trees and bound for Kahili.

Lanphier did not wait for an invitation. He broke sharply into a dive with his engines wide open. He soon realized this was a mistake. His greatly increased airspeed would not only cause him to overshoot Yamamoto, it would also very likely plant him among the trees. He cut back on his engines and went into a skid to brake his dive. Then the Zeros he had loftily snubbed joined him, their feelings obviously hurt. They came in fast, slightly to his right, and headed for Yamamoto's flagship. They obviously planned to block any attempt by Lanphier to get to the admiral, at the cost of their own lives if necessary. Looking ahead and mentally gauging his speed and that of the Zeros and the Mitsubishi, Lanphier could see a spot in space where they would almost certainly meet — with dire results for all concerned. The destruction of Yamamoto was the reason for the attack; the downing of an occasional covering Zero was only a requisite to the destruction of Yamamoto. The demise of Capt. Lanphier did not figure in either his or the War Department's plans. It was either pull out of his descent now, or stick it out and trust to luck.

Unfortunately for Adm. Yamamoto,

A pictorial representation of the air battle in which Admiral Yamamoto met his death.

Lanphier made the latter choice. He stayed on his course until the "Betty" loomed large ahead of him. He opened with a long and steady blast, firing across the bomber's flight pattern from a 90-degree angle. Almost immediately the right engine of the Mitsubishi burst into flames that were soon engulfing the right wing.

Escape was impossible. Once a Japanese plane caught on fire, it was doomed. And this plane was too close to the ground for the admiral to bail out.

The Zeros were still bearing down on Lanphier, and he was coming dangerously close to the firing range of the Mitsubishi's tail cannon. Although mortally wounded, the Betty, like a jungle beast, was still capable of dealing a dying blow. The Zeros, on their present course, were coming in too hard to risk anything but a suicidal encounter. The sight of the flaming Mitsubishi forced them to a last-minute change of stratagem. The admiral was lost. Rather than throw their lives away for a futile cause, they elected to regroup and attack the offending Lightning under more auspicious circumstances. They veered sharply, passed over Lanphier, and began to climb.

Lanphier was unable to alter his course. As he came within the range of the bomber's cannon, the flaming wing ripped off. The Mitsubishi faltered and then lunged into the jungle. An explosion marked the end of Isoroku Yamamoto. The mission was accomplished. Yamamoto's fate, signed by Knox in Washington, sealed by the precision of Mitchell's timing, was delivered by Lanphier.

This was no time for him to compliment himself if he ever hoped to talk to anyone else about it. He'd slowed so much to insure his accuracy that he almost hung in the air, moving at slower than normal cruising speed, at an altitude of ten feet!

Both Zeros returned, with vengeance in their hearts. If they had hoped to enlist aid from their cohorts, they had found them busily engaged with Lt. Barber. The remaining Mitsubishi had already fallen prey to his guns.

They dived repeatedly at the lumbering Lockheed from right angles. It began to look as if it would only be a matter of minutes before he would follow Yamamoto! Lanphier reached for his radio mike for the first time that day.

"Hey, Mitch! Get these monkeys off my tail!"

"Be right down," was the reply.

Other than observing the proceedings below, Mitchell's section had had little to occupy them. The expected resistance had not materialized, for not one Jap plane stuck its nose above 5,000 feet that day.

Lanphier continued his hedgehopping with skidding and sideslipping motions as he tried to escape his tormentors. He led them across a corner of the Kahili airdrome where he could see frenzied activity as the Japs scrambled to get fighters into the air. At last he made the harbor and open sea. A quick climb took him to 20,000 feet where he lost the Zeros, escaping with only two bullet holes in his rudder.

Mitchell's flight, meanwhile, had dispersed the remaining Zeros and headed east to join Lanphier for the trip home. Barber had joined Hines and Holmes, the latter still plagued by his extra tanks. On their return they were jumped by a gang of Zeros and Lt. Hines was shot down, the only American casualty of an encounter that saved countless American lives.

As the victorious flight winged in low over Henderson Field, those pilots whose guns had tasted Japanese blood banked their ships up and over in victory rolls. Lanphier was one of these, and as he leveled out of his rolls, he jauntily reported to the tower, "If Yamamoto still figures to dictate the peace terms from Washington, he'll have to go by way of a hole in the bottom of the ocean!"

By the summer of 1944 the Allied advance toward Japan had reached Saipan in the Mariana Islands. In mid-June the American fleet was protecting the landings on Saipan, the first of the Marianas to be occupied. Because the loss of any of the islands in the Marianas was extremely serious for Japan, she sent her navy to engage the American fleet. The result was the greatest carrier battle of the war.

Hellcat at the Turkey Shoot

Edward H. Sims

ONE OF THE NAVY's greatest days in World War II was June 19, 1944, the date of the now legendary "Marianas Turkey Shoot" when U.S. Navy fighters and antiaircraft gunners of the ships of Task Force 58 shot down 346 enemy aircraft.

These were fighters, dive bombers, and torpedo bombers from a Japanese fleet that included six carriers, the first time the enemy had committed his main fleet to battle since the Battle of Midway, two years earlier. It had been provoked into action by the U.S. invasion of Saipan, in the Marianas.

The resulting battle is known as the First Battle of the Philippine Sea and is still the subject of controversy. Although the Japanese lost three carriers, and other ships, and almost 400

223

aircraft, some believe Task Force 58 could have won a greater victory — and destroyed most of the enemy's fleet.

The critical decision of the battle was whether the massive U.S. fleet protecting the amphibious operation at Saipan should have steamed west to meet the enemy (whose approach was known) sooner than it did. On the night of June 18, as a result of submarine sightings and a radio intercept, Adm. Marc A. Mitscher, commanding U.S. carriers aboard *Lexington,* proposed to turn his ships west, to bring them within 200 miles of the enemy by 5:00 A.M. on June 19.

That would have allowed the potent U.S. carrier force to strike the enemy a devastating blow that morning. However, the decision of Adm. Raymond A. Spruance, overall commander of the fleet, was that the carriers should remain close to the landings on Saipan, the protection of which was the fleet's primary obligation. This was the safe course to follow and Spruance's decision has been supported in most of the postwar memoirs and evaluations by the Navy's highest officers.

Nonetheless, in retrospect, knowing what we know now, it is probable that, had Mitscher been allowed to steam west on the night of the 18th, the result would have been the most spectacular carrier victory of the war, on the 19th.

As it turned out, carriers of Task Force 58 found themselves waiting for the enemy's air attack on the morning of June 19 — an attack which developed on schedule and resulted in a great defensive victory — the above mentioned "Turkey Shoot."

One can readily understand Mitscher's desire to close with the approaching enemy fleet on the night of the 18th. He and then Capt. Arleigh Burke, who, also aboard *Lexington* shared Mitscher's sentiments, had read reports of Japanese fleet movements with growing anticipation. At last the enemy's main fleet had come out, and if Task Force 58 could utterly devastate it in full engagement, the war might be appreciably shortened.

The enemy had ample military justification for committing his fleet in June — in an effort to smash the U.S. invasion of the Marianas. The Marianas are part of a chain of islands which stretch almost due south of Tokyo for over 1,000 miles. They are the steppingstones to the south, to the great naval base at Truk, and to the Carolines. In the hands of an enemy they would provide air bases and a staging area for further advances north up the island ladder to Japan itself.

Saipan was the first U.S. invasion target in the Marianas. Guam and Tinian were to follow. The following year, as the island-hopping march toward Tokyo continued, Iwo Jima, to the north in the Volcano Islands would similarly be invaded, and six Marines would earn immortality by raising the flag on Mount Suribachi, on February 23, 1945.

224

The invasion of the Marianas, in 1944, was viewed by the Japanese as a critical test for the Imperial Navy. The commander in chief, Adm. Soemu Toyoda, had decided, before the landings on Saipan began, to commit the Japanese fleet if the Marianas were invaded. Opinions in higher echelons of the U.S. Navy were divided — as to whether or not the enemy fleet would make an all-out stand in the Marianas.

On June 13 the U.S. submarine *Redfin* reported heavy enemy fleet movements into the Sulu Sea. Two days later coast watchers in the Philippines reported a major enemy fleet, composed of battleships and carriers, headed toward San Bernardino Strait. Another submarine report confirmed this, and still another told of another fleet 200 miles east of Surigao Strait — apparently heading for the Marianas. The last two submarine reports, from *Flying Fish* and *Seahorse,* were instrumental in convincing Mitscher the Japanese were committing their fleet.

As a result of the impending fleet action, the invasion of Guam — scheduled for June 18 — was postponed, and Mitscher's carrier force was beefed up by the addition of ships from the actual landing operation at Saipan and by the recall of carrier forces then raiding enemy airfields on the Volcano and Bonin islands.

By the night of June 17-18, it was clear the enemy fleet was steaming toward Saipan, and when, in the early morning hours of the 18th, Burke awoke Mitscher to inform him of the latest submarine report from *Cavalla,* to that effect, Mitscher concluded a carrier strike might be possible late that afternoon if Task Force 58 proceeded west immediately.

But the dangers involved in leaving the vicinity of the largest amphibious operation of the war, and in risking a night engagement, were considered too great by Spruance and Adm. Willis Augustus Lee, commanding the battleship force. Even that night, when Pacific Fleet Comdr. Chester Nimitz reported that monitoring stations had picked up a broadcast from the Japanese fleet commander, Adm. Jisaburo Ozawa, indicating the enemy's fleet was now 355 miles to the west-southwest, Task Force 58 was not ordered to close the distance.

And so it was that dawn on June 19 found the massive naval force of Task Force 58, comprising some 15 carriers and an estimated 900 aircraft, waiting expectantly for an attack from the enemy's approaching carriers. It was to come, that day, as expected.

On flying duty aboard *Lexington,* Mitscher's flagship, was a fighter pilot destined to end the war as the Navy's fourth-ranking fighter ace, Lt. Alexander Vraciu, of East Chicago, Indiana.

Vraciu had been a flying enthusiast before enlisting in the Navy. He qualified for a civilian pilot's license before joining the service in June of 1941 — just six months before Pearl Harbor. Within a month of the country's entry into the war, the Navy ordered him to Corpus Christi for flight training as

Lt. Alexander Vraciu in a picture taken after he had scored nineteen victories in aerial battles with the enemy.

an aviation cadet.

But it was to be almost two years before Vraciu would shoot down his first enemy aircraft, in October of 1943. He completed cadet flight training in August of 1942, two months after the Battle of Midway and at the onset of the long struggle for Guadalcanal, but he was not sent overseas at that time.

Instead, he went to Melbourne, Florida, for further flight instruction in carrier flying. It was in 1943 that he was ordered to San Diego and shipped out from that bustling World War II port for combat duty. He was fortunate in being assigned to the wing of the late Lt. Comdr. Edward H. ("Butch") O'Hare, skipper of Fighting Squadron 3. At Wake Island, on October 5, Vraciu shot down his first enemy plane and on another mission at this time he helped sink a Japanese tanker — winning air medals for both actions.

But the enemy caught up with O'Hare. An enemy bomber got him at night, and for Vraciu O'Hare's death was a bitter blow. He had learned his flying and fighting trade from O'Hare, whom he admired in many ways and on whose wing he had flown. Vraciu reacted intensely to O'Hare's death; he resolved to shoot down ten of the enemy for Butch. From then on he hated as few fighter pilots did, and was out to repay the debt. He paid the largest installment during the Marianas Turkey Shoot on June 19, 1944, about which we shall now learn.

Pilots aboard *Lexington* had been

226

aware of the impending battle for days. They had been disappointed when *Lexington* and other task force carriers did not steam west during the night of the 18th, toward the approaching enemy fleet, in order to launch a dawn strike. No strike went off next morning. And search planes had found nothing. It was nine o'clock.

Vraciu was one of 12 VF 16 fighter pilots on the alert. The squadron commander, Lt. Comdr. Paul Buie, would lead any scramble, Vraciu leading the second division (the second four-plane unit). But there had already been an aerial battle that morning. Japanese fighters based on Guam swarmed into the air at approximately 7:15. They were met by fighters from *Belleau Wood,* orbiting above Guam for that very purpose, and by fighters scrambled by other carriers. The score had been impressive: thirty-five enemy aircraft had been destroyed for the loss of one Hellcat! It was an omen of bigger things to come.

Though search planes had not located the Imperial fleet, it was nevertheless within range and had already launched an all-out strike at the U.S. fleet. At approximately 9:50 radar screens on various ships began to reflect the images of a large raid. At four minutes past ten, general quarters was sounded aboard *Lexington,* and as the warning bell sounded throughout the ship, Vraciu and the other pilots on alert dashed for their fighters. There was no question about it. This was it.

On the flight deck the scene was action in color. Engines were beginning to roar as plane handlers in blue hurried chores. Plane directors were dressed in yellow, hookmen in green, chockmen in purple, fire fighters in red, and there were two monsters in asbestos suits.

In a few minutes Buie was roaring off the end of *Lexington,* now plowing through the sea at close to 30 knots, into the wind. After Buie had cleared, and three others, Vraciu, making an "end" speed of 90 knots, pulled back on the stick and dragged the F6F off the end of the flight deck.

Soon the 12 F6F's from *Lexington* were climbing into the west, Buie far out front and the others strung out behind. Vraciu had difficulty keeping up; his engine was throwing oil and Buie had a new engine, which could outperform his own. The skipper was going hell-for-leather for the enemy, as he should have been, but he was pulling away from Vraciu in the process.

Apparently some of the other Hellcats couldn't keep pace either. Vraciu noticed the skipper had lost his wingman, and several others were dropping back. He found himself with several additional fighters, which gave him six in all. Buie pulled away steadily, out front, as the fighters of many carriers streaked into the west, the morning sun at their backs.

The sky was full of contrails. It was a clear day, with a westerly wind and a bright sun as the blue-gray F6F's bit their way up into the higher altitudes.

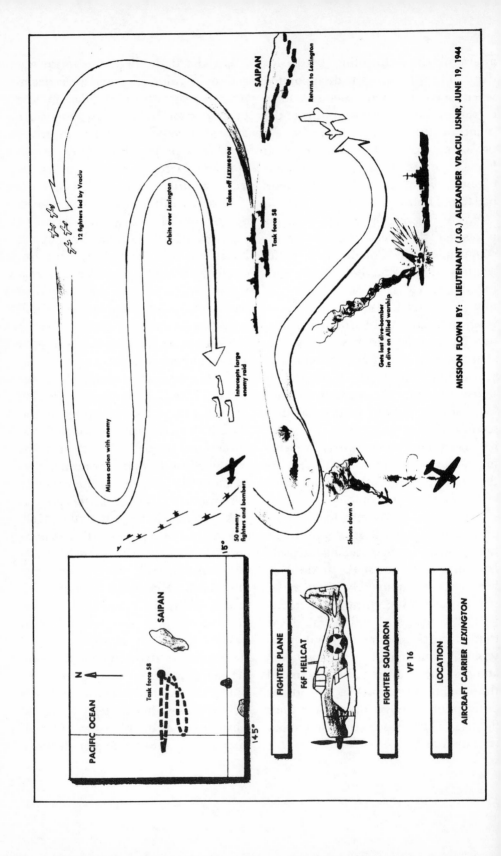

MISSION FLOWN BY: LIEUTENANT (J.G.) ALEXANDER VRACIU, USNR, JUNE 19, 1944

SAIPAN

Returns to Lexington

Task force 58

Takes off LEXINGTON

Gets last dive-bomber in dive on Allied warship

12 fighters led by Vraciu

Orbits over Lexington

Misses action with enemy

Intercepts large enemy raid

Shoots down 6

50 enemy fighters and bombers

15°

145°

PACIFIC OCEAN

N

SAIPAN

Task force 58

FIGHTER PLANE

F6F HELLCAT

FIGHTER SQUADRON

VF 16

LOCATION

AIRCRAFT CARRIER LEXINGTON

Radar scanners had indicated the enemy's altitude at 24,000 feet, and the defending fighters were straining to reach that height. First reports had indicated the enemy was 100 miles west, bearing 260 degrees.

At this moment the first interception of the enemy was made, not by *Lexington* fighters, but by those of Comdr. David McCampbell's VF 15, from *Essex*. (During the day this squadron destroyed over 60 enemy aircraft.) After the first interceptions there was a lull in the battle.

Vraciu, meanwhile, had seen no enemy planes and no action. He now experienced trouble with his supercharger. As he reached 20,000 feet and attempted to put the engine in high blower, it cut out every time he pushed the throttle handle forward.

Dismayed, and disappointed because he had been unable to intercept the enemy, Vraciu reported to the fighter director aboard *Lexington*. He was ordered to orbit near the carrier with his six fighters. The F6F's circled their floating base in a wide arc, and waited. Vraciu had time to check his instruments, guns and gunsight. The engine gauges were normal. The engine was smooth and running cool, though it wouldn't shift into high blower. Vraciu could see other fighters orbiting above other ships in the distance. He continued circling . . . for ten, twenty, twenty-five minutes.

Another large enemy air armada is now on the way, unknown to Vraciu

at the moment. Aboard *Lexington,* below, the radar screen detects the ominous spots. Suddenly, as the F6F's orbit above *Lexington,* the fighter director breaks in over the radio: "Vector 265!" Vraciu knows by the tone of voice that this is something big.

He banks into a 265-degree heading and quickly pushes the handles which charge his six .50-caliber guns. He checks the gunsight, which is operating properly, and glances behind to see if his comrades are in proper formation. To the side he can see other Hellcats pointed in the direction he is flying, obviously vectored by other carriers to the bogeys approaching from the west.

For ten minutes the Hellcats streak westward . . . down below fighter directors warn the enemy gaggle is very close. Vraciu estimates he is 25 miles west of *Lexington*. At that instant he sees them! Three unidentified specks in the sky ahead! "Tallyho!" he yells into the mike. He is not sure of the identity of the three strangers. They're slightly below the Hellcats ahead. And this can't be the enemy armada.

Vraciu, known for keen eyesight, scans the sky, up and down. The three specks are ten miles in the distance. He looks all around them, then he takes a long look at the air space beneath them. Faintly . . . specks . . . dots . . . a mass of dots! It must be 50. Vraciu again calls in over the mike: "Tallyho, 11 o'clock low!"

Now the tempo of events picks up. Other carrier interceptors spot the

Japanese and rush to meet them. The enemy planes are dangerously close to the U.S. carriers. There is not a minute to lose.

Nerves tingle as the Hellcat pilots watch the silhouettes of the oncoming enemy planes grow larger and larger. They come closer and closer and still the two opposing forces continue on converging courses; the Americans want to intercept as far away from ships of the fleet as possible. Vraciu is so close he can see that the enemy planes are painted in a light color, not the usual dirty greenish-brown. There are Judys, Jills, and Zeros in the enemy gaggle . . . dive bombers, torpedo bombers, and fighters! He reports this to *Lexington.*

Now the distance between the several groups of Hellcats and the big enemy formation closes and the Hellcats begin to rack into tight turns as they arrive overhead and prepare to make deflection or six o'clock passes on the enemy planes, which are at about 17,000 feet.

Vraciu spots one of the enemy planes off to the side. He stands on his left wing and carves an arc, reversing his course, and rolls out on an approach from the rear port quarter of the enemy. He checks the sky above for the three enemy fighters; they're nowhere in sight.

The big gaggle is so close to the fleet every Hellcat races to a target and the sky is soon filled with individual actions. Now the enemy aircraft ahead is almost in range of Vraciu's

guns. But . . . off to the right, another Hellcat, moving up on the enemy's tail! Vraciu has spotted him just in time. The two pursuers are on converging courses! Vraciu slaps his stick right and down. The Hellcat sticks its nose down and with added speed roars beneath most of the enemy aircraft. Vraciu pulls clear, and turns back toward the melee.

He sees a Judy to the left of the enemy gaggle and slices in behind, pouring on throttle and closing the gap fast. This time he is determined to get the job done; the Judy widens in his gunsight glass and the victim ahead comes within range. Vraciu's finger is on the trigger. His canopy is smeared with oil, his vision obstructed, and he wants to make sure of this one. He is on him . . . 300 feet, 200!

Now! He squeezes the trigger. The shock and thunder of the Hellcat's six guns silence the engine. Shells converge into such a close pattern that the Judy immediately begins to fly to pieces. Vraciu has only a second or two left, being so close. The F6F's guns throw a murderous stream of shells into the Judy's fuselage.

It's too much. The dive bomber in the sight circle erupts in a fiery explosion. Vraciu manages to steer clear of the smoke and bits of wreckage. In the excitement he shouts into the mike, triumphantly: "Splash one Judy."

But the enemy is close to the fleet. No time is to be lost. Vraciu pulls the stick into his belly and back out and then back in. He clears his tail and then picks out two more Judys flying side by side. He will make another dead-astern approach. And this time he will try to knock down two on one pass. Checking the sky behind, and finding his tail clear, he dips the stick and starts down on the enemy gaggle, now so low that some of the dive torpedo bombers are letting down in preparation for the attack on the fleet.

The air is full of calls and shouts, as other F6F's maneuver desperately to knock the enemy planes out of the sky before they can deliver their bombloads on the U.S. carriers. The Judys and Jills, meanwhile, seek to avoid the U.S. fighters so they can carry out their attack.

The two Judys ahead fly on. Vraciu will first close the one on the right. He rams the throttle all the way forward. The big Hellcat roars and steps up on the Judys from behind. The rear gunner this time sees the F6F approach, however, and twinkles from his 7.7 machine gun catch Vraciu's eye. Responding, Vraciu opens with his six guns. The rear gunner continues his fire but the accuracy and volume of Vraciu's shooting immediately dooms the Judy, which staggers and begins to fall off on the right wing.

Vraciu keeps up with the fire. A long trail of black smoke stretches backward. As the second victim wings over, the Jap gunner in the rear cockpit is still firing away. He goes down still firing; the burning Judy plunges to the sea at the bottom of a vertical column of smoke. Without a moment's hesitation, Vraciu slips left, with left rudder and stick, and is on the other.

The battle everywhere is fast and furious. Two enemy torpedo bombers reach *Lexington* at this time, drop torpedoes intended for Mitscher's flagship. *Lexington* nimbly dodges them. But *South Dakota* and *Indiana,* in the battleship force farther west, are not so lucky. *South Dakota* takes a bomb and *Indiana* receives a suicider.

But most of the Japanese planes have failed to penetrate the fighter defense. Vraciu is working on victim No. 3 as the battle reaches a climax. Following up his second kill, he is now within firing range of the third Judy, to the left. A short burst produces quick results; the Judy instantly catches fire. Flames and smoke streak backward.

Vraciu follows with another short burst at point-blank range, and watches the burning enemy bomber wobble out of formation and take the fatal dive. Three victories in a matter of minutes! But the attackers continue on course. Vraciu takes time to radio *Lexington*: "Don't see how we can possibly shoot 'em all down. Too many!"

With that sentiment he plunges back into the fray. He had pulled up to radio *Lexington*; now he leans forward in a dive at a fourth Judy!

The Judy ahead is breaking away from the formation. Vraciu curves in behind him, once again closing from the rear. Neither the enemy pilot nor the tail gunner seems to have caught sight of the F6F swooping down from the rear. In seconds, Vraciu is only several hundred feet behind his fourth victim. Carefully lining him up in the gunsight circle, Vraciu again squeezes the trigger.

The effect of his fire is even more devastating than before. The Judy immediately bursts into flame and wobbles wildly to the right. Victory No. 4! It is deadly accurate gunnery. Out the side of his eye Vraciu sees most of the Judys pulling to one side or the other, preparing for runs on the ships of the fleet, now clearly visible ahead and below. The Jills, down low, begin shallow glides, preparing to drop torpedoes at selected targets. Vraciu immediately turns away from his fourth burning victim, now out of control. With full throttle he points his nose at three Judys about to wing over into dive-bombing runs on a ship below.

Vraciu wonders if he can reach the three in time. The distance is short, but the first of the three Judys is almost over the ship target ahead. The Pratt and Whitney strains, and the F6F steadily closes. The blue-gray Hellcat is on the last of the Judys, but the first is over the target. Five-inch flak begins to dot the sky as Vraciu readies his aim to open fire on the third plane. He squeezes the trigger. Aim is accurate. Shells instantly strike the Judy and, as he closes the distance, pieces of the dive bomber's engine fly backward. As the fifth victim disinte-grates, he can see the first of the three Judys diving on a big ship below.

Still at full throttle, he banks away from the fiercely burning Judy and aims at the second in the three-bomber formation. Down below, Vraciu sees the first Judy still diving. The Judy now wings over into his dive-bombing run on a destroyer. Vraciu stands on a wing and starts down after him. He'll risk antiaircraft fire in an effort to bring down the dive bomber in a vertical dive. It's a dangerous feat.

The wind screams as the big F6F plunges straight down at ever-increasing speed. Ahead, the diving Judy is zeroing in on the U.S. destroyer. Vraciu sees five-inch bursts all around him, and as the altitude decreases the flak gets thicker. He will have to finish the job in seconds. The heavy fighter rockets straight down. He is rapidly overtaking the Judy. At terrific speed, he glances through the gunsight glass and waits . . . seconds. Now! the F6F's guns thunder and tracers streak straight down into the enemy dive bomber. Vraciu hangs on for a few seconds, wondering how long he can fire. At that instant he blinks at a bright explosion — where the Judy had been. The enemy's bomb must have detonated. Vraciu yanks back on the stick, blood draining from his head, and pulls out of the screaming dive.

As he levels out, and draws away from the destroyer, he glances behind to see what's happening below. The first Judy in the formation is now directly over a U.S. battleship, farther away. Vraciu watches, frozen, to see if the enemy pilot will succeed in crashing into the battlewagon. He picks up the mike and radios *Lexington*: "Splash No. 6! One more dive bomber ahead — diving on a battleship." However, the curtain of iron thrown up by the battleship's antiaircraft guns explodes the dive bomber. A bright flash at 1,000 feet! Vraciu breathes a sigh of relief.

Climbing for altitude again, he scans the sky for other enemy planes. Almost miraculously, the sky seems completely cleared of the enemy. In every direction he sees only Hellcats. The enemy formation has been received by the fighters of many carriers.

Still, there must be some of the enemy left; Vraciu looks down on the surface below to see if any Jills are closing the ships just above the water. He can find no enemy planes, either directly on the water or in the sky in any direction. The big enemy gaggle has been wiped out, probably to the last plane. Vraciu himself hasn't done badly: six dive bombers and 12 enemy airmen sent to a watery grave. This was a day Butch O'Hare would appreciate!

On board the carriers below, radar screens show the sky cleared of enemy aircraft. Judys attacked *Lexington, Enterprise,* and *Princeton,* but all escaped injury. The fleet is in good condition. Losses suffered by the enemy are staggering. The air battle had raged up and down the line of ships,

and the attackers were slaughtered as in no other interception of the war.

Jubilation reigns aboard many of the ships as Vraciu turns toward *Lexington,* the sky now clear, and prepares to land. Some pilots are already putting down on their carriers. Many have great tales to tell. Air Group 15, aboard *Essex,* destroyed more than 60 aircraft. VF 16, from *Lexington,* accounted for 44, for a loss of four. Vraciu's total of six is high for the squadron.

Now Vraciu is approaching from his assigned sector, and as he reaches the outer screen of ships around *Lexington,* American antiaircraft gunners open fire on him.

Startled, Vraciu jinxes immediately, turns away from the fire. His "IFF" is operating normally. Why have the ships fired on him? IFF is a radar device designed to identify him as a friendly aircraft. Rather than take further chances, Vraciu detours around the fire, and heads straight for *Lexington.* Over the radio he offers some philosophy to the antiaircraft gunners — too strong for print.

Soon he is approaching *Lexington,* which plows through the seas into the wind, undamaged, taking aboard Hellcats. Vraciu prepares to come down, circling to the left, banking into the landing approach, tail hook extended. He is now to be the center of one of the great human-interest moments of the war. Ahead, the landing signal officer gives him the "cut," and Vraciu pulls throttle back all the way, feels

233

himself settling toward deck. The oil-spattered fighter bangs the deck, bounces, and then the tail hook engages. Vraciu is snapped to a stop. The cable is disengaged. He taxis to the parking area, canopy back, looking up toward the bridge, a grin on his wind-blown face. Mitscher looks down from the bridge. Vraciu holds up six fingers. Mitscher gets the message.

Vraciu cuts the engine, unbuckles belt and harness, and climbs out on the wing. His crew chief and other deck personnel rush to his side. They beam when he relates how the six enemy aircraft had fallen before his guns. Another well-wisher hurries up to the 25-year-old ace. It is the small, tanned face of Marc Mitscher that catches Vraciu's eye.

By now, photographers and other pilots are crowding around. Mitscher comes right up to Vraciu and congratulates him personally for flaming six Japs. He shakes the smiling pilot's hand feelingly, then steps to one side. Vraciu answers questions for the others.

The photographers go to work, and Vraciu's "flight of six" becomes history. Comparatively unnoticed, to the side, Mitscher enjoys the scene. Then, embarrassed, he asks to pose with the young flyer, with a qualification: "Not for publication. To keep for myself."

The carrier pilots of Task Force 58 had missed their best chance to destroy the enemy fleet by not being in posi-tion to launch a dawn strike that morning. However, the enemy was not to get away unscathed. By three o'clock that afternoon it was apparent the enemy's offensive punch had been spent. Adm. Spruance signaled Mitscher he was free to go after the enemy fleet. Mitscher immediately conferred with Burke and other senior officers.

The carriers, it was decided, would launch a strike at the fleeing enemy fleet. The decision was reached only after much soul-searching; there was a grave risk that the attacking planes could not complete the return trip to their carriers before darkness set in. Never had a major air strike been launched with the knowledge that many of the planes might have to find their way back to the carriers in darkness. But this was the only chance to hit the enemy fleet. Mitscher ordered the strike.

By 4:30 that afternoon the first deckloads of fighters were away. Mitscher was launching everything he had. A few minutes before sunset, far to the west, Task Force 58 pilots spotted the first ships of the enemy fleet. The enemy had lost most of his fighters in the day's operations, but launched what he could as American dive bombers and torpedo planes went in to the attack.

The failing light was perhaps the enemy's best defense, although carrier *Hitaka* was sunk and many other ships were hit. The loss of *Hitaka*, along with two carriers sunk by U.S. submarines, brought Japanese carrier losses in the battle to three, a major naval disaster.

The drama of the day, however, was not yet over. Night settled over the Pacific, and aircraft from the U.S. carriers straggled east, searching for their ships in the darkness. Mitscher had made the decision to carry out the strike, though he knew a night recovery might turn into a disaster. Therefore, as he walked the bridge and glanced at his watch, the tension mounted. At 8:30 the first returning planes were sighted. But to the south there was lightning, and some pilots, mistaking this for the fleet, turned south.

The fuel supply of most of the planes was extremely low. In the sky above, returning pilots who had already spotted ships of the fleet were unable to identify them in the darkness. The ships were blacked out, according to standard operating procedure, designed to protect them from submarine attacks. Mitscher now made one of the stirring decisions of the war, one which will long be remembered in naval history. As returning planes began to stray southward, and mill about, pilots thoroughly confused by an inability to identify the ships below, Mitscher was in agony. In Flag Plot with him at the time was Capt. Burke. He looked Burke in the eye and calmly said, "Turn on the lights."

Suddenly the entire task force burst into light as if to say to heck with the enemy submarines. Searchlight beams fingered the sky, cruisers threw up star shells, and the fleet was visible for miles and miles away. And the planes began to land.

Of 216 planes launched, about 100 managed to make it back to the carriers, though all but 16 pilots and 22 crewmen were rescued from what had threatened to be the Navy's worst carrier aviation disaster.

The Vraciu story had a happy ending. For his gallant performance on June 19, the Indianan was awarded the Navy Cross. The citation was for "extraordinary heroism" and said, in part: "With his task force under attack by a numerically superior force of enemy aircraft, Vraciu struck furiously at the hostile bombers and, despite vigorous fighter opposition, succeeded in shooting down six and contributing to the breaking-up of a concentrated enemy attack.

"His outstanding leadership, superior flying ability and daring tactics maintained in the face of tremendous odds contributed materially to the success of our aerial operations . . ." it continued. At the end of the war Vraciu's total number of confirmed kills was 19, and there were additional victims he did not claim as victories.

During World War II, Charles A. Lindbergh, the man who made the famous 1927 solo flight across the Atlantic, was a technical representative of an American plane manufacturer. In that civilian capacity he visited the Pacific theater of operations in 1944. While there he shot down one Japanese plane and was almost shot down himself. Here is the story.

Lindbergh's Air Battles

Gen. George C. Kenney, USAF (Ret.)

IN FEBRUARY, 1954, President Eisenhower commissioned Charles Augustus Lindbergh a brigadier general in the United States Air Force Reserve. It was a long-delayed recognition of his services to the Air Force and his country over the last 30 years, and a partial recompense for being deprived of his reserve commission of colonel, when his opinions as to the advisability of our becoming involved in World War II clashed with those of the Roosevelt administration.

This experienced aviator, who had done so much to focus attention on the possibilities of long-range air operations by his solo flight from New York to Paris on May 20, 1927, and who had done a lot of work for the Army Air Forces since that time, was deprived of any chance to serve his country in uniform.

He had flown practically every type of military and civilian aircraft of that day and was a recognized student and authority on the subjects of airplanes, aircraft engines, and accessories. He was an experienced navigator as well as pilot. He was only 39 years old when Pearl Harbor put us in the war. Many combat flyers and many more air commanders and staff officers were of that age or older. I could have used his services with profit in the Pacific.

Lindbergh above everything else is a patriotic American. He wanted to serve his country in some capacity regardless of his personal opinions before we got into the conflict.

His talents were in the field of aviation. As long as he was not allowed to fight, he did the next best thing and became a technical representative of one of our aircraft companies.

I had met "Slim," as the air crowd called him, many times since his historic transatlantic flight in 1927 and had the highest respect for his flying ability, his courage, and his judgment on aviation matters.

The more I got to know this shy, retiring, self-confident, but unobtrusive individual, the more I liked him as a fellow aviator and as a person. I hadn't liked it when he was kicked out of the Army Air Force and I don't know any of the air crowd that did, but there wasn't anything we could do about it. We hadn't been able to do anything about keeping Billy Mitchell in the service after his opinions had clashed with those of the people "higher up."

In July, 1942, I had gone to Australia to head the Allied Air Forces under Gen. MacArthur. By midsummer of 1944 we had defeated the Japanese Air Force and were moving fast. I was getting ready to move my main headquarters to Hollandia in Dutch New Guinea which we had captured on April 23.

On July 4, 1944, one of the war correspondents just back from Nadzab came into my office in Brisbane, Australia, and told me that he had seen Lindbergh up there the day before. It was Lee Van Atta the INS man assigned to MacArthur's Southwest Pacific area. I asked him how long Lindbergh had been there. He said he wasn't sure, but he thought only a few days, and he understood that a Marine flyer had brought him in from Guadalcanal.

I was quite sure that MacArthur's headquarters didn't know anything about it, so I sent word to Gen. Whitehead, my commander at Nadzab, to have Lindbergh flown to Brisbane immediately and report to me. He arrived the next morning.

It took about two minutes' conversation to confirm my suspicions. He had no authorization to come into the theater, and if I didn't fix up some orders to legalize his entry, he could get into all kinds of trouble. In time of war you simply don't roam around in a theater of operations without authority as you would in peacetime.

"Slim" told me that he was affiliated with one of the aviation companies, and had gotten permission from the Navy Department to visit and make observations in the South Pacific theater where Adm. "Bull" Halsey was in command. He was particularly interested in the efficiency in combat of the two-engined fighter plane versus the single-engined job. The two-engined P-38 was being used in both the South Pacific and Southwest Pacific theater.

After spending a few weeks flying with both Navy and Marine pilots in the Solomon Islands, Lindbergh thought it would be a good idea to come over to my area where the P-38's were not only more numerous but where at that time there was much more air action. Without bothering to get clearance or permission from anyone, he had simply thumbed a ride to New Guinea and had been staying with Whitehead since July 1.

I listened to his story and then said, "Come on, Slim, let's go upstairs to General MacArthur's office, pay a call on him and see if I can't get a legal status for you before we do anything else."

237

Lindbergh and General George C. Kenney in the general's office. General Kenney was commander of the Allied air forces in the Pacific area.

We went directly to the general's office where I introduced Lindbergh. MacArthur was the soul of cordiality and, after chatting for a while, asked Lindbergh if there was anything he could do for him. I butted in and said that I wanted to look after him as I had an important job that would keep him busy every minute that he could spare.

If anyone could fly a little monoplane all the way from New York to Paris and have gas left over, he ought to be able to teach my P-38 pilots how to get more range out of their airplanes. If he could do that, it would mean that we could make longer jumps and get to the Philippines that

much quicker, so I wanted to take him under my wing, issue the necessary orders, and put him to work. Lindbergh nodded with that charming kid grin of his that is one of his best assets. Gen. MacArthur said, "All right, Colonel. I'll just turn you over to General Kenney, but I warn you, he's a slave driver."

As soon as we got back to the office I got Lindbergh fixed up with enough pieces of paper to legalize his status, and then we talked about the job. He was quite enthusiastic about its possibilities and thought that with a little training he could increase our operating radius of action nearly 50 per cent. We were now operating the P-38's to

238

a distance of about 400 miles from our airdromes. If Lindbergh was right, we could stretch it to 600.

The first hitch came when I told him that I didn't want him to get into combat. He was actually a civilian, with a lot of headline possibilities. Those headlines would not be good, if he should get shot down, and they would be still worse if by any chance the Japanese should capture him.

He thought that it would be hard to check on how well the pilots were absorbing his teachings if he couldn't go along to watch them and besides he wanted to observe the P-38 in combat to get the answers in regard to the comparison of single-engined versus two-engined fighters.

I said that the enemy aircraft were not flying over New Guinea any longer, except for an occasional night bomber, so I'd let him go along with the fighter escort to the bombers and strafers making attacks anywhere except on Halmahera. Up there, a fight would be a certainty.

I reiterated I didn't want him to get into combat. My top priority, as far as he was concerned, was to show the P-38 pilots how to get more range out of their airplanes.

Lindbergh went back to New Guinea and went to work. For the next six weeks he did a superb job for me. Flying constantly with the P-38 squadrons, he preached and practiced his technique of economical operation of the engines. The 600-mile radius of action soon became a reality and the kids got more and more enthusiastic about Lindbergh and his ideas. He spent most of his time with Col. Charles H. MacDonald's 475th Fighter Group and pretty soon that outfit was beginning to talk about the possibility of even 800 miles as an operating radius of action.

During the early part of August the group, then based at Biak, was covering a bomber raid on the Japanese oil depot at Boela, on the island of Ceram. It was a very successful, although rather uneventful raid except that a lone enemy airplane suddenly loomed up directly ahead of observer Lindbergh's P-38.

I had told him that, of course, if it came to a matter of self-defense, I could not expect him to refrain from shooting. How much elasticity his conscience suddenly acquired in regard to the business of self-defense I don't know and never asked him, but anyhow Lindbergh fired a burst and the enemy went down.

I knew about the story shortly after the group landed, but as long as no one put in a claim for official credit for the destruction of an enemy airplane I pretended that I hadn't heard of the occurrence.

A week or so later, to prove the long-range capabilities of the P-38, Lindbergh, accompanied by Col. MacDonald, Lt. Col. Meryl Smith, and Capt. Danforth P. Miller, headed off for Palau, a little over 600 miles to the north of Biak, their departure point.

239

They arrived over the main island of Babelthuap at 15,000 feet, dived to the treetops, strafed a patrol boat, and headed south over the main Japanese airdrome. Several Japanese fighters took off and Lindbergh gained the shocking information than an enemy airplane on his tail was something he could not get rid of. Luckily he had three experts at the art of handling such situations.

They extricated him from his dilemma by the simple method of shooting down the Japanese before the Japanese shot down Lindbergh. MacDonald got two, Meryl Smith got one, and Miller probably destroyed another, which went down on fire but was not seen to crash by the quartet hurriedly extricating themselves from the aroused hornets' nest. The little episode over Ceram had made shooting down an enemy look easy. Lindbergh knew better now. He mentally filed the picture away somewhere in his brain. The next time he wouldn't get caught like that at low altitude by an enemy airplane that could outmaneuver him.

There wasn't to be any next time, however. I told him he couldn't go out on any more combat missions and I wished he would go home. I was, and still am, exceedingly fond of Charles Lindbergh, but I was getting worried. I owed him a debt of real gratitude for increasing the combat range of our fighter planes.

It was going to pay heavy dividends for the rest of the war and I appreciated what he had done, but I was getting worried for fear he would get shot down. If that happened it would hurt the Air Force and it would certainly bring down a lot of criticism on MacArthur and on me for allowing him to go on such missions.

Lindbergh agreed. He said he had taught the kids all that he could, had learned the answers about fighter tactics that he had come out to get, and was ready to return to the United States.

I asked him not to tell anyone back home about being in combat as long as the war lasted and said that if the story leaked out, I would tell the newspapermen that there was no record of his ever having flown on combat missions, let alone having shot down a Japanese airplane. Lindbergh said he had no intention of telling the story as he too was anxious not to have any publicity in regard to his activities in the Pacific, particularly while the war was on. And thanking me for the opportunities I had allowed him and for legalizing his status, he left for home on August 21.

Many times since the war I have been asked how many Japanese Lindbergh shot down and how many missions and combat hours he flew during the six weeks he was with me in that summer of 1944 in New Guinea. I don't know. My instructions were that no official record was to be kept of any "combat time" which by definition was, "flying time over any area in which combat is probable or expected." There is no official record that "Slim" ever took part in a combat mission or ever shot down a Japanese.

Besides that, we all tried to change the subject whenever the matter came up and forget anything we heard about him except that he was doing a grand job of teaching the fighter pilots cruise control methods that would let them operate at greater distances than they had before he arrived.

There was no thought of depriving him of recognition. We were trying to protect him and incidentally everyone else in the theater from Gen. MacArthur on down. Civilians are not supposed to fight in wars. The uniform is supposed to offer some protection to the combatant, but the man in civilian clothes has no rights under military law if he is caught in combat.

If Lindbergh had been shot down or had a forced landing and had been picked up by the Japanese they would have been justified in shooting him on the spot. If any news about his combat activities in the Southwest Pacific leaked out, it certainly would not be good for him back in Washington, and it would not be good for the rest of us. If he had been killed in an accident under me there would have been a lot of explaining to do, but if he had been captured or killed in combat, the questions that would have been asked would have been at least embarrassing.

I know that he shot down one Japanese airplane over Ceram. I know that he nearly got shot down during a flight to Palau just before I sent him home. As far as I know those are the only combats he ever got into although there may have been others that the "grapevine" did not communicate to me. I didn't ask too many questions about it during the war and I haven't since.

Lindbergh has always appreciated my position during the war and, several times since, has stood smiling by me when in answer to some interviewer about the story of his shooting down Japanese airplanes, I have answered, "There is no official record of Lindbergh ever having flown a combat mission in the Southwest Pacific area."

Now that the war is over and beginning to be forgotten in the light of our present troubles, I see no reason for denying that as far as I am concerned, Charles Augustus Lindbergh was one of the unsung heroes of World War II, whose devotion to his country has too long gone unrecognized. I hope that this story will serve at least partially to give him that recognition.

November 24, 1944, was a big day on Saipan in the Mariana Islands. One hundred and eleven B-29 Superfortresses of the XXI Bomber Command, taking off from the new United States base on Saipan, made the first attack on Tokyo since the Doolittle raid in 1942. It was followed by a series of attacks by the big bombers on industrial targets in Japan. The results were disappointing.

The B-29 had been heralded as the perfect plane for the bombardment of Japan. It had the necessary range and speed; it could carry 20,000 pounds of bombs and it was heavily armed. In spite of repeated attacks, Japanese industry was not being knocked out. At the same time B-29 losses were heavy, much too heavy.

The problem was solved with a dramatic change in tactics. The B-29 had been committed to battle using the daylight precision bombardment methods that had been developed against Germany. On March 9, 1945, Gen. Curtis E. LeMay, in one of the greatest military decisions of the entire war, sent over 300 of his big bombers on a nighttime, low-level incendiary strike against Tokyo. That strike was a turning point in the strategic campaign against Japan. An unbelievable 15.8 square miles in the heart of Tokyo were completely destroyed, and only 14 Superforts were lost to enemy antiaircraft fire. To Gen. Le May it meant that Japan could be conquered from the air without the tremendous loss of life that would necessarily accompany an invasion. The March 9 raid had been a gamble but it had shortened the road to victory.

Tokyo Fire Raid

Glenn Infield

OUTLINED BY a dark, brooding sky overhead and by brilliant orange flames that flickered below, the B-29 made a perfect target for the Japanese antiaircraft gunners defending Tokyo. Near-hits rocked the bomber and made flying difficult. "God Almighty," the pilot, Capt. Robert Carrier, yelled to bombardier Lt. Philip Smith, "how much longer? We've got to scram out of here or we're going to be blown to pieces."

"Give me one more minute," Smith requested.

"No can do."

As they crossed the city, Carrier could see sweat glistening on the face of Lt. Harold Javens, his copilot across the aisle. Carrier's own flying suit was soaked. It clung to his body like a wet towel. But there was nothing he could do except hold the plane on course and wait.

They had come all the way from

This picture was taken from the nose of a B-29 Superfortress during the first attack on Tokyo since the famous Doolittle raid in 1942. The weather over the target was bad and bombing results were poor.

Guam to drop their incendiaries at low level as part of the "LeMay Gamble," and the future of the XXI Bomber Command — in fact, the future of the entire air war in the Pacific — depended upon the outcome of the mission. Cigar-smoking, surly-countenanced Curtis LeMay was staking his career, $400 million worth of aircraft and equipment, and the lives of 3,000 men, that it would be a success. There could be no mistakes.

Carrier winced as a flak shell cracked outside the cockpit window, and he fought to keep the big plane level.

"They have our track," he yelled to Javens. "The next barrage will cut us in half . . ."

"Bombs away!" Smith intoned gleefully.

Carrier felt the plane lift as the twenty-four 500-pound bombs, each filled with clusters of six-pound M69 incendiaries, fell from the bomb bay and dropped toward the roaring inferno 5,000 feet below. "Hold tight. We're going to get the hell out of here fast," he yelled, twisting the control wheel to the left and slamming in enough left rudder with his foot to

243

keep the B-29 from skidding.

Since the "LeMay Gamble" involved the bombing of Tokyo individually, instead of in formation, Carrier had no other aircraft on his wing to be concerned about. He stood the big plane on the left wing tip and, dodging the exploding fireballs of antiaircraft, headed toward the Pacific. When the compass needle pointed east, he kicked the bomber straight and with the four 18-cylinder Wright engines each delivering their maximum horsepower, raced for the coast of Japan.

Halfway across the fire-streaked area of Tokyo, though, there was a thunderclap burst of flak and the control column jerked completely out of his hands. Instantly the B-29 rolled to the right, the nose dipping below the horizon.

"No. 4 engine is burning!" the right scanner screamed. "It's burning bad!"

Carrier couldn't answer. The B-29 was in a perilous vertical dive now and the right wing was tucking back and turning gradually as it threatened to throw the big plane into a death spin. "Help me on the wheel," he yelled to Javens across the aisle. "Pull! Pull!"

The two men strained at the control wheel, trying desperately to force it back into their laps; but the Superfort continued its suicidal dive toward the flames beneath them. "The control cables must be cut," the copilot said. "The nose won't come up." There was panic in Javens' voice now as the engines roared like scared banshees, a re-

sult of the propellers overspeeding.

Carrier shook his head. Although the big plane was not responding to their efforts, he could feel pressure against the control wheel. If the cables had been shot away, the wheel would have been limp in his hands. "Pull, dammit, pull. It has to come out."

At 3,000 feet Carrier gave up. He couldn't wait any longer. "We'll have to jump," he bellowed, reaching for the bailout bell. "We're running out of space!"

But even as his fingers found the bell, the greenhouse nose of the B-29 began a slow arc upward to the horizon; and the airspeed needle, which had been pushing the peg, began going back to the green.

Out of his window, Carrier could see the tremendous strain bending the huge wings, could hear the aluminum creaking and protesting at the overload. His arms ached until tears of pain ran down his cheeks but he refused to release the wheel. Inch by inch, the nose of the bomber reluctantly rose toward the horizon until, finally, the plane flew level once again.

Quickly trimming the aircraft for straight flight, Carrier rubbed his numb fingers and muttered, "That was close. I thought we had it." Picking up the microphone he asked, "How's No. 4?"

"Still burning, I think we . . ."

The scared voice of the tail gunner cut the right scanner's message short: "Pilot, there's a Baka on our tail!"

A shiver ran down the spine of

244

Capt. Carrier. A Zero or Raiden would have been bad enough. But a Baka, the Jap rocket plane loaded with explosives and manned by a suicide pilot intent on ramming his target, was a death sentence with wings.

Carrier could feel his hands shaking on the controls, his shoulder muscles tightening as he gripped the wheel, waiting for the collision he anticipated. This was the end. They didn't even have a gun to fight back. LeMay had ordered all guns removed so extra bombs and fuel could be cached aboard, deciding that the low-level raid would be such a surprise there would be no fighter opposition. Now, with a Baka pilot hurtling his rocket plane directly at them, there was nothing Carrier could do.

Suddenly the words of the briefing officer swept through his mind: "If you are crew members of a B-29 then you must expect to receive the roughest sort of treatment from the Japanese if you are shot down. Your chances of living are not too good."

"He's coming!" the tail gunner screamed.

Carrier took one final look at the burning Jap capital below him and reached for the bailout bell switch for the second time within a few minutes. There was no choice, although jumping into the inferno beneath the plane would be suicide.

They were doomed. Either the Baka would ram them or they would hurtle earthward in a fiery parachute — and if by some miracle they did get down alive, the Japs would execute them.

At the same moment Carrier's hand flicked the bailout bell switch over Tokyo, a husky full-faced man with jet-black hair and a fat cigar between his teeth paced his office on Guam. "Iron Pants" LeMay was worried. He had just taken the biggest gamble of his career, a daring stroke that could wipe out the entire XXI Bomber Command and destroy American airpower in the Pacific theater of operations.

The load was entirely on LeMay's two shoulders. He had made the decision. Washington, London, Paris — the top brass in these Allied capitals knew nothing of his plans until the field order was under way. It was the "LeMay Gamble" from planning board to execution, and as the general looked out into the night, on March 9, 1945, his teeth chewed hard into the end of his cigar, nearly cutting the Havana in two.

"It's early yet, General," said Brig. Gen. August Kissner, LeMay's chief of staff. "Take it easy." The 39-year-old Kissner knew the general intimately, having flown with him back at Kelly Field in 1929 and served with him in England earlier in World War II.

LeMay shook his head. As usual the taciturn CO spoke little. "What time is it?" he finally said.

"0100."

"We ought to hear from Power within the next half-hour." LeMay's brow furrowed and he began pacing

Major General Curtis Le-May (left), who sent 334 B-29's on a radically different, low-level, incendiary attack on Tokyo, and Brigadier General Thomas S. Power, the man who led the highly successful mission.

the floor again. "We better hear from him by then," he added significantly.

Across the room, Col. James D. Garcia, 31-year-old intelligence officer of the XXI Bomber Command, watched the worried general a few minutes, then said, "Everything will turn out O.K. If you hadn't been convinced of that you wouldn't have sent the boys out tonight, General. You know that."

"We all make mistakes." LeMay stopped his pacing and sank wearily in the small chair behind his desk. He looked tension-ridden and ten years older as he stared at the wall maps through his black, overhanging eyebrows . . . once again going over every detail of the planning, every factor for

and against the success of the low-level night attack. "I know I'm right. I have to be right," he muttered, as though trying to convince himself.

LeMay had been training all his life to make decisions. He never wanted to be anything but a soldier, even as a boy back in Ohio. The oldest of six children of a Columbus, Ohio, laborer, he had struggled every inch of the way to the position he now held.

With no family connections or influential politicians backing him, LeMay couldn't get into West Point. Undaunted, he made an end run to fulfill his military ambitions. He enrolled at Ohio State University and joined the Army Reserve. It was a tough grind. One semester he worked in a foundry from 5:30 P.M. until 2:30 A.M., in addition to attending classes all day and cramming in his homework whenever he found a spare moment.

In 1928 he still lacked a few credits for a diploma but, fully qualified as far as ROTC was concerned, he promptly put in for pilot training.

At March Field he graduated not only as a pilot, but also as a navigator . . . and in the next few years learned about engines, radios, and bomb-aiming techniques; then he went back to Ohio State for his degree in engineering.

In 1937, one of the best-qualified aviators in the Army, he was assigned to the first B-17's. From that time on Curtis LeMay was a big-bomber man. Early in World War II he put his knowledge to work in the ETO. As commander of the Third Division of the 8th Air Force, he sent out his small, outnumbered B-17's to fight the mighty Luftwaffe at its peak.

Before his heavy-bomber forces were finally reinforced in numbers great enough to fight on even terms, it had been his skill in planning and techniques that brought many a pilot home safely. But the losses hurt LeMay emotionally. After that experience in Europe, he thought nothing could be worse. Now he knew he had been wrong.

"No report from Power yet?" he asked. Brig. Gen. Thomas S. Power, of the 314th Bombardment Wing, was leading the Tokyo mission.

Garcia looked at his watch. "Not yet."

Almost talking to himself, as if to prop up his own faltering convictions, LeMay said, "If I had left the guns aboard they'd be shooting each other down in the darkness. Besides, we needed the extra bombs."

Justification. Rationalization. Appraisal. Reappraisal. The old torture rack of command.

LeMay remembered how the flyers had gaped at him, horrified, when he first told them that the next raid against the Jap mainland would not be by daylight, but at night. It would be against Tokyo and at low level. But the biggest shock treatment of all had come when he told them to remove the guns from the planes and replace their weight with extra fire bombs. In the dark the gunners couldn't do any real good, but those bombs could.

Now, as he sat in the chair and waited for some word from the flyers, he reconsidered his decision from every angle and still felt justified. Sixteen times since he had taken command of the XXI Bomber Command in January, he had sent his bombers to Japan and not one important target had been destroyed — although they had dropped 5,000 tons of bombs. To boot, losses had been high: enemy planes and flak had accounted for nine fighters and 29 Superforts; mechanical difficulties had resulted in the loss of 21 B-29's, and 15 other big babies were lost to unknown causes, perhaps

Baka attacks.

LeMay had tried every tactical trick he had learned in the ETO while the crews cursed him. Nothing had worked. Then, early in March, he had made his bold move.

Garcia stared at LeMay for a minute, then said, "All our reports indicate there will be few, if any, enemy fighters in the target area."

"What about the new Matsuyama Wing?"

"It's a good unit, General, but even with their new planes, they can't stop a force of 300 Superforts at night."

"By God, they better not be able to stop them or we are out of business." He looked at his watch for the hundredth time since dusk. It was exactly 0115 hours. "If we don't hear soon, they must be in trouble . . ."

The B-29's were in trouble. Bad trouble. Closing on the target city, several of LeMay's planes were trailing smoke from smashed engines, and men were bleeding and dying on the air decks as the Jap antiaircraft cut into their thin-skinned bombers. Fires bloomed from gasoline tanks, small red dots in the black sky compared to the blazing holocaust below.

Lt. George Baker's *Top-of-the-Cloud* was hit in the left aileron and slid off in a steep dive. With little altitude to spare, it seemed doomed until the B-29 suddenly began drifting upward and passed in front of Carrier's aircraft. The captain, fighting desperately to keep the wings of his own Superfort level so the crew could bail out, stared in amazement at the antics of Baker's plane. "What the hell is . . ."

Carrier stopped talking in midsentence as an unbelievable thing happened. His own B-29 was suddenly lifted from its piece of sky and tossed upward like a scrap of paper in a hurricane. One minute the bomber was below 3,000 feet, and next it was at 9,000!

The floorboards were uprooted and loose equipment was hurtled around inside the plane like shrapnel. Carrier, helpless at the controls, saw the B-29's nose flare higher and higher until finally the bomber seemed to be standing on its tail. It teetered there momentarily, threatening to go one way, then another — until it suddenly went over on its back.

Even with his safety belt fastened tight, the captain was jostled hard against the glass canopy above his head. Fire extinguishers, parachute packs, water containers, dirt — everything not tied down went flashing past his face or thudded against him. Across the aisle the copilot hung limp from his safety belt, blood streaming from a gash in his head, a victim of the accurate antiaircraft fire which smashed into the cockpit as the B-29 careened crazily through the sky.

"We're upside down," the tail gunner screamed. "We're going to crash!"

"The — wings will come off!"

Carrier, shocked at events, cursed softly as the B-29 completed its screaming loop and nosed straight down toward the burning Japanese capital. "Jump! Clear out . . ."

He fought to maneuver the bomber out of its death dive and this time he had an ally — the same superheated thermal wave that had tossed his and Baker's plane around like a toy.

Out of the corner of his eye, Carrier could see other B-29's diving and climbing crazily over the city, completely out of control. The thermals that soared upward from Tokyo that night were fantastic. Sixty-ton bombers were mere specks of dust to them. The skies over the city became a sea of violence, a devil's caldron, boiling and raging. Prodigious, hurricanelike blows smashed against the B-29's while waves of heat danced and shimmered visibly outside the cockpits.

Carrier was slammed down hard in his seat as the big plane suddenly checked its dive and started to climb again at a tremendous rate. This time, though, the captain was not caught by surprise. Neutralizing the controls, he permitted the plane to ride the soaring thermal. He knew that if he attempted to hold his altitude and fought the vertical column of superheated air, he would exceed the structural limitations of his plane.

At 8,500 feet the thermals dissipated, and as the Superfort began to drop, the captain gunned the engines in an effort to hold his altitude. The bomber settled to 7,000 feet . . . then started to fly out of the turbulent superheated air toward the east coast of Japan.

By this time Carrier was near exhaustion. So many things had happened in such a short length of time that he was confused. He had given the bailout signal — but how many of the crew had been able to get out of the hurtling plane? What had happened to the Baka that had been so intent on ramming him? And the No. 4 engine — was it still burning? All these questions raced simultaneously through the pilot's mind as he fought to get the crippled Superfort out over the Pacific.

"Pilot to crew. Pilot to crew. Is anyone still back there? . . ."

"The Ninth Air Force got the hell shot out of themselves at Ploesti," LeMay muttered. "That was supposed to be the end of the low-level missions. Now I've sent the entire XXI Bomber Command over Tokyo and didn't even get a radio message back from them." He walked over to the window and looked out at the dark skies. "Not one radio call."

Garcia was beginning to fidget in his chair. Was it possible that all 334 planes had been wiped out? He remembered the intelligence report he had read two days ago — a report that at the time seemed insignificant; but now, in this hushed office, it suddenly took on dreadful importance.

The Japanese army and navy had been ordered to keep its planes on the ground, hidden beneath camouflage and scattered in dispersal areas, so that when the expected invasion of the mainland came, they would be

249

ready to go into action. It was estimated that this last-ditch air fleet consisted of 5,130 planes, of which 3,000 were Kamikazes, navy suicide planes, and Bakas. What if this hoarded armada had been ordered into the air this night against the low-flying, unarmed B-29's? It is doubtful if there would have been time for any of the Superforts to send a radio message in that case.

The A-2 officer shook his head slightly at the thought and muttered, "Surely not all of them would be shot down?"

LeMay turned quickly to Garcia. "What did you say, Colonel?"

Garcia, embarrassed, replied, "I was just thinking out loud, sir. Sorry." He hoped the general hadn't been able to make out his words.

LeMay turned back to the window. "Well, if I failed I certainly haven't any alibi. I know what the Nips are capable of doing. I know what our boys can do. I thought we could go in and drop the incendiaries and get away without heavy losses." He sighed ponderously. "I must have been wrong."

The room was silent after he finished. What could be said? It was late, very late, and every man on Guam knew that if the mission had gone as expected, Power should have sent a message by this time.

Something went wrong. What? There were so many factors involved in the daring gamble: winds, gas loads, navigation over dark seas, typhoons, enemy interception, engine trouble, espionage — the list was endless, and one mistake would mean tragedy.

"I'm going over to the MCR," Garcia said. He couldn't stand the tension any longer and wanted to get every bit of information available. The mission control room would have it.

Yet, once there, he learned very little. A blackboard listed the story known thus far in figures: the number of planes that took off, the aborts, the early returns. After studying the scoreboard for a few seconds, Col. Garcia stepped over to the radio operator who was monitoring the bomber frequency. Static, whines, screeches and other odd sounds buffeted Garcia's ears — but no human voice or keyed message.

"Nothing?" he asked.

The radio operator shrugged. "Nothing but static, sir. Not one damn word."

"Thanks."

He returned to the general's office. As soon as he opened the door LeMay turned and looked at him questioningly. Garcia shook his head. "Not a word."

The cigar in the general's mouth drooped and the heavy eyebrows sagged until his eyes were mere slits. He ran a hand through his hair, wiped some sweat from his forehead, then turned and faced the assembled staff officers. "This decision was completely mine and naturally I will shoulder all the blame. I'll notify the Pentagon that..."

Suddenly the office door burst open and a sergeant hurried in with a sheet of paper which he handed to LeMay. The general read the message silently and those sitting in the room couldn't tell whether it was good or bad news. LeMay's expression never changed and his cigar still dangled precariously from his lips, giving him a depressed look. After an interminable period he looked up.

"It's from Power," he said. "Came at 0121. 'Bombs away. General conflagration in target area. Flak moderate to heavy. Fighters few.' "

A collective sigh sounded in the room. "Thank God," Garcia murmured. "They made it . . ."

The battle of Tokyo was 15 minutes old now as pilot Carrier headed east. *K for King*, with Lt. William Johnson at the controls, crossed underneath the captain's crippled plane, outlined clearly in the glow from the flame in Tokyo. Although one engine was on fire, Johnson — headed for Saipan — maintained level flight as if he were on a Sunday cross-country joyride. Carrier spotted another B-29 flying about 150 feet off the water, its tail section ripped to shreds and the rear of the fuselage nearly cut in half; but it, too, continued on course toward home.

"Pilot to crew. Is anybody back there?"

When there was no answer to his call, Carrier glanced across the aisle at Javens. The copilot lay slouched in his seat, not moving a muscle. Up front in the greenhouse nose Carrier saw the dim outline of the bombardier, Lt. Philip Smith. "You O.K., Smith?" he asked over the intercom.

"Roger."

"Can you see No. 4 engine?"

There was a pause. Then Smith said, "Negative."

Carrier swore. He had to know whether No. 4 was still burning or not. If it was, time was running short for anyone left aboard the aircraft. The flames might reach the fuel tanks at any second and blast them all to eternity. Still, he didn't want to ask the bombardier to crawl back to the scanner's position through the tunnel connecting the front and rear of the plane. If anything happened while Smith was in the tunnel, he would be trapped.

"Hey, anybody up front? This is the right scanner. You all right?"

"Feel like I've gone through a meat grinder, but I guess I'm still all in one piece."

"How's No. 4?"

"Smoking but I don't see any flames."

"Good."

Carrier twisted in his seat to see if the flight engineer was still at his instrument panel. He wasn't. Evidently he had jumped before the thermals had tossed the plane around the sky. The captain knew the terrific buffeting might have extinguished the fire, but he couldn't afford to take a chance. Quickly he closed the throttle on No. 4, feathered the propeller and put the mixture in idle cutoff. After he had shut off the boost pump and fuel valve, set the cowl flaps at 10 degrees, and the nacelle fire extinguisher to No. 4, he pulled first one and then the other extinguisher handle.

"How does it look now, scanner?"

"I think the smoke is dying away. Looks a lot better."

"Keep an eye on it. Anyone else back there with you?"

"Negative. The CFC (central fire control gunner) and the left scanner jumped."

"Roger."

Carrier next tried to contact the tail gunner but there was no answer. Nor was the navigator or radio operator still aboard. After determining the crew status, Carrier made his decision. With the fire in No. 4 engine temporarily under control and the Baka evidently no longer a threat, lost in the wild thermal caldron over Tokyo, the captain headed the bomber southeast. "Smith, get back to the navigator's table and plot a course to Iwo."

"Will do," the bombardier replied.

A minute later, as Carrier was trimming the B-29 for the flight to Iwo, Smith walked past on his way from the nose to the navigator's position.

"Think we'll make it?"

The captain shrugged. "We'll give it a good try."

Iwo Jima, still not completely free of Japs, was the halfway point between Tokyo and Guam. A volcanic island with a short emergency strip for crippled B-29's unable to make it back to home base, it was a mere speck in the Pacific; but that speck could mean the difference between life and death to an aircrew — and on March 9 it was just that to Carrier and his companions.

"How does that right wing look, scanner?" the pilot asked.

"The fire is practically out, but there is a hell of a big hole outboard of No. 4 engine where the flak hit. Every time we hit rough air, I can see the wing tip wobble in the moonlight. Think it might break off?"

"We'll have to take that gamble."

As they neared the Bonin islands, Carrier made his first attempt to contact Iwo. "Iwo tower, this is B-29 'Square 76.' Do you read me?"

There was no answer. He tried three times again but still Iwo didn't answer, and the captain decided that his radio transmitter must have been knocked out by the flak over Tokyo. "I'll have to . . ."

"Flames shooting out of No. 4 again. Worse than ever." Panic trebled the voice of the right scanner now.

Carrier shuddered involuntarily at the words. He had used both nacelle extinguishers to put the fire out the first time. Now he had nothing left. "Smith, how far are we out of Iwo?"

"Fifty miles dead ahead."

"Get up here fast."

When the bombardier arrived at the cockpit, Carrier motioned for him to remove Javens from the right seat and take it himself. Quickly Smith unloosened the copilot's safety belt and dragged the limp body to the nose compartment. He then returned and slipped into the vacated seat.

Carrier had already started his descent for Iwo. Pointing to the airspeed dial he said, "I want you to call out the airspeed on the approach, and don't make any mistakes. We won't have one mile to spare either way. That strip is only 4,000 feet long."

He had 60 tons of airplane to barrel in at 110 mph and to get stopped in less than a mile. There was no run out space as there was at Guam on the 8,500-foot strip. He had to hit the edge of the strip at exactly the right speed and height and the brakes had to hold. If they had been shot out over Tokyo . . .

Underneath him he suddenly spotted the B-29 that had been clipping the waves as it left the coast of Japan earlier. Only now it was weaving from side to side as though the pilot was having trouble controlling it. Parts of the ripped tail section were tearing loose. "He's going to be lucky to get in," Carrier muttered.

The words were no sooner out of his mouth than the bomber slowly and gracefully tipped up on its nose, did half a wingover, and hit the water. There was no explosion, probably because there wasn't enough fuel remaining in the tanks to cause one. Capt. Carrier stared at the wreckage. Then, tearing his eyes away, he whispered, "I hope we're not next."

"Iwo, can you read me?" he called.

There was a long silence. Carrier was getting ready to call again when a voice came through his earphones. "Plane calling Iwo. We read."

"This is 'Square 76.' Engine on fire. Coming in. Is the runway clear?"

"Roger, 'Square 76.' Cleared to land. Runway 4,000 feet, under mortar fire. Width 50 yards with deep craters on left. Good luck."

There was no time to circle the strip even once to look it over. The flames were again shooting out of No. 4, reaching halfway back to the tail. It was a race with time. Carrier reached over and flipped the landing gear switch to the down position. "Gear going down, scanner. Give me a call when it's locked."

A few seconds later the three green lights flashed on in the cockpit and the scanner called, "Gear down and locked. Gee, Captain, the flames go clear back past my bubble. The wing is going to burn off and we'll . . ."

Carrier shut his ears to the crewman's panic and turned the crippled plane onto the approach, knowing he had only one chance to land. There could be no go-around, no foul-up. "Give me half flaps," he ordered. Then, remembering that the bombardier wasn't familiar with the copilot's duties, he reached over and put them down himself.

"Flaps going down." Although he was scared so bad his voice trembled, the scanner stayed on the job.

"Airspeed?" Carrier asked.

"One-sixty . . . 155 . . . 150 . . . 145 . . ." the bombardier called.

Carrier was committed now. From

253

This is what a Japanese city, hit by incendiaries and burning, looked like to the crews of General LeMay's B-29's.

here on in there was no margin for error. Despite the fact that every muscle in his body ached with weariness he kept his feet, legs, arms, and hands moving constantly as he pulled, pushed, nudged, and turned the wheel and rudders, trying to keep the big bomber lined up with the strip.

"One-forty . . . 135 . . . 125 . . . 115 . . . 105 . . ."

"My God, it's dropping out from under me," Carrier cried, shoving all three throttles forward and feeling the plane swing violently to the right into the dead engine. Skidding, a mere fraction above stalling speed, the three engines roaring at full power, he crossed the edge of the runway five feet high, then cut everything off.

With the airspeed now increasing due to his last-moment application of power, Carrier thought the B-29 would never touch down. It floated inches above the strip for several hundred feet, hit, skipped, hit again, and started to fishtail to the left where the craters loomed in the darkness. Carrier hit the brakes hard, heard them screech in protest, held them on for a second until smoke billowed from the expanders, then jerked his feet from the pedals to allow the brakes to cool. Instantly the bomber swerved to the left.

"We're going into the craters!" the bombardier screamed.

" 'Square 76,' watch the bomb craters on your left! Look out . . ."

Carrier tapped the right brake hard enough to pull the B-29 back onto the strip, and when he saw the end of the runway rushing toward him, stood up hard on both brakes. Rubber burned from the tires as the giant plane slid, tearing at the ground in a Herculean effort to stop. The 60 tons of metal refused to quit racing down the strip; and at the last second, when it seemed the bomber was going to pile up at the end of the field, Carrier did the only thing possible. He kicked right rudder and gunned both engines on the left wing.

This sudden action swung the B-29 violently to the right in a ground loop. Dust billowed around the plane as it tried to flip over on its back, but finally, in a gesture of defeat, it rocked back on its wheels, trembled a few times — and stopped dead.

"Get out. Get the hell out before it explodes!" the quivering captain yelled.

The three men jumped from the plane, dragging copilot Javens' body with them.

The strip was under heavy shelling from Japanese forces still dug in on the perimeter of the base, but the airmen made it to the dugouts without getting hit. Just as they dived into the nearest hole, flames from the burning engine broke through a fuel-tank wall and the B-29 exploded in a huge cloud of fire.

Less than one minute had separated Carrier and his companions from death. Javens, the copilot, was not so fortunate. The flak burst that had hit him during the wild ride in the thermals over Tokyo proved fatal.

Nine of the Superforts fell into the flaming city of Tokyo that night, their gasoline and bombs adding to the already savage flames. Another five, damaged but still able to fly, managed to stagger away from the city and reached the water, where they ditched. All five crews were saved. Forty-two of the B-29's which reached home safely were damaged by the heavy and accurate antiaircraft fire over Japan.

The raid, though — despite the losses and damage — was a spectacular epic success. Recon photos, taken shortly after completion of the "Le-May Gamble," showed that 15.8 square miles of Tokyo had been burned to the ground. This included 18 per cent of the industrial area, 63 per cent of the commercial area, and the heart of the residential district. Also, 22 industrial targets which the XXI Bomber Command had on its strike list were destroyed.

Even the great British air missions over Hamburg were overshadowed by the Tokyo fire raid. During a ten-day period, 12 square miles of the German city had been burned out; but at Tokyo, in less than six hours, nearly 16 square miles were wiped out and more than 100,000 people were killed.

Gen. Power said later, "The March 9 fire-bomb raid was the greatest single disaster in military history. It was greater than the combined damage of the A-bomb drops on Hiroshima and Nagasaki. In that fire raid there were more casualties than in any other military action in the history of the world."

Enola Gay *and* Bock's Car, *the B-29's that dropped the atomic bombs on Hiroshima and Nagasaki were engaged in a new kind of aerial combat, a combat in which a single plane carrying a single bomb did tremendous damage to the enemy. The bomb that was dropped on Hiroshima destroyed 4.7 square miles of that city. The bomb that fell on Nagasaki completely demolished an area 2.3 miles long and 1.9 miles wide. There is little doubt that these attacks hastened the surrender of Japan.*

The awesome new weapon delivered by the two B-29's had been under active development since late in 1939 when the noted physicist, Dr. Albert Einstein, suggested to President Franklin D. Roosevelt that such a bomb was possible. Dr. Einstein thought the bomb might prove to be too large to transport by air. As time went on its size was reduced, but it remained a big bomb. As it happened, the United States had an airplane big enough to carry it, the B-29 Superfortress.

In 1944 a special combat unit, the 509th Composite Group, went into training at Wendover Field in Utah. Under the leadership of Col. Paul

W. Tibbets, Jr., the members of the select group, flying B-29's, practiced high-altitude bombing and overwater navigation. By May, 1945, they were ready to move to Tinian in the Mariana Islands.

Intensive training continued on Tinian culminating in a series of strikes at Japan to familiarize crews with target areas in that country. By the beginning of August, the 509th was ready and so was the first atomic bomb.

A list of possible targets had already been selected. It included Hiroshima, Niigata, Kokura, and Nagasaki, all relatively undamaged by previous bombing and each one "a military installation or war plant surrounded by or adjacent to houses and other buildings most susceptible to damage." Hiroshima was named as the primary target for the first atomic bomb.

Three B-29's were chosen for the momentous mission: the Enola Gay *to carry the bomb and* The Great Artiste *and No. 91 to act as observation planes. The date was set at no earlier than August 3 and as soon thereafter as weather would permit. The weather had to be good because the bomb was to be dropped visually. It was August 5 on Tinian when the weather forecasts looked right. Three B-29's, one of them carrying the bomb, took off early the next morning.*

A Tale of Two Cities

Gene Gurney

THE CREW STARTED to assemble at the *Enola Gay* at two o'clock. Besides Col. Tibbets there were Capt. Robert A. Lewis, who was acting as copilot; Maj. Thomas W. Ferebee, the bombardier; Capt. Theodore J. Van Kirk, the navigator; Lt. Jacob Beser, a radar countermeasures officer; Master Sgt. Wyatt E. Duzenbury, the flight engineer; Staff Sgt. Joe S. Stiborik, radar operator; Sgt. George R. Caron, the tail gunner; Sgt. Robert A. Schumard, the waist gunner; and Pfc. Richard H. Nelson, radio operator. Also making the trip were Navy Capt. William S. Parsons, who had worked at Los Alamos and was in charge of the bomb, and his assistant, Lt. Morris R. Jeppson.

After Army photographers had taken their pictures of the plane, the ground crew, and the crowd gathered to see them off, one by one the men climbed into the Superfort. Tibbets appeared at the pilot's window; he waved and started the four powerful

General Carl Spaatz (second from right), who controlled all B-29 operations in the Pacific area, awaits the return of the "Enola Gay."

engines one after another. Slowly the *Enola Gay* taxied to her runway. The camera plane, piloted by Capt. George W. Marquardt, and Maj. Charles W. Sweeney's *The Great Artiste,* which had been transformed into a flying laboratory, were waiting for their takeoff time. The *Enola Gay* left the ground at 2:45 to be followed at two-minute intervals by the other two planes. The "Little Boy" was on its way to Japan.

The bomb was still not armed. There had been a series of bad takeoff crashes which had made everyone worry about having the *Enola Gay* take off with a live bomb on board. Capt. Parsons had decided to put off the final assembly of the bomb until after they were safely airborne. To make sure that he would be able to do it smoothly when the time came, he had practiced putting the explosive charge in the end of the bomb over and over again. Now, as the *Enola Gay* leveled out over the Pacific, Parsons and Jeppson went to work in the bomb bay. The charge was inserted and the final connections made. The bomb would now explode after it had dropped to an altitude of 1,850 feet.

At Iwo Jima the *Enola Gay* began a slow climb to the altitude from which the bomb was to be dropped. The decision to strike the primary or the alternate targets rested with Col. Tibbets and was to be made on the basis of information transmitted by the weather ships flying ahead of the *Enola Gay*.

At 8:15 the report on Hiroshima was received: "2/10 lower and middle lower, and 2/10 at 15,000 feet." Visual bombing conditions at the primary target! The decision was quickly made. Hiroshima!

The doomed city, Japan's eighth largest, was exactly what the Interim Committee had recommended as a target for the first atomic bomb — a military installation surrounded by houses and other buildings. It was an important army transport base and contained large ordnance, food, and clothing depots. It also had a ship-building yard, textile mills, oil-storage facilities, electrical works, and a large railroad yard. Because Hiroshima was on the list of targets reserved for the 509th, it had received so little damage that some of its residents had come to believe they were going to be spared the fate of Tokyo and Yokohama.

As the *Enola Gay* flew toward Hiro-shima with her deadly cargo, the crew passed the time in various ways. Some of them tried to sleep, some read, some just sat and thought about the job that lay ahead. They were all a little awed by the bomb that rode in the forward bay. It was gray and long — close to ten feet — and about a yard in diameter. It was the biggest bomb they had ever seen.

Col. Tibbets crawled back through the tunnel from the pilot's compartment to give the men in the rear a final briefing on the bomb. He asked the tail gunner, Sgt. George Caron, if he had figured it out yet.

Caron asked, "Is it some chemist's nightmare?"

Tibbets said it had nothing to do with chemistry. Then Caron recalled something he had read about a cyclotron and asked if it was a physicist's nightmare.

To this Col. Tibbets replied, "I guess you could call it that."

As he started to return to the pilot's compartment Caron stopped him with another question: "Are we going to split atoms?"

The colonel just smiled and went back to his flying.

As the *Enola Gay* neared the Japanese coast, Capt. Parsons went back to take one last look at the bomb. With Jeppson he had been keeping an electronic check on it from the forward compartment. Everything seemed to be all right. The bomb run was begun 25 miles out. Each man had his goggles ready to pull over his eyes when he heard the bombing signal. When they were 12 miles from target, Ferebee, the bombardier, took over. Below he could see Hiroshima on the delta of the Ota River.

It was 8:15 in Hiroshima when the bomb was released. The continuous tone of the signal cut off, warning the crew and those in the accompanying Superforts that the bomb was away. The *Enola Gay* was at 31,600 feet, traveling at 328 mph. It was clear and sunny. There were no enemy aircraft visible and the flak was far below them. The men sat behind their dark goggles and waited.

The bomb, set to go off above the ground to increase the effect of its blast, exploded in less than a minute. By that time Tibbets had put the *Enola Gay* into a steep, tight turn — the same turn he had practiced so often — and was leaving the target behind.

Far below, the 245,000 people who had not been evacuated from Hiroshima were up and beginning a new day. There had been an air-raid alert when the weather planes had passed over, but the all clear had sounded. War workers were either en route or had already arrived at their destinations while others were busy building firebreaks and removing valuables to safety in the country. Probably few heard the *Enola Gay* as it passed over Hiroshima. The Japanese jammed in the vast Bushido Arsenal or hurrying through the heart of town to their jobs had no warning of the holocaust that was to envelop them.

Suddenly a light brighter than a thousand suns filled the sky. The world's first atomic bomb had exploded. At that moment, air became fire, walls crumbled to dust, and lives flickered out by the thousands.

The explosion started hundreds of fires almost simultaneously — fires whose intense heat sucked in air from all directions, creating a fire wind which helped to spread the numerous blazes. An area measuring 4.7 square miles in the heart of the city was completely destroyed. According to Japanese figures, 71,379 residents of Hiroshima were either dead or missing as a result of the bombing; almost that many more were injured. Many of the casualties were among the personnel of the Second Army and the Chucogu Regional Army units stationed in Hiroshima.

When the bomb exploded, the *Enola Gay* was racing away from Hiroshima. In spite of the bright sunlight, the flash of the explosion lit up the inside of the Superfort. The crews of the two escort planes, observing the explosion through their protective goggles, reported that the flash after the explosion was deep purple, then reddish. It reached to almost 8,000 feet. The cloud, shaped like a mushroom, was up to 20,000 feet in one minute. Then the top part broke from the stem and eventually reached 40,000 feet.

Sgt. Caron, riding in the tail of the *Enola Gay,* was in the best position to view the effects of the blast. He saw a flash followed by a tremendous buildup of light which grew and then faded out.

"After what seemed like an eternity," Caron reported, "I saw shock waves coming up. I reported this to the colonel and started taking pictures. He called back and told me to keep talking. I added that the shock waves resembled a series of circles like those caused from dropping pebbles in water. Seconds later they struck the airplane and one of the pilots asked if we had been hit by flak.

"Colonel Tibbets kept asking me what was going on. Then I saw the cloud and was never so busy in my life — trying to take pictures and keep the colonel and the rest of the crew up to date on the blast.

"By the time the cloud rose slightly into the air we were far enough away and I could see the entire city. I commented that the whole area was covered with a thick, purplish mass that looked like fluid. It looked like it was a hundred or more feet thick and flooding out over the city from the center of the blast. Then flames started breaking up through the smoke and dust. The colonel asked me to count them. I tried but lost track. In the meantime I was still taking pictures.

"Then Colonel Tibbets turned the *Enola Gay* so all crewmen could see and each gave his impression over the intercom and into the wire recorder. As we headed for home, the colonel told me to keep my eye on the 'mushroom' and tell him when it disappeared from view. The crew for the most part was quiet on the return. I just sat there and watched that cloud. Finally, I called up that I was losing sight of it. We then were 363 miles from Hiroshima."

Capt. Parsons later described what he was able to see: "A few fires were visible around the edges of the smoke, but we could see nothing of the city except the dock area where buildings were falling down. The boiling dust and debris continued for several minutes, as a white cloud plumed upward from the center to 40,000 feet and an angry dust cloud spread all around the city."

The crew felt a sense of relief that the bomb had been dropped successfully after their many months of training. But it was relief tinged with awe at the unearthly flash, the shock of the distant explosion, and the sight of a city disintegrating before their eyes.

The Superfort whose single bomb had destroyed Hiroshima sped back to Tinian, 1,600 miles away. So did *The Great Artiste,* whose instruments had measured the blast, and the B-29 camera plane. Messages had preceded them that the bomb had been dropped sucessfully.

The trip back was uneventful. Capt. Lewis described their landing:

"I looked at 'Ole Bull (Col. Tibbets) and his eyes were bloodshot and he looked awful tired. He looked like the past ten months at Wendover and

261

After her momentous journey into the atomic age, the "Enola Gay" is returned to the parking area on Tinian in the Mariana Islands.

Washington and New Mexico and overseas had come up and hit him all at once. I said to him, 'Bull, after such a beautiful job, you'd better make a beautiful landing.' And he did."

The *Enola Gay* touched down at 2:58 P.M., 12 hours and 13 minutes after she had taken off on her momentous journey into the Atomic Age. Close to 200 people were waiting as the Superfort taxied to her hardstand. Among them was Gen. Spaatz, who pinned the Distinguished Service Cross on Tibbets' flying suit.

President Truman received news of the successful dropping of the bomb as he was returning from Potsdam on board the *Augusta*. His public announcement of the bombing was released in Washington 16 hours after it happened — still August 6 in the United States because of the time difference. The President again warned the Japanese people of what was in store for them.

The men in the Marianas received their first word of the powerful new bomb that had been dropped on Japan from the President's message. The 509th now became the center of attention, but the other B-29 units still had work to do. On the 7th, 131 Superforts struck at Tokokawa. The next day there was an incendiary attack on Yawata.

When no offer of surrender came from Japan the decision was made to drop a second atomic bomb on the 9th. This time the primary target was to be Kokura in northern Kyushu, the site of a large army arsenal. Nagasaki was the secondary target. It was an industrial city covering a series of hills and valleys on the west coast of Kyushu.

"Fat Man," the plutonium bomb that had been tested at Alamogordo on July 16 and found to be more powerful than the one dropped on Hiroshima, was made ready and placed aboard the Superfort, *Bock's Car*. Maj.

262

Charles W. Sweeney, who had been in charge of one of the observation planes on the Hiroshima mission, was the pilot; his copilot was Lt. Frederick Olivi; the bombardier was Capt. Kermit K. Beahan; and Capt. James F. Van Pelt, Jr., was the navigator. Lt. Comdr. Frederick Ashworth was in charge of the bomb, which this time had to be armed before the plane took off.

Sweeney's regular B-29, *The Great Artiste,* which had been filled with instruments, accompanied *Bock's Car* as an observation plane and was flown by Capt. Frederick Bock, who usually flew *Bock's Car.* This switch of planes between Sweeney and Bock led to confusion in stories about the dropping of the second atomic bomb. For years afterward there were accounts of the mission that had *The Great Artiste* carrying the bomb to Nagasaki.

Once more, in the early hours of an August morning, Superforts were prepared for takeoff. Two observation planes went with *Bock's Car;* two weather planes were sent to check bombing conditions at Kokura and at Nagasaki. A spare B-29 would be waiting at Iwo Jima in case *Bock's Car* couldn't make it all the way with the bomb.

The strike force got safely off at 3:39 A.M., much to the relief of the scientists, who feared a crash with the armed bomb would destroy half of Tinian. At 9 A.M. the report received from the Kokura weather plane indicated visual bombing conditions over the primary target. With orders that called for a visual drop, Sweeney headed for Kokura.

But by the time *Bock's Car* arrived over the target, the weather had closed in and visual bombing was impossible. In his report Maj. Sweeney described what happened:

"The navigator made landfall perfectly. We passed over the primary target, but for some reason it was obscured by smoke. There was no flak. We took another run almost from the IP. Again smoke hid the target. 'Look harder,' I said to the bombardier, but it was no use. Then I asked Commander Ashworth to come up for a little conference.

"We took a third run with no success. I had another conference with the commander. We had now been 50 minutes over the target and wanted to drop our bomb in the ocean. Our gas was getting low. Six hundred gallons were trapped in one of the tanks.

"We decided to head for Nagasaki, the secondary target."

The report received from the Nagasaki weather plane at 9:19 had been "ceiling and visibility unlimited," but when *Bock's Car* reached there the target had a 8/10 cloud cover. Because of their fuel shortage Sweeney and Ashworth had decided to make one run and drop the bomb by radar if they had to. Comdr. Ashworth took the responsibility for the change in procedure.

The big ship was on instruments for 90 per cent of the bomb run. At the last moment Capt. Beahan, the bombardier, called out, "I can see it, I can see the target!"

He took over and made a visual release of the bomb. It was 10:58 Nagasaki time. As the thundering Superfort turned in a tight arc and sped south, the city vanished in a sky-searing flash of light.

Nagasaki had had an air-raid alert at 7:45 A.M.; the all clear had sounded at 8:30. When *Bock's Car* was sighted, the raid signal was given again but few people bothered to go to the shelters. If they had, the loss figures would have been less than the estimated 35,000 killed, 5,000 missing, and 60,000 injured.

The Nagasaki bomb's blast effect seemed greater than that at Hiroshima because of the difference in topography and the type of bomb used. The area totally destroyed was an oval 2.3 miles long and 1.9 miles wide; every building in it was destroyed, with severe damage extending in an irregular pattern beyond that. Over 68 per cent of Nagasaki's industrial area was destroyed.

The men in *Bock's Car* had donned their polaroid glasses before the bomb was dropped, but they were nearly blinded by the flash. Sgt. Raymond C. Gallagher, the assistant flight engineer, told of a tremendous white flash such as he had never seen before; this was followed by a black cloud which billowed up like a balloon.

The tail gunner, Staff Sgt. Albert T. Dehart, saw what looked like a big red ball coming up at him. On the ground was a big black cloud and out of it came a huge white cloud.

The shock of the explosion was felt by those in the strike plane. "The turbulence of the blast," said Maj. Sweeney, "was greater than that at Hiroshima. Even though we were prepared for what happened, it was unbelievable. Seven or eight miles from the city shock waves as visible as ripples on a pond overtook our plane, and concussion waves twice thumped against the plane, jolting it roughly.

"The underside of the great cloud over Nagasaki was amber-tinted, as though reflecting the conflagration at least six miles below. Beneath the top cloud mass white in color, there gradually climbed a turbulent pillar of black smoke and dust which emitted a second fireball less vivid than the first. It rose as solid as a stump, its base dark purple, with a reddish hue in the center that paled to brown near the top."

The last look they got at Nagasaki showed a thick cone of dust covering half the city. On its rim near the harbor great fires were raging.

Aboard *Bock's Car* there was serious debate as to whether to bail out over an air-sea rescue craft in the Pacific or to try to reach Okinawa's Yontan airfield on their shrinking fuel supply. The decision was to make a run for Okinawa. As *Bock's Car,* practically dry of gasoline, descended to land at Okinawa, Sgt. Dehart, the tail gunner, saw smoke from Nagasaki 385 miles away.

All the Superforts of the Nagasaki mission were safely back at Tinian by midnight of August 9. They were not the last B-29's to make the trip to Japan because the expected surrender did not come. On the 10th, 114 B-29's were airborne and a total of 828 on the 14th. Before the last of these planes returned to the Marianas, Japan had agreed to an unconditional surrender.

The *Tokyo Hitchhiker*, 398th Squadron of the 313th Wing, had become the last Superfort to drop bombs on Japan. The target had been Nobeoka, a small town near Bungo Strait, where the Superfort had covered a mine-laying mission. While returning to their base at Tinian, the *Hiker*'s radio operator picked up a message announcing the capitulation of the Japanese Empire.

The B-29 had dropped 147,000 tons of bombs on Japan in a little more than a year, with results that convinced the Japanese their cause was hopeless and the AAF that strategic air power was of the utmost importance to the future defense of the nation. Although the B-29 attacks on Japan had been planned as a prelude to invasion, invasion had not been necessary; the million or more casualties expected from such an operation were never lost.

The 509th Composite Group's pictorial history carried this tribute to the B-29 and the men who made it:

"To the builders and designers of the B-29, the best, the biggest, the fastest bomber, for bringing our crews safely from each mission, for helping conclude the war from the skies, and making unnecesary an invasion into Japan itself."

PART FIVE

GREAT AIR BATTLES OF THE KOREAN WAR

Introduction

THE FIRST JET air war was fought in Korea between November, 1950, and July, 1953. It was characterized by aerial combat at speeds and altitudes far greater than those of World War II. The fighter tactics developed during that war were used again in Korea with allowances for the changes brought about by the jet engine.

Hostilities began on June 25, 1950, when the Republic of Korea was invaded by the North Koreans. American air, ground, and naval forces were directed to support the Republic's army and the United Nations sent additional assistance. At the end of October it appeared that the North Koreans were facing defeat. This situation was changed drastically when the Chinese Communists entered the conflict in force in November. Instead of coming to an end, the fighting dragged on for 32 more months.

In the struggle for superiority in the air over Korea the Communists had the Russian-built MIG, a jet fighter that performed especially well at altitudes over 35,000 feet. The United Nations had the F-86 Sabrejet of the United States Fifth Air Force. These were the planes that battled it out in the world's first jet air war. When the conflict ended, Sabrejets had shot down 802 MIG's with a loss of only 56, a ratio of 14 to one in favor of the Sabrejet.

It wasn't an easy victory. The jet fighter placed great demands on the pilot. He approached the enemy at speeds that ranged from 500 to 650 mph with little time for decision and action. The enemy, traveling at the same high speed, could get into a position to attack almost before he was seen and identified, especially at high altitudes where planes were difficult to spot against the deep blue of the sky. This was aerial combat at the beginning of the jet age when the airplane could often outperform the pilot who flew it.

A formation of F-86 Sabrejet fighters.

The ground rules of the Korean War, dictated by political necessity, made it a hard war to fight for the airmen on both sides of the conflict. United Nations air forces were forbidden to cross the Yalu River into Manchuria. To do so would be a violation of the air space of the Communist Chinese. This enabled the Chinese to operate from completely safe Manchurian air bases. On the other hand, if they were used for attacks on United Nations ground positions, it was understood that there would be reprisals against the Manchurian bases. The Communists would have been free to launch such attacks from North Korean bases, but these had been destroyed early in the conflict.

As a result of these restrictions, Communist MIG's flew across the Yalu River toward the Chongchon River in northwestern Korea looking for United Nations aircraft. This was the area known as "MIG Alley" where many of the battles between the MIG and the F-86 took place.

Here is an account of an aerial battle in "MIG Alley" by the man who commanded the United States Fourth Fighter-Interceptor Wing from November 1, 1951 to October 2, 1952. During that time he shot down five MIG's and became the 16th jet ace of the Korean War.

Air-to-Air Combat in Korea

Col. Harrison R. Thyng

LIKE KNIGHTS of old the F-86 pilots ride up over North Korea to the Yalu River, the sun glinting off silver aircraft, contrails streaming behind, as they challenge the numerically superior enemy to come on up and fight. With eyes scanning the horizon to prevent any surprise, they watch avidly while MIG pilots leisurely mount into their cockpits, taxi out onto their runways for a formation takeoff.

"Thirty-six lining up at Antung," Black Leader calls.

"Hell, only 24 taking off over here at Tatungkou," complains Blue Leader.

"I see dust at Fen Cheng, so they are gathering up there," yells Yellow Leader.

Once again the Commie leaders have taken up our challenge, and now we may expect the usual numerical odds as the MIG's gain altitude and form up preparatory to crossing the Yalu.

Breaking up into small flights, we stagger our altitude. We have checked our guns and sights by firing a few warm-up rounds as we crossed the

271

bombline. Oxygen masks are checked and pulled as tight as possible over our faces. We know we may exceed eight "G's" in the coming fight, and that is painful with a loose mask. We are cruising at a very high Mach. Every eye is strained to catch the first movement of an enemy attempt to cross the Yalu from their Manchurian sanctuary into that graveyard of several hundred MIG's known as "MIG Alley." Several minutes pass. We know the MIG pilots will become bolder as our fuel time limit over the "Alley" grows shorter.

Now we see flashes in the distance as the sun reflects off the beautiful MIG aircraft. The radio crackles, "Many, many coming across at Suiho above 45,000 feet." Our flights start converging toward that area, low flights climbing, yet keeping a very high Mach. Contrails are now showing over the Antung area, so another enemy section is preparing to cross at Sinuiju, a favorite spot.

We know the enemy sections are now being vectored by GCI (ground-controlled interception), and the advantage is theirs. Traveling at terrifically high speed and altitude, attackers can readily achieve surprise. The area bound by the horizon at this altitude is so vast that it is practically impossible to keep it fully covered with the human eye.

Our flights are well spread out, ships line abreast, and each pilot keeps his head swiveling 360 degrees. Suddenly MIG's appear directly in front of us at our level. At rates of closure of possibly 1,200 mph we pass through each other's formations.

Accurate radar ranging firing is difficult under these conditions, but you fire a burst at the nearest enemy anyway. Imediately the MIG's zoom for altitude and you break at maximum "G" around toward them. Unless the MIG wants to fight and also turned as he climbed, he will be lost from sight in the distance before the turn is completed. But if he shows an inclination to scrap, you immediately trade head-on passes again. You "sucker" the MIG into a position where the outstanding advantage of your aircraft will give you the change to outmaneuver him.

For you combat has become an individual "dogfight." Flight integrity has been lost, but your wingman is still with you, widely separated but close enough for you to know that you are covered. Suddenly you go into a steep turn. Your Mach drops off. The MIG turns with you, and you let him gradually creep up and outturn you. At the critical moment you reverse your turn. The hydraulic controls work beautifuly. The MIG cannot turn as readily as you and is slung out to the side. Quickly closing the brakes, you slide onto his tail and hammer him with your "50's." Pieces fly off the MIG, but he won't burn or explode at that high altitude. He twists and turns and attempts to dive away, but you will not be denied. Your "50's" have hit him in the engine and

Colonel Harrison R. Thyng, one of the jet aces of the Korean war, waves from the cockpit of his F-86 Sabrejet.

slowed him up enough so that he cannot get away from you. His canopy suddenly blows and the pilot catapults out, barely missing your airplane. Now your wingman is whooping it up over the radio, and you flash for home very low on fuel. At this point your engine is running very rough. Parts of the ripped MIG have been sucked into your engine scoop, and the possibility of its flaming out is very likely. Desperately climbing

for altitude you finally reach 40,000 feet. With home base now but 80 miles away, you can lean back and sigh with relief for you know you can glide your ship back and land, gear down, even if your engine quits right now. You hear over the radio, "Flights re-forming and returning — the last MIG's chased back across the Yalu." Everyone is checking in, and a few scores are being discussed. The good news of no losses, the tension which

273

gripped you before the battle, the wild fight, and the "G" forces are now being felt. A tired yet elated feeling is overcoming you, although the day's work is not finished. Your engine finally flames out, but you have maintained 40,000 feet and are now but 20 miles from home. The usual radio calls are given, and the pattern set up for a dead-stick landing. The tower calmly tells you that you are No. 3 dead stick over the field, but everything is ready for your entry. Planes in front of you continue to land in routine and uninterrupted precision, as everyone is low on fuel. Fortunately this time there are no battle damages to be crash-landed. Your altitude is decreasing, and gear is lowered. Hydraulic controls are still working beautifully on the pressure maintained by your windmilling engine. You pick your place in the pattern, land, coast to a stop, and within seconds are tugged up the taxi strip to your revetment for a quick engine change.

Debriefing begins at once, and the excitement is terrific as the score for the mission mounts to four MIG's confirmed, one probable, and four damaged. A quick tally discloses that we had been outnumbered at least three to one, but once again the enemy had been soundly racked up.

This mission is the type most enjoyed by the fighter pilot. It is a regular fighter sweep, with no worries about escort or providing cover for fighter-bombers. The mission had

been well planned and well executed. Best of all, the MIG's had come forth for battle. Our separate flights had probably again confused the enemy radarscope readers, and, to an extent, nullified that tremendous initial advantage which radar plotting and vectoring gives a fighter on first sighting the enemy. We had put the maximum number of aircraft into the target area at the most opportune time, and we had sufficient fuel to fool the enemy. Our patrolling flights at strategic locations had intercepted split-off MIG's returning toward their sanctuary in at least two instances. One downed MIG had crashed in the middle of Sinuiju, and another, after being shot up, had outrun our boys to the Yalu, where they had to break off pursuit. But they had the satisfaction of seeing the smoking MIG blow up in his own traffic pattern. Both instances undoubtedly did not aid the morale of the Reds.

It is a hard bitter air war, with the cards all stacked in favor of the enemy. It is difficult to describe one's personal feelings about being unable to strike the enemy in his vulnerable spots with our great air capability. This is modern-day fighting, yet in its code it parallels knightly warfare of the Middle Ages. Imagine patrolling up and down the Yalu, watching the enemy form up only three miles away on his field at Antung. From one end to another the place is just loaded with aircraft which one good strafing would put out of commission forever. Supply targets and rail centers also within view could be destroyed and the enemy's capability of continuing war made impossible. But we are learning valuable lessons. We are training many pilots. We are proving to the enemy that American youths are not soft, but have the courage and the ability which was so apparent in their forefathers.

A captured MIG is flight tested by American Air Force pilots.

MIG Maneuvers

A Picture Story

HIT-AND-RUN. During the early months of history's first jet warfare Communist MIGs confined their air operations largely to the immediate vicinity of the Yalu River, rarely venturing more than a few miles into North Korea. As USAF pilots approached the Yalu at 38,000 to 40,000 feet, enemy jets swooped across the border in flights of four at altitudes of 40,000 to 50,000 feet, breaking into elements of two for the attack. One diving pass began and ended the battle. Then followed a race for Manchuria and safety.

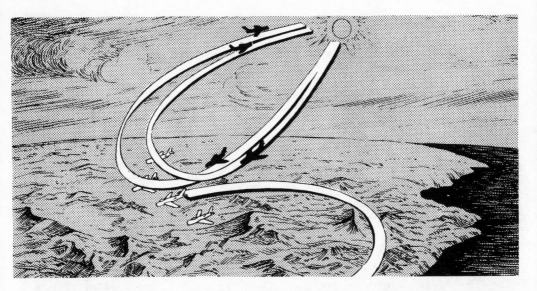

ZOOM AND SUN. Beginning in April 1951 MIG pilots became bolder and more aggressive. As their numbers increased, they ventured as far south as Sinanju. Employing a refined version of the hit-and-run, MIGs lingered over North Korea, hiding in the sun at 48,000 to 50,000 feet. When Sabres patrolling the Yalu at 40,000 feet were sighted, the Communists dived on them for one firing pass, pulled up sharply, evaded back into the sun with aid of the MIG's exceptional rate of climb.

YO-YO. By May and June 1951 the number of MIGs had increased tremendously, and Red pilots were venturing as far south as Pyongyang. Communist pilot proficiency and aggressiveness had improved. A typical maneuver of this period was the Yo-Yo. Twenty or more MIGs orbited in a Lufberry 5000 to 6000 feet higher than the Sabres on Yalu patrol. Single MIGs dived in a firing pass on the Sabre formation, then climbed into another Lufberry to await a second turn after the other MIGs had repeated the routine.

PINCER AND ENVELOPMENT. From September 1951 through April 1953 the enemy accented the mass employment of MIGs against small Sabre formations. The mass attack phase was attended by noticeable pilot inefficiency and poor gunnery, although the enemy was bold enough to send mass flights of MIGs down to Pyongyang, and lone MIGs occasionally even ventured south of Seoul. Formations generally contained as many as 180 MIGs. A typical maneuver of this period was the pincer and envelopment. A formation of 60 to 80 MIGs would cross the Yalu at 35,000 feet and head southeast, dropping off small units to engage U.N. air patrols north of the Chong-chon River. Scouting flights were dispatched to the Wonsan area for high-altitude flank patrol. A similar MIG force would head down the West Coast at 35,000 feet dropping off intruder and scout units near Chinnampo and Chodo Island. As these forces converged on Pyongyang, they dropped to 15,000 to 20,000 feet and swept back north over the main supply routes in search of U.N. fighter bombers and homeward-bound Sabres. An additional MIG force came straight down the jaws of the pincers to Sinanju to trap any aircraft caught in the pincer. This force also provided cover for the other MIGs who were by then homeward-bound to Manchuria and running low on fuel.

END RUN. From May to July 1952, increased Communist aggressiveness and pilot proficiency indicated that the enemy was committing his better-trained pilots to battle. A typical maneuver of this period was the end-run made around Sabres on the Yalu patrol to decoy them from their patrol and allow a second Red force to slip south and attack U.N. fighter bombers and reconnaissance aircraft. The enemy could use this device because the Sabrejets were so close to the Yalu that the Communist ground radar system in Manchuria could locate the F-86s and direct their own aircraft into position.

THE DECOY. Enemy pilots displayed wide diversity in aggressiveness and aerial maneuvers. They made every attempt to position themselves so that their superior numbers would gain them the edge. But once locked in individual combat, the Reds sought every means of escape—cloud cover, violent maneuvers, and protection north of the Yalu. Prominent in this period was the "decoy." Sabres patrolling at 27,000 to 30,000 feet would sight two MIGs at 18,000 to 25,000 feet and dive to the attack. Large flights of MIGs flying high cover in rear of the decoy at 38,000 to 40,000 feet dived on attacking Sabres from behind as the lower MIG decoy element escaped.

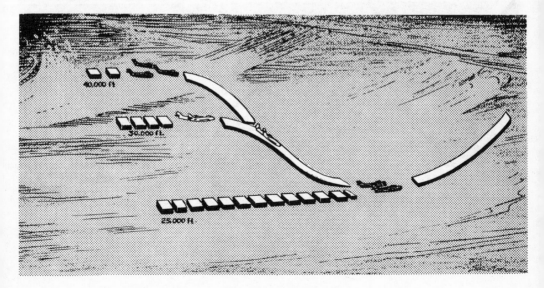

THE JAWS. Sabres, sighting MIGs flying below them in line-abreast formation, dived to the attack. The end MIG peeled off, came around, and went straight up the middle as the remaining MIGs split into two elements, one group going high and the other low. If the Sabres pursued the single MIG which baited the trap, the high and the low MIG elements would close on them from above and below.

THE UPPERCUT. A flight of Sabres on patrol south of the Yalu at 30,000 to 35,000 feet spots two MIGs flying at 20,000 to 25,000 feet. As the Sabres dive to the attack, a large flight of MIGs, camouflaged to blend with the terrain and flying well below and to the rear of the original two, climb and close in from behind.

THE STAIR CASE. A formation of eight or more MIGs would cruise in elements of two. The elements were camouflaged to blend with the landscape and were stepped down and back 1000 to 2000 feet from each other. The leading MIG element was at 8000 to 15,000 feet and might be well out in front to act as a decoy. When Sabres dived on the lead element, trailing MIG elements climbed rapidly and closed from behind. In all maneuvers against Sabrejets, the Red pilots relied heavily on two basic advantages: the MIG's superior rate of climb and superior numbers—sometimes as much as 25 to 1. To the enemy's consternation both failed to produce. For each Sabrejet shot down, 14 MIGs lay smashed and burning on North Korean countryside.

The first attempt to negotiate an armistice in Korea got underway on July 10, 1951, at Kaesong. There and later at Panmunjom the only result was a stalemate. This led to a decision to use United Nations airpower to destroy selected targets in North Korea in an attempt to force the Communists to accept truce terms. One of those targets was the North Korean hydroelectric power generating complex. Irrigation dams were another important target.

Here is an account of the attack on the irrigation dams, an attack which many experts think hastened the end of the war.

The Attack on the Irrigation Dams in North Korea

An Air University Staff Study

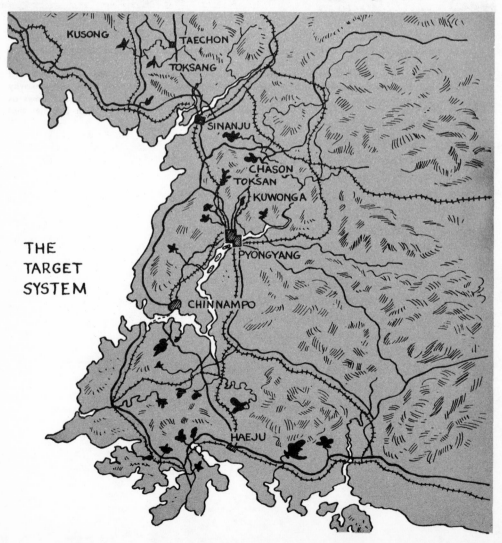

THE TARGET SYSTEM

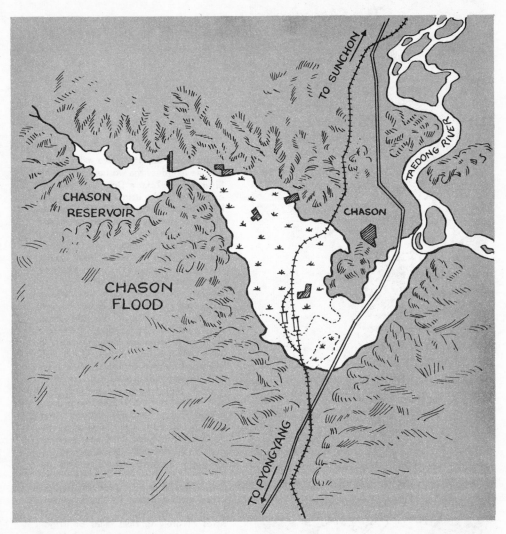

Outline of the principal area washed out by the Chasan flood, from the foot of the dam to the Taedong River. One of two main rail and highway lines connecting Pyongyang with Sunchon, Kaechon, Sinanju, and the Manchurian supply areas extended for several miles across the broad, flat valley. With the Toksan strike completely cutting one main north-south transportation artery and the Chasan strike cutting the other, UNC estimated that all south-bound supplies destined for the western part of the front lines would be stopped for two to three weeks. Total damage caused by the Chasan flood included: 2050 feet of rail track completely washed out; 9000 feet of rail track undermined and weakened by inundation; 2000 feet of rail by-pass washed out; two major railroad bridges destroyed; three miles of highway weakened or washed out by inundation; 18 buildings destroyed, 50 seriously damaged; miles of irrigation canals and connecting irrigation network washed out or silted; tremendous destruction of the rice crop and damage to flooded agricultural lands. The flood water surging down the Taedong River inundated large parts of the North Korean capital city of Pyongyang.

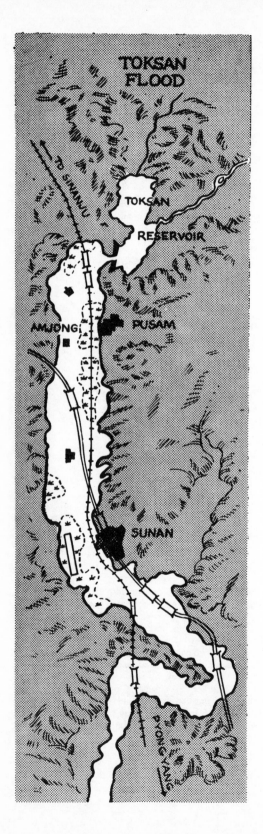

This graphic depicts twelve miles of the 27-mile length of the washed-out Potong River valley. Toksan Dam was selected as the first of the irrigation dam attacks because of the strategic value of the valley below the dam. The important Kyongui main line railroad, connecting Sinanju with Pyongyang, ran the complete length of the valley from Toksan Dam to Pyongyang. The main highway route from Sinanju to Pyongyang also entered the valley south of Amjong below the dam and ran down the valley through Sunan to Kangdaedong, just north of Pyongyang. Complete statistics of damage included: over 6 miles of rail line destroyed, 5 rail bridges destroyed or damaged; 2 miles of highway destroyed, 5 highway bridges destroyed or damaged; 700 buildings destroyed, 877 buildings damaged; Sunan airfield flooded and washed out; part of the town of Sunan flooded; 8 occupied AAA gun positions and an unidentified underground installation flooded; many sections of rail line and highway and many rail and highway bridges probably undermined or weakened by flood waters; inestimable damage to thousands of acres of growing rice; miles of irrigation canals washed out or silted. Flood conditions extended as far downstream as Pyongyang, causing considerable damage to the capital city.

Index

286

287

288